Philosophy and Language

Steven Davis

THE BOBBS-MERRILL COMPANY, INC.
Indianapolis

First Edition
First Printing 1976

Excerpts from *Word and Object* by W. V. O. Quine, copyright
1960 by the M.I.T. Press, are reprinted here with the permission
of the author and the publisher.

Excerpts from "On the Reasons for the Indeterminacy of
Translation" by W. V. O. Quine, *Journal of Philosophy* LXVII:
179–181, 183, are reprinted here with the permission of the
author and the publisher.

Library of Congress Cataloging in Publication Data

Davis, Steven.
  Philosophy and language.

  (Traditions in philosophy)
  Bibliography: p.
  Includes index.
  1. Languages—Philosophy. I. Title.
P106.D3   401   75–15910

For My Mother and Father

Contents

IV.   Transformational Linguistic Theory—
      N. Chomsky   86
      1. The Goals of Transformational Linguistic
         Theory   86
      2. Transformational Syntactic Theory   88
      3. Transformational Semantic Theory   114
      4. Ross's Performative Thesis   122
      5. A Critical Appraisal of Transformational
         Semantic Theory   130
      6. Jackendoff's Revision of Transformational
         Linguistic Theory   136

 V.   Behaviorism, Inscrutability of Reference,
      and Translational Indeterminacy—
      W. V. O. Quine   141
      1. Quine's Behaviorism   141
      2. Language Acquisition and Use   142
      3. Radical Translation and Behavioristic
         Semantics   150
      4. Translational Indeterminacy of Terms   167
      5. Translational Indeterminacy of Standing
         Sentences   184
      6. Translational Indeterminacy and
         Propositions   188

VI.   Transformational Linguistic Theory and
      Translational Indeterminacy   203
      Introduction   203
      1. Quine on 'Analyticity', 'Synonymy', and
         'Necessity'   204
      2. Katz on 'Analyticity' and 'Synonymy'   207
      3. A Reconsideration of the Translational
         Indeterminacy of Standing Sentences   212
      4. Transformational Linguistic Theory and
         Translational Indeterminacy   216
      5. Some Criticisms of Quine's Argument for
         Translational Indeterminacy   220

Preface

In the chapters which follow I shall describe in some detail three theories about language and speech which are among the most influential in contemporary linguistics and analytical philosophy. Two of the three have been proposed by philosophers, J. L. Austin and W. V. O. Quine, and the third by the philosopher and linguist, N. Chomsky. Beside describing these theories, my goal is to cast light on the nature of language and the connection between language and certain philosophical questions about meaning, truth, action, and the human mind.

There are many to whom I owe a debt of gratitude, especially Lewis White Beck who introduced me to philosophy and Charles E. Caton and Leonard Linsky who introduced me to the philosophy of language. In writing the book, I am grateful to Dale Beyerstein, Marilyn Frye, Charles E. Caton, Richard Gale, Arnold Herschorn, Stephen Darwall, Richard Garner, Alice Harris, Dorothy Grover, Charles H. Lambros, Christopher Hill, Gerald Massey, and Norman Swartz for their valuable criticisms which helped me avoid many errors in content and style. And I thank Marsha Miner, Judy Ayoub, and Fern Wilkinson for patiently typing and retyping the various versions of the manuscript.

The book is intended for students of philosophy and linguistics. Though the formal notation has been kept to a minimum, it would be helpful if the students had a first course in symbolic logic. And it would aid the philosophy students if they knew some linguistics and the linguistics students if they knew some philosophy. But my hope is, of course, that they will learn a bit of both by reading this book.

Throughout I use the standard conventions for quotation marks. Single quotation marks indicate that an expression is being mentioned rather than used; double quotation marks indicate quotation. I have italicized key words on their first introduction.

Steven Davis

Burnaby, British Columbia
January 1974

Philosophy and Language

I

Philosophy and Language

Introduction

Language and its bearing on philosophical problems has interested Western philosophers, at least from the time of the ancient Greeks. But until the latter part of the nineteenth century, interest in language was not central to philosophy, although almost every major Western philosopher has written on the subject. The important change came when philosophers saw that many philosophical problems can be made clearer when they are rephrased in the linguistic mode. For example, instead of asking what it is to be moral, the question in part has been recast into a set of questions about the meaning or the use of such expressions as 'good,' 'ought,' 'right,' 'duty,' 'obligation,' 'justification,' and so forth. Some have taken this concern with language, in what is called the *analytic* tradition, either as indicating a lack of interest in the classical issues in philosophy or as trivializing them. Of course, it is unconvincing to anyone who sees analytical philosophy as concerned with 'merely semantic' questions to be told simply that the linguistic turn helps in understanding many of the central problems of philosophy. I believe that a more convincing case can be made by analyzing some philosophical problems and showing how paying attention to language illuminates and helps to solve them. In the following, this is one of the tasks which I hope to accomplish.

But an interest in language as a tool for doing philosophy has led philosophers to raise questions about the nature of language itself. If, for example, we think it important to know what the meaning or the use of 'good' is, then we should be clear about what it is for a word to have a meaning or a use. And to raise questions about meaning and use in their most general form has led philosophers to ask, on the one hand, about the relationship between language users and language and, on the other, about the relationship between language and the world. These questions about language have come to be grouped into a separate area of philosophy called *philosophy of language*. A second purpose of this book will be, then, to consider these central questions in the philosophy of language and to investigate several attempts to answer them.

Philosophy of language and analytical philosophy should not be confused. Philosophy of language is an area of philosophy, on a par with other areas of philosophy, such as philosophy of art, philosophy of religion, and philosophy of mind, each with its own, but not separate, subject matter. In contrast, analytical philosophy is a method of doing philosophy which involves certain linguistic concepts which are used for analyzing and hopefully solving many philosophical problems from different areas of philosophy. Since philosophy is a self-reflective activity, one of the tasks philosophers of language have set themselves is to understand the linguistic concepts used within analytical philosophy in order to come to a clearer understanding of the methods which it employs.

Obviously, philosophy is not the only field in which language is studied. Research on various aspects of language is carried out in several areas among which are literary criticism, sociology, anthropology, computer science, mathematics, logic, psychology, and linguistics. In fact the leading questions within philosophy of language can be distributed across these fields. Psychology, sociology, anthropology, and linguistics consider questions about the relationship between language users and language and also between language and the world. And all the fields to a greater or lesser extent ask questions about the nature of language. However, in the fields of psychology, logic, and linguistics, both the questions about and the research on language coincide most closely with those in philosophy of language. An additional purpose of this book, then, is to show the interconnection between these fields and philosophy of language, and the bearing that the work in these areas has had on philosophical problems.

Within the analytic tradition there are many philosophers and linguists who have made major contributions to the philosophy of language among whom are Frege, Russell, Wittgenstein, Carnap, Tarski, Austin, Chomsky, and Quine.[1] In a book of this size, however, it is impossible to consider the views of all of these philosophers. Consequently, of these, I have selected to expound critically the views of Austin, Chomsky, and Quine. However, since Russell's theory of definite descriptions is the *locus classicus* of philosophy of language, I shall begin with its exposition, but I shall not attempt a full treatment of Russell's theory of language.

Hence, this book has four purposes. First, it is an essay in the philosophy of language touching on some of the main themes in this field. Second, it attempts to show the connection between philosophy of language on the one hand and logic, linguistics, and psychology on the other. Third, it tries to show how the linguistic turn in philosophy illuminates and helps to solve some of the traditional philosophical problems about truth, meaning, mind, and action. And lastly, it is an exposition of the views on language of Austin, Chomsky, and Quine. But let us begin with Russell's theory of definite descriptions.[2]

1 Russell's Theory of Definite Descriptions

Suppose I say

(1) Caroline has hepatitis.

(1) appears to consist of a subject, 'Caroline,' and a predicate, 'has hepatitis.' It is natural to suppose that (1) is about Caroline who is designated by the subject of (1) and that what is meant by 'Caroline' is what it designates. That is, the meaning of 'Caroline' is Caroline. Russell seems to adopt this view about proper names in his *Introduction to Mathematical Philosophy* where he takes ". . . a name [to be] a simple symbol which directly designates an individual which is its meaning."[3] As we shall see, it turns out that for Russell proper names are not names in his sense of 'name.' However, for the moment we shall suppose that they are. The question I want to consider is whether the meaning of other expressions which can function as subjects of sentences can be the objects which they designate. In particular, can an expression of the form, 'the ϕ', which Russell calls a *definite description,* have as its meaning the object which it designates? That is, can definite descriptions, except for not being simple, be Russellian names? For example, in

(2) The author of *Waverley* wrote more books than you can shake a stick at.

can 'the author of *Waverley*', which is the subject of the sentence, designate Scott? Can Scott, then, be the meaning of 'the author of *Waverley*'?

There is a difficulty in taking definite descriptions to be Russellian names. This problem is posed by *negative existentials,* which are sentences that deny the existence of something. Suppose someone says

(3) The jolly green giant does not exist.

Now what is said is true and meaningful. And for it to be meaningful all its parts must have a meaning. But what is the meaning of the subject of (3)? If we hold that the meaning of a definite description is the object it designates, then we shall be forced to take it that 'the jolly green giant' designates some object, namely, the jolly green giant, which is its meaning. This seems to commit us to the existence of the jolly green giant and to the falsity of (3). We can avoid this consequence by making a distinction between different kinds of existence. We could say that objects, such as the jolly green giant, will not be taken to exist in the sense in which you and I exist, but *subsist* in the way in which figments of the imagination, fictional characters, and mythological figures exist.[4] But 'subsist' seems to be a label for a philosophical problem rather than its solution.

Russell's way around this unpalatable consequence is to deny that the meaning of a definite description is the object which it designates. His argument that definite descriptions cannot be Russellian names is the following. Consider:

(4) (a) Scott is Scott.
     (b) Scott is the author of *Waverley*.

which differ in meaning. On the assumption that 'the author of *Waverley*' is a Russellian name, its designation, Scott, is its meaning. But, then, (4) (b) should mean the same as (4) (a). Since it does not, 'the author of *Waverley*' cannot be a Russellian name.[5]

How are expressions of the form, 'the ϕ', to be treated, if they are not names? Russell's theory of definite descriptions, one of the most influential theories in the analytical tradition, offers a solution to the problem engendered by negative existentials such as (3).[6]

Consider the *positive existential*

(5) The jolly green giant exists.

which appears to be of the subject-predicate form in which the subject 'the jolly green giant' putatively designates some object and to which the predicate 'exists' attributes existence. It might seem that (5) is *about* the jolly green giant and, thus, for (5) to be meaningful there must be a jolly green giant for it to be about. This raises a paradox for positive existentials parallel to that for negative existentials. Russell's solution to the paradox is to deny that (5) is of the subject-predicate form. Instead, on Russell's theory of definite descriptions the logical form of (5) is the conjunction

(6)   There is a jolly green giant and no more than one jolly green giant.

And since there is no jolly green giant, the first conjunct of (6) is false. And hence, (6) itself is false. Moreover, since (6) is not of the subject-predicate form, 'the jolly green giant' cannot occur as its subject. In fact 'the jolly green giant' does not even occur as a constituent of (6). Because of this, (6) need not be about the jolly green giant to be meaningful. And furthermore, since (6) is the logical form of (5), we should neither take 'the jolly green giant' to be the logical subject, nor even a constituent of (5). Armed with this analysis of positive existentials, the analysis of negative existentials is rather straightforward. On Russell's theory the logical form of (3) is

(7)   It is not the case that there is a jolly green giant and there is no more than one jolly green giant.

And since in (7), as in (6), 'the jolly green giant' does not occur as a constituent, (7) does not have to refer to the jolly green giant to be meaningful. And since (7) is the logical form of (3), to be meaningful it too need not be about the jolly green giant.

Russell's theory of definite descriptions allows us to solve rather neatly the following logical puzzle.[7] Since there is presently no king of France

(8)   The present king of France is bald.

is false. Now the *law of excluded middle* tells us that either a statement or its negation is true. Since (8) is false, (9) should be true.

(9)   The present king of France is not bald.

But it is not. Russell's theory of definite descriptions allows us to solve this difficulty without abandoning the law of excluded middle. On Russell's theory, the logical form of (8) is

(10)   There is a present king of France;
       There is no more than one present king of France;
       and
       Whatever is present king of France is bald.

There are two negations of (10), the first of which is true.

(11)   It is not the case that (there is a present king of
       France; there is no more than one present king of
       France; and whatever is a present king of France
       is bald).

There is, then, no incompatibility between (10) and (11)
and the law of excluded middle, since (10) is false and (11)
is true. But what about (9)? The negation of (10) which
corresponds to (9) is

(12)   There is a present king of France;
       There is no more than one present king of France;
       and
       Whatever is a present king of France is not bald.

And because there is no present king of France, (12) is false.
Consequently, so too is (9) for which (12) is the analysis.
Thus, (8) and (9) turn out to be false and the law of ex-
cluded middle need not be abandoned.

2   Russell's Theory of Proper Names

We have assumed that 'Caroline' is a Russellian name.
That is, 'Caroline' designates Caroline which is, then, the
meaning of the name. Problems arise, however, when we
attempt to treat all proper names as Russellian names. For
Russell, as we have seen, a name is a simple symbol which
directly designates an individual. But 'Pegasus' and 'Santa
Claus' cannot be Russellian names, since they do not designate anything. How, then, are we to account for the meaningfulness of

(13)   Pegasus does not exist.

Russell's solution is to give up the assumption that proper
names are names in his sense. Rather, Russell construes
proper names to be "abbreviated descriptions."[8] That is,

in (13) 'Pegasus' can be replaced by 'the winged horse of Greek mythology', yielding

(14)   The winged horse of Greek mythology does not exist.

which can be analyzed utilizing Russell's theory of definite descriptions. On this analysis, (14) is meaningful without there being a winged horse of Greek mythology. In turn because (13) and (14) mean the same, (13) can be meaningful without there being something called 'Pegasus'.

Russell's theory of proper names has the advantage of being able to account for the meaningfulness of negative existentials which appear to contain a proper name as subject. As well, Russell's theory is able to offer an explanation for the connection between a proper name which designates an object and the object which it designates. To provide an account of the connection I shall introduce the technical notion of *denotation*. Suppose we have a proper name, 'A', which is an abbreviation of 'the ϕ'. Now A is the denotation of 'the ϕ' if and only if A is the unique individual which is a ϕ. Suppose A is the denotation of 'the ϕ'. Since 'A' is an abbreviation of 'the ϕ' we can take A too to be the denotation of 'A'. That is, the denotation of a proper name, if it has one, is given by the denotation of the definite description with which the proper name is associated.

There are difficulties both with Russell's theory of definite descriptions and his theory of proper names. I shall begin with criticisms of the latter theory. As we have seen, Russell's argument against definite descriptions being names in his sense rests on his claim that

(15)   (a)   Scott is Scott.

(b)   Scott is the author of *Waverley*.

do not mean the same. But if 'Scott' is an "abbreviated description" for 'the author of *Waverley*', replacing 'Scott' in (15) (a) and (b) with this description gives us in both cases

(16)   The author of *Waverley* is the author of *Waverley*.

Hence, Russell's theory of proper names leads us to the contrary to fact conclusion that (15) (a) and (b) have the same meaning.

'Caroline' raises further problems for Russell's theory of proper names. There is no dictionary entry for 'Caroline', which contains a definite description, which we can associate with the name, as there is for 'Pegasus'. How, then, are we to provide the definite description for which 'Caroline' is an abbreviation? One possibility is that the definite description be obtained from each person who uses the name. But this creates the following difficulties. The first is that two people might connect different definite descriptions with 'Caroline'. For example, you might associate it with 'the vice-chairperson of the school board' and I might associate it with 'the lawyer for the university'. 'Caroline' would not, then, abbreviate the same definite description for the two of us and consequently, on this view, we should understand different things by 'Caroline has hepatitis'. But obviously we do not. The second difficulty is that a speaker might be able to provide more than one definite description to associate with a proper name. For example, I can supply more than one definite description which denotes Caroline and, thus, which I could associate with 'Caroline', for example, 'the sister of Alice Hart', 'the smartest person in the graduating class of 1960 at U.S.C.', and 'the senior partner in the firm of Hart, Shaffner and Bullock'. Which of these is *the* preferred definite description which I am to associate with 'Caroline'? Russell's theory gives no principled way of determining this.

I think both these criticisms can be turned aside by making Russell's theory a bit more sophisticated. Instead of associating one definite description with a proper name, we could associate a set of definite descriptions with it. And instead of taking the set of definite descriptions to be the one which a single individual associates with a proper name, we could take the set to consist of the common definite descriptions which all or almost all users associate with the proper name.[9] These changes in Russell's theory require us to amend our account of the way in which a proper name which denotes an individual is connected with that individual. We shall say that a proper name, '*A*', denotes *A* just in case *A* is the denotation of a sufficient number of the definite descriptions which are commonly associated with '*A*'. Now the reason that *A* need not be the denotation of every definite description associated with '*A*', for '*A*' to denote *A,* is that it is possible for everyone who uses '*A*' to be wrong about one or two of the definite descriptions which they associate with '*A*'. For example, everyone, including Caroline, might think that she was the smartest person in the graduating class of 1960 at U.S.C. and because of this, associate 'the smartest person in the graduating class of 1960 at U.S.C.' with 'Caroline'. But, it might turn out that they were all mistaken and consequently, that 'the smartest person in the graduating class of 1960 at U.S.C.' does not denote Caroline. If it were necessary for Caroline to be the denotation of every definite description associated with 'Caroline', for 'Caroline' to denote Caroline, 'Caroline', then, would not denote Caroline. But it seems a bit extreme, if Caroline were the denotation of a substantial number of the definite descriptions associated with 'Caroline', not to take Caroline to be the denotation of 'Caroline'. For this reason we shall not require that Caroline be the denotation of all of the definite descriptions associated with 'Caroline', but only of a sufficient number for 'Caroline' to denote Caroline.

3   Russell's Theories Criticized

Even with this revision of Russell's theory of proper names, it is open to criticism. First, it is perfectly possible for there to be no set of definite descriptions common to the users of a proper name. Suppose half the people who know Caroline knew her up until the time she was ten years old, but know nothing about her after that time. And the other half of the people who know 'Caroline' met her when she was twenty-five years old and know nothing about her earlier years. It might well be the case that there is no overlap in the sets of definite descriptions which these two groups associate with 'Caroline'. And hence, there is no set of definite descriptions common to all, or almost all, the users of 'Caroline' which they associate with that name. Were this the case, on the theory being considered these two groups would mean different things by 'Caroline has hepatitis'. Second, it is possible for the definite descriptions associated with a name to denote an individual which is not named by that name.[10] Suppose that Socrates was not the ancient Greek philosopher who was accused by the Athenians of subverting the youth of Athens and who was forced to drink hemlock. Instead, he was Plato's fishmonger. The actual Greek philosopher who was accused of subverting the youth of Athens was really Thrasymachus. And Plato was using Socrates' name in his dialogues to protect Thrasymachus' family from any reprisals from the Athenian government. If this story were true, I believe that 'Socrates' in Plato's dialogues would name Plato's fishmonger and that in using 'Socrates' we would be naming or referring to Socrates and not Thrasymachus, although Socrates would have none of the properties commonly attributed to him. But, since we would not know that Plato was using Socrates' name in this way, we would associate with 'Socrates' 'the ancient Greek philosopher who was accused of subverting Athenian youth', etc. However, these definite descriptions would denote Thrasymachus and not Socrates. And on the theory of proper names we are considering, 'Socrates' also would denote Thrasymachus and not Socrates. Consequently, this theory does not give a correct account of the relationship between a name and what it names. The last criticism of the theory is that it is possible for a name to name an individual, but for it not to be the case that users of the name be able to supply a set of definite descriptions which uniquely pick out that individual. Suppose we find an ancient manuscript describing a rather lavish Roman party at the end of which appears the names of all those present, including the name 'Diogenes'. Sometime after reading the

manuscript, I am asked about Diogenes. All that I can remember is that he is one of the people reported to have
been at the party described in the ancient manuscript. And
so in answer to the question I say

(17)   Diogenes was one of the people reported to have
been at the party described in the manuscript.

In so saying I believe that I have named or referred to
Diogenes, but there are no definite descriptions which I can
associate with his name, since I know nothing which describes him uniquely. And let us further suppose that I am
the only one who has read the manuscript and, thus, that
I am the only user of Diogenes' name. On the theory of
proper names we are considering there would be no account
of the connection between my use of 'Diogenes' and Diogenes or between the name 'Diogenes' and what it names.

These criticisms of a more sophisticated version of Russell's theory of proper names show, I believe, that the relationship between a use of a name and what is named and between a name and what it names cannot be provided by
the definite descriptions which users of the name commonly
associate with it. And as a consequence, proper names cannot be "abbreviated descriptions."

I now want to turn to one of P. F. Strawson's criticisms
of Russell's theory of definite descriptions.[11] Suppose the
light bulb in the bathroom is broken and referring to it I
say

(18)   The light bulb is broken

According to Strawson, on Russell's theory of definite descriptions the analysis of (18) is

(19)   (a)   There is a light bulb
(b)   There is no more than one light bulb
(c)   Whatever is a light bulb is broken

Now (19) (b) and (c), and hence (19) as a whole, are pal-
pably false, though (18) is true. According to Strawson what
is missing from Russell's analysis is that in saying (18) one
and only one light bulb is being referred to. The difficulty

is that there is no satisfactory way to add this to Russell's analysis of (18). One attempt is

(20) (a) There is a light bulb being referred to
     (b) There is no more than one light bulb being referred to
     (c) Whatever is a light bulb being referred to is broken

However, there are difficulties with (20) as an analysis of (19). Were I to say (20), I would be asserting that a light bulb is being referred to, but in saying (18) I am not asserting that a light bulb is being referred to, but rather I am referring to a light bulb. As Strawson puts it, "To refer is not to say you are referring."[12] And so, (20) cannot be the correct analysis of (18). The upshot is that Russell's theory of definite descriptions does not provide a correct analysis for every definite description.

Strawson's own theory of definite descriptions is based upon a distinction he makes between the expressions in a language and the uses to which they are put.[13] Consider the sentence

(21) The fig juice has turned sour.

This sentence is neither true nor false, but it can be *used* to make a true or false statement. And the subject of (21), 'the fig juice', does not mention or refer to anything, but a speaker in uttering (21) can *use* this definite description to refer to something. In this book I shall not discuss Strawson's theory of reference, but the interested reader should consult Strawson's "On Referring" and *Introduction to Logical Theory* and the discussion of Strawson's theory in L. Linsky's *Referring*.[14] However, in the next chapter I shall have a great deal to say about the uses speakers make of the sentences of their language.

II

Speech Act Theory

1 Reichenbach's Cognitive and Instrumental Usage

As the Greeks have taught us, to know what some things are is to know what they are used for. This is especially true of those things whose existence depends upon human creativity. Consider a chair. We would hardly know what it is, unless we knew it was used to sit on. It is similar for human languages. To understand their nature, one of the purposes of this book, we must know how they are used. There is a long and important tradition of philosophers and literary critics who have attempted to catalogue the different uses of language. Most of this work has been influenced by C. K. Ogden and I. A. Richards' *The Meaning of Meaning*.[1] I have chosen as representative of this tradition Hans Reichenbach's treatment of the different uses of language in his *Elements of Symbolic Logic*.[2] I shall first briefly discuss his views and, then, contrast them with those of J. L. Austin[3] who, I believe, offers a deeper analysis of the uses of language than those who stand in the Ogden-Richards tradition.

What are the uses of language? According to Reichenbach the uses of language can be divided into two kinds: the *cognitive* and the *instrumental*. The cognitive usage of the language is ". . . for the purpose of expressing true statements. Cognitive usage of language belongs to semantics since truth is a relation between signs and objects."[4] And the instrumental usage of language has as its aim ". . . influencing the listener . . . for certain purposes intended by the speaker."[5] Reichenbach, then, attributes two distinguishing characteristics to cognitive and instrumental usage. First, cognitive, but not instrumental usage, is true or false.[6] And second, instrumental usage is using language with the intention of producing an effect on a listener, while cognitive usage is using language with the intention of saying something true.

There are many actions we can perform by and in using language which fall under Reichenbach's instrumental usage. For example, by using language we can persuade, convince, dissuade, alarm, frighten, and anger someone. And in saying something we can warn, apologize, congratulate, thank, command, entreat, and order. In performing both sorts of actions we have the intention of producing some effect on our audience. When we persuade someone of something, our aim is to influence them to believe something. And when we order someone to do something, our aim is to get them to do it. But, there is a difference between the two which is marked by 'in using language' and 'by using language'. Let us suppose that I intend to persuade you that my uncle was Jesse James and I intend to do so by saying 'My uncle was Jesse James'. I have persuaded you that he is only if you come to believe it. That is, only if my words have my desired effect on you. Suppose, now, that my intention is to order you to fetch Jesse James and I intend to do so in saying 'Fetch Jesse James'. In saying 'Fetch Jesse James' I have, thereby, ordered you to get him. And I have ordered you to do so even if my words do not have my desired effect on you; that is, if you do nothing. So in both persuading someone of something and ordering someone to do something the speaker has the intention of influencing his listener for certain of his purposes. But the difference is that a speaker can do the former only if this intention is fulfilled, whereas he can do the latter without its being fulfilled. To mark this distinction between these two species of instrumental usage we shall borrow terminology from Austin. Those actions, such as persuading, which are done by using language will be called *perlocutionary acts* and those, like ordering, which are done in using language will be called *illocutionary or performative acts*.[7] We have, then, a distinction between cognitive and instrumental usage. And instrumental usage can be further subdivided into using language to perform perlocutionary and illocutionary acts. The question I want to raise is whether Reichenbach's cognitive usage is a kind of illocutionary act. But before broaching this question we must have a fuller understanding of the nature of illocutionary acts.

2   Illocutionary Acts

According to Austin, illocutionary acts have at least three properties. First, they are acts we perform in uttering sentences in appropriate circumstances.[8] For example to say

(1)   I promise to be there.

in appropriate circumstances is thereby to promise to be there. In contrast, to say

(2)   (i)   I admire you.
     (ii)   I believe you.

is not thereby to admire or to believe someone. Second, illocutionary acts cannot be done unless we utter a sentence or sentence fragment.[9] We cannot make a promise or give an order without saying something. But we can admire someone or believe something while sitting quietly in a corner. Third, characteristically, illocutionary acts have associated with them performative verbs. For example, in English 'promise' is associated with promising. According to Austin, the function of such performative verbs, when they occur as the main verb in a present, first person, active indicative sentence, is to make explicit the illocutionary act a speaker intends to be performing in uttering the sentences in which they occur. For example, 'congratulate' makes explicit the illocutionary act a speaker intends to be performing in uttering

(3)   I congratulate you on your fine performance.

Notice that in uttering (3) a speaker is not telling his hearer that he is congratulating him, but in an appropriate context he is thereby congratulating him. And 'congratulate' makes clear his intended act. Compare an utterance of (3) with

(4)   I am tuning the double bass.

In uttering (4) a speaker is telling us that he is tuning a double bass and, clearly, in uttering (4) no matter what the circumstances are, he is not, thereby, tuning a double bass.

Although illocutionary acts have associated with them performative verbs, it is not necessary that a sentence contain a performative verb for it to be used in an illocutionary act. We can make promises and give orders in uttering

(5)   (i)   I will be there.
      (ii)   Close the door.

But these sentences can be used in performing other illocutionary acts as well, (5) (i) in making a prediction and declaring one's intention and (5) (ii) in making a request. Because of this, in contrast to (1) or (3), it is sometimes less clear or explicit what illocutionary act a speaker intends to be performing in uttering these sentences. I say 'sometimes' because quite often the context makes it clear what illocutionary act a speaker intends to be performing.

How can we distinguish performative from non-performative verbs? There are no sure fire tests, but there are two which roughly mark the distinction. First, 'hereby' can be inserted in verb phrases which contain performative verbs without oddity.[10] Compare

(6)   (i)   I hereby promise to pay you $5.00.

(ii)   I am hereby running a race.

Second, substituting a performative verb in the following schema yields a true statement.

(7) In saying 'I x . . .' I was x-ing.[11]

Applying (6) to 'promise' and 'run', we get

(8)   (i)   In saying 'I promise' I was promising.

(ii)   In saying 'I run' I was running.

Thus, 'promise', but not 'run', is a performative verb. There are difficulties with these tests. The first is too narrow. It excludes verbs such as 'commiserate', 'plead', and 'ask' which seem to be straightforward performative verbs. And the second is too broad, for it includes verbs like 'think' which is not a performative verb. One can think, after all, without saying anything. These difficulties aside, illocutionary acts have three characteristics. They are performed in saying something; they cannot be performed unless language is used; and they have connected with them performative verbs the occurrence of which as a main verb in a present tense, indicative, active, first person sentence makes explicit what act a speaker intends to be performing in uttering the sentence.

In describing illocutionary acts we characterized them as acts performed in uttering certain words in appropriate circumstances. But 'circumstance' is notoriously vague. As Austin points out,

> Besides the uttering of the words of the so-called performative, a good many other things have as a general rule to be right and to go right if we are to be said to have happily brought off our action.[12]

Instead of concentrating on the things which must be right and go right, Austin draws our attention to the things which can be wrong and go wrong with illocutionary acts. Austin fittingly calls his taxonomy of the kinds of unhappiness which beset illocutionary acts *the doctrine of the infelicities*. There are two kinds of infelicities which plague illocutionary acts, *misfires* and *abuses*.[13] Other kinds of actions, especially those involving rules, are also subject to these difficulties. For example, if I bid out of turn in a bridge game, then my bid misfires; it does not come off. On the other hand, an abuse occurs if I sneak a look at an opponent's hand before I bid. My bid comes off, but I am open to criticism. By concentrating on the types of unhappiness which can befall illocutionary acts, we obtain a clearer picture of the kind of acts they are. In turn this will enable us to contrast them with Reichenbach's cognitive usage.

Examples make it easier to understand the different kinds of infelicities. There are four kinds of misfires. I do not suppose I can go up to any young woman I might fancy and say

(9) I marry you

and, thereby, be married to her. There is no convention for doing this, in this country at least. Similarly, I cannot promise you anything by saying

(10) I promise to make you Captain in the army of the People's Republic of China.

I can promise you no such thing because I am, at the moment, in no position to promise anything of this sort. To change the example a bit, let us assume I am in a position to make you captain, and you, not being inclined to take on such responsibilities, decline to be appointed to the position, if it comes your way. In this case the promise has not been completed. Lastly, you, realizing what the world situation is, accept my offer and I, being an unreconstructed Nationalist, in conferring the rank on you, say

(11) I appoint you Captain in the army of the Republic of China.

In saying this I have not appointed you Captain in the People's Army of China. I have not gone through the procedure to do this correctly. The above examples illustrate four conditions which must be satisfied for a performative to come off:

(A.1)   There must exist an accepted conventional procedure having a certain conventional effect, that procedure to include the uttering of certain words by certain persons in certain circumstances.

(A.2)   The particular persons and circumstances in a given case must be appropriate for the invocation of the particular procedure invoked.

(B.1)   This procedure must be executed by all participants both correctly and

(B.2)   Completely.[14]

There are two kinds of abuses. The first kind of abuse depends upon whether the speaker has the thoughts, intentions, or feelings appropriate to the illocutionary act. Suppose I promise to meet you at Scotty's, but I have no intention of doing so. I still have promised, but have made an insincere promise. Or similarly, I apologize for having slighted you at the ball, but I do not feel sorry. I have apologized, but done it insincerely. Lastly, I compliment you on your beautiful painting, when I think it is ugly. I have complimented you, although it is an insincere compliment. The second kind of abuse applies only to illocutionary acts which commit a speaker to future action, such as promising. If I promise, then I should keep my promise. However, as with the first kind of abuse, my not keeping my promise does not mean that I did not promise. The two kinds of abuses illustrated above occur, according to Austin, when the following conditions are broken:

(Γ.1)   Where, as often, the procedure is designed for use by persons having certain thoughts or feelings, or for the inauguration of certain consequential conduct on the part of any participant, then a person participating in and so invoking the procedure must in fact have those thoughts or feelings and the participants must intend so to conduct themselves and further,

(Γ.2)   Must actually so conduct themselves subsequently.[15]

If an abuse occurs, the intended performative comes off, but the speaker is open to criticism.

We have made an initial distinction between Reichenbach's cognitive usage on the one hand and Austin's illocutionary acts on the other. According to Reichenbach, the former is characterized as using language for the purpose of saying something which is true or false. A plausible way of interpreting Reichenbach's cognitive usage is to identify it with stating. The question I want to raise is whether stating is a kind of illocutionary act.

First, stating is an act we perform in uttering a sentence. Second, it cannot be performed unless a speaker uses language. And third, it has associated with it a verb, 'state', which can be used to make explicit what speech act a speaker intends to be performing. For example, uttering

(12)   I state that this country is going to pot.

in appropriate circumstances is to state that this country is going to pot. And 'I state' makes explicit what act a speaker intends to be performing in uttering (12).[16] Moreover, 'state' passes both tests for performative verbs.

(13)   (i)   I hereby state that this country is going to pot.
         (ii)   In saying 'I state' I was stating.

Consequently, stating is characterized by the same traits as illocutionary acts.

In addition, some of the conditions in Austin's doctrine of infelicities apply to stating. However, not all the ills which Austin thinks infect statements do in fact plague them. Austin maintains that condition (A.2)—the circumstances and persons must be appropriate for the invocation of the particular performative—applies to stating. Let us begin with 'circumstances'. There are two different sorts of cases where purported statements fail to come off because the 'circumstances' are not appropriate. First, if I say

(14)   The dean of students is a liberal.

then I have presupposed that there is a dean of students. And if there is none, then I have not stated that anyone is a liberal. The same failure can befall bequests, a straightforward illocutionary act, when for example, I bequeath a watch which no longer exists.[17]

Second, there are things which must be appropriate about the linguistic context for a speaker to be able to make certain statements. Suppose you say (14) to me, I understand you, and you know that I understand you. Then, I am not in a position to state immediately to you what you have just stated, although I can agree or disagree with you or deny or affirm what you have said.[18] Denying and affirming, both illocutionary acts, are subject to similar ills. I cannot go up to someone who has said nothing and deny or affirm anything. In order to deny or affirm one must deny or affirm what someone has said. Let us now turn to the second part of A.2—the person must be appropriate for the invocation of the performative. Austin holds that this applies to stating; that is, there are some things some people are not in a position to state.[19] According to Austin, I am not in a position to state at the present time that there are exactly thirty-seven people in the White House. But suppose, quite mistakenly, I believe that I am; I believe that I have special powers which enable me to determine such things. Have I not stated that there are exactly thirty-seven people in the White House? It is certain that I do not know that there are. But this is not at issue. Regrettably, people make statements about many things they do not know and are in no position to know. So, against Austin, even though some people should not make certain statements, because they are in no position to do so, they nevertheless do make them without a misfire occurring. Perhaps this should be included under abuses, since if people make statements they are in no position to make, they are open to criticism.

Austin claims that defects of the (B.1) variety—the procedure must be executed correctly—also infects statements. For example, if I say

(15)   Joan is a bat.

when I mean to say 'cat', then I have not stated Joan is a cat—nor that she is a bat.[20] But, contrary to Austin, my mistake here does not consist in performing the act of stating incorrectly, but in failing to say what I mean. In fact there is a whole host of infelicities which apply to our utterances of sentences, rather than to our illocutionary acts. We must avoid slips of the tongue, misusing words, mispronouncing them, and garbling our syntax.[21] There is a relationship between saying what we mean on the one hand and illocutionary acts on the other. Usually, if we do not do the former, then our intended illocutionary act does not come off. But, not always. However, it is unnecessary for us to consider cases of this sort. The important point is that (B.1) does not apply to statements, at least not in the way Austin thinks it does.

(Γ.1) obviously applies to statements. When people make statements, we usually take them to believe what they say. But, people sometimes lie. And when they do, they are open to criticism in the same way someone is open to criticism who offers congratulations when he believes what was done was done poorly.

It seems clear enough, then, that stating and consequently Reichenbach's cognitive usage is a species of illocutionary act. It has the characteristics which illocutionary acts have and many of the conditions in Austin's doctrine of infelicities apply to it. But possibly we have been unfair to Reichenbach. In distinguishing between instrumental and cognitive usage Reichenbach maintains that 'true' and 'false' apply to the latter, but not the former. Perhaps this gives a way to save the distinction between illocutionary acts and statements. We can say that statements, but not illocutionary acts, are assessed as being true or false. However, this will not do, for when we say that a statement is true or false, or even when we say that it is rough or an exaggeration, what we are doing is assessing its fit with the facts.[22] Similarly, an estimate of something's length or an assessment of its monetary value, can be correct or incorrect and a warning can be false, if what we warn about is not the case. And to say of an estimation or an assessment that it is correct or incorrect or of a warning that it is false is to assess their fit with the facts. Moreover, in saying either

(16) (i) I estimate this table to be three feet long.

     (ii) I assess the table to be worth $5.00.

     (iii) I warn you that the market will crash.

in appropriate circumstances is to perform an illocutionary act. Conseqeuntly, illocutionary acts can also be assessed as to their fit with the facts. And, thus, our being able to say of statements that they are true or false does not give us a way to distinguish between them and illocutionary acts.

There is still a nub of truth in Reichenbach's distinction, which I am afraid we have overlooked. The reason Reichenbach gives for his claim that cognitive usage, but not instrumental usage, can be assessed as true or false is that

> These predicates express a semantical relation . . . between signs and objects, but since instrumental usage . . . includes the sign user, it cannot be judged as true or false.[23]

But, if 'true' and 'false' are predicated of signs, then it cannot be the act of stating which is true or false. What, then, is true or false? There is an ambiguity in the use of 'statement'. It can be used to refer to the act of stating and, also, to what can be called the *content of the act of stating* or what is stated. These two must be kept distinct. For actions, and thus 'statements' in this sense, are neither true nor false. Notice that we do say such things as

(17) (i) What he stated was true (false).

     (ii) The truth (falsity) of what he stated is obvious.

'True' and 'false', thus, are predicated of what is stated, rather than of acts of stating.

To illustrate the difference between statements as acts and as contents, consider the following case. It is quite possible for me to utter a sentence the utterance of which I intend to be a statement, but which fails to be one because it violates one of Austin's felicity conditions and also possible for what I uttered to be true. I, having the position I presently have, happen to walk before a set of television cameras which are prepared for a high ranking Israeli official. The reporters, thinking I am the official, ask me for my statement on the number of atom bombs Israel currently has. (This, by the way, is the characteristic situation in which statements are made. We do not ordinarily make statements to people when we talk with them.) Thinking that this is the skit I was asked to be in, faking an accent, I say

(18)   Israel has several bombs.

I have, of course, no idea whatever whether they have any. Moreover, my impersonation is immediately discovered and rectified by the Israeli official who says

(19)   Israel has no bombs.

It is clear in this case that he, and not I, has made a statement to the press. In uttering (17) I have not made a statement, even in the full-blown philosophers' sense of 'statement'. Much to the surprise of everyone, it turns out that when I said (17) Israel in fact had several bombs. This does not now make my utterance of (17) a statement to the press; I still have done no such thing. But yet what I said was true.

Since I did not make a statement and what I said was true, it cannot be my statement, the performative sense of 'statement', which is true. It seems we have reached the paradoxical conclusion that statements are neither true nor false. But this paradox trades on the ambiguity of 'statement'. I said above that 'statement' refers both to the *act* of stating and what is *stated*. 'True' and 'false' do not apply to the former, but to the latter. In the example being considered no illocutionary act is performed; no statement is made in this sense of 'statement', but what I say in uttering (17) is true or false and it is this sense of 'statement' which is applicable to my utterance of (17). Since there is a difference between the act and content sense of 'statement', there is a difference between an illocutionary act and a statement when considered as the content of an act of stating. But there still is a paradox. How can there be a content of an act of stating when there is no such act? How can what I state be true, if my act of stating does not come off? There is still an act which has been performed. I have uttered a sentence. And perhaps it is the content of this act, the sentence uttered, which is true. I shall return to this point.

In light of the above, we can recast Reichenbach's point. So-called cognitive usage is to be identified with what is stated, rather than with the act of stating for it is the former which is true or false, not the latter. But if this is what Reichenbach has in mind, it will not do to call what is stated 'cognitive usage'. What is stated is not a use to which language is put. Rather, it is the content of an act of stating. So, on the one hand we have the act of stating and on the other the content of an act of stating. As we have seen, the former is a species of illocutionary act, but the latter is not. This, then, allows us to draw a distinction between statements (what is stated) and illocutionary acts.

We can generalize this distinction. Suppose I utter the following sentences:

(20) (i)   I state that Johnson is dead.
      (ii) I maintain that Johnson is dead.
      (iii) I conclude that Johnson is dead.
      (iv) I warn you that Johnson is dead.
      (v)   I claim that Johnson is dead.

In uttering each of these what I am doing is stating, maintaining, concluding, et cetera. But if in uttering these sentences I mean the same thing by 'Johnson is dead' and am referring to the same Johnson, then what I am stating, maintaining, concluding, is the same thing, namely, that Johnson is dead. That is, I am performing different sorts of illocutionary acts, but the content of the acts is the same. It should be noted that it is this content, i.e., that Johnson is dead, and not the illocutionary acts, which is true or false. Thus, the distinction generalized is between *illocutionary act contents*—what is stated, what is concluded, what is claimed, and so forth—and illocutionary acts. What, then, of Reichenbach's cognitive usage? On the one hand Reichenbach considers it to be a use of language and on the other what is true or false. But, this conflates statement acts and statement contents. So, Reichenbach's cognitive usage must go by the board.

3 *Perlocutionary Acts*

Our discussion has centered on cognitive usage and illocutionary acts. In doing so we have given short shrift to perlocutionary acts which have as their purpose the production of certain changes in the thoughts, desires, actions, beliefs, etc., of the listener and which are performed only if these purposes are fulfilled. For example, by saying

(21) I am going to hit you.

I might cause you to bolt out of your chair or I might upset you. Austin takes great pains to distinguish perlocutionary acts from illocutionary acts. Perlocutionary acts are acts we perform *by* saying something, whereas illocutionary acts are performed *in* saying something. This distinction can be brought out more clearly by considering the relationship between our saying what we do and certain effects and consequences of what we say.

Perlocutionary acts should not be confused with the effects or consequences of what we say. My saying (21) might have the effect of upsetting you. But your being upset is not something I do or have done. Rather, what I do is say that I am going to hit you and, thereby, I have upset you. And the perlocutionary act I have done is that I upset you. There is a way of reporting what I have done which includes both what I have said and its effect on you.

(22) By saying that I was going to hit you I upset you.

It follows from (22) that I said that I was going to hit you, that I upset you, and that you were upset. But (22) does not bring out the causal relationship between my saying that I was going to hit you and your being upset. (23) which I take to be equivalent to (22) does bring this out.

(23)   By saying that I was going to hit you I caused you to be upset.

This shows quite clearly that my saying that I was going to hit you does not cause *my* upsetting you, but causes *you* to be upset. Hence, my upsetting you by saying that I was going to hit you, a perlocutionary act, is identical to my causing you to be upset by saying that I was going to hit you. We can, then, schematize perlocutionary act descriptions in two ways:

(24)   (i)   *S*'s φ-ing *H* by saying that *p*.
       (ii)   *S*'s causing *H* to be φ by saying that *p*.[24]

'*S*' is to be replaced by a designation for a speaker, '*H*' by a designation for a hearer, 'φ' by a verb, and '*p*' by a sentence.

Even with this analysis, it should not be thought that perlocutionary acts are simple. The relationship between my saying what I do and your being upset involves many factors. First, you understand what I mean by what I say. Second, you believe that I said it seriously. Third, you must believe that I am capable of carrying out my threat. Lastly, you are the sort of person who is upset by someone's threatening to hit you. What is the relationship among these conditions? Does it constitute a causal chain which begins with my saying what I do and ending with your being upset? It is true that my statement caused you to be upset and involved in this are the conditions above, but my statement did not *cause* you to understand what I said and it is doubtful that your understanding what I said *caused* you to believe that I would hit you. That is, there is not a causal chain which has as its starting point my statement and as its end your being upset. Rather, the set of conditions enumerated above is a set of sufficient conditions for your being upset. If we are to speak of my remark as being *the* cause of your being upset, we mean that it is the cause against a set of background conditions. The situation is similar to other causal ones. Placing a lighted match to a sheet of paper causes it to burn. But without the presence of sufficient oxygen there would be no fire. Hence the lighted match in the presence of sufficient oxygen is the cause of the fire. Suppose we have the following sufficient causal conditions:

(25) S's saying that p
      H's understanding 'p' $\Big\}$ c
      H's believing that p
          etc.

A perlocutionary act occurs if and only if c causes e, where e is a perlocutionary effect on the hearer. That is

(26) S ϕ's H by saying that p if and only if S's saying that p against certain background conditions causes H to be ϕ.

(26) gives us a test for perlocutionary act verbs.

(27)   'A-ing' designates a perlocutionary act if and only if substituting 'A' for ϕ renders (26) true.

However, (27) does not capture all perlocutionary acts. Making someone happy by telling them something is a perlocutionary act, but 'happy' cannot be grammatically substituted in (26). I believe (26) can be amended to meet this objection, but I shall not attempt to do so here.

This analysis of perlocutionary acts is very sketchy and does not begin to touch on very important philosophical problems connected both with the nature of human action and causation. For example, it assumes that perlocutionary acts can be analyzed in terms of our saying something and the effects our remark has on our hearers. However, we sometimes talk about the results and consequences of saying something. We might wonder whether the distinction among effects, results and consequences bears on the analysis of perlocutionary acts.[25] In addition we have not discussed in any detail whether your taking what I say seriously causes or is a reason for your belief that I am going to hit you, and whether this belief causes or is a reason for your being upset. Of course, this would involve us in a discussion of the distinction between causes and reasons. I think, however, that the analysis is sufficient to enable us to distinguish between perlocutionary and illocutionary acts.

First, for a perlocutionary act to come off, the speaker must produce some effect on his hearer by saying something. Take my upsetting you by saying

(28) I am going to hit you.

My saying (28) causes you to be upset. Contrast this with an illocutionary act. Suppose I am in a position to fine you and I say

(29) I fine you $10.

If the circumstances are appropriate, I have fined you whether or not my intended effect is produced; i.e., whether or not you pay the fine. Moreover, the relationship between my saying (29) and your being fined is not causal. For an event to be a cause of a state of affairs, the state of affairs must occur after or simultaneously with the event. If I upset you by saying (28), I say (28) *and then* you are upset. But if I fine you in saying (29), I do not say (29) and then you are fined. Nor is it true that I say (29) and at the same time you are fined. Rather, my saying (29) in appropriate circumstances *counts as* fining you and as a result you are fined. The second difference between illocutionary and perlocutionary acts, obviously related to the first, is that no illocutionary act verbs are true substitution instances of (26). In fact, some illocutionary act verbs cannot be substituted in (26) with grammaticality preserved, for example, 'maintain', 'define', 'deny', and 'agree'. Third, perlocutionary acts do not have associated with them verbs which, when they occur in a sentence, make explicit what act is being performed in uttering that sentence. Suppose I say

(30) I frighten you.

It is quite possible that you might be frightened by my saying (30). But, 'frighten' does not make explicit what I am doing in or by uttering (30). Rather in saying (30) I am saying something about myself. If 'frighten' were replaced by 'promise' in (30), I would not be saying something about myself, but would be making a promise. Fourth, there is an asymmetric relation between perlocutionary and illocutionary acts. I can perform perlocutionary acts by performing illocutionary acts, but I cannot perform illocutionary acts by performing perlocutionary acts. I can frighten you by fining you, but I cannot fine you by frightening you.

Lastly, let us imagine that we have been brought up in a society called 'Glum' where people are very serious and where they do not amuse one another. In fact, Glum is so serious that people in it do not know what it is to amuse one another. We, serious minded and all, come to 'Glee', another society. Now it is possible for us to amuse someone in Glee even though we do not know that we are amusing them—and more importantly even though we do not know what it is to amuse someone. This contrasts quite sharply with illocutionary acts. We can bid four spades even if at the moment we are not paying attention, but we cannot do it if we have no idea what it is to bid in a game of bridge. So we can say that it is a necessary condition for performing an illocutionary act that the person performing that act knows how to perform acts of that type. On the other hand it is possible to perform perlocutionary acts, even if we do not know what it is to perform acts of that type.

I have presented the distinction between illocutionary and perlocutionary acts as if there were no connection between the two.[26] There is, however, a complicated interrelation between some illocutionary acts and an intention to perform some perlocutionary acts. To illustrate this by example suppose that I say

(31) I request you to get me the pliers.
with the intention of getting you to fetch the pliers. Let us call this intention the *primary perlocutionary intention* of my request. Obviously, I need not have this intention to make my request. For example, I can request you to get the pliers in order to divert your attention, even though I have

no interest in your getting the pliers. So, the perlocutionary act I intend to be performing in making my request is to divert your attention and my intention is fulfilled regardless of whether you get the pliers. Let us call intentions of this sort, *secondary perlocutionary intentions.* The point about my request is that I must at least have some secondary perlocutionary intentions in order to make it. That is, to make a request one must have the intention to perform some perlocutionary act. Although there is no necessary connection between making requests and their primary perlocutionary intention, it must generally be the case that when speakers make requests that they have such intentions. Were this not the case, requesting would lose its point. That there is such a connection between making a request and intending that the request be carried out is borne out by the oddity of 'I request you to get the pliers, but I do not intend to get you to fetch them'. There are other illocutionary acts which are connected with perlocutionary acts in the same way as requesting, for example, making a statement, asking a question, and offering an apology. In contrast, other illocutionary acts require no perlocutionary intentions, for example, vetoing a motion, sentencing someone to a jail term, or appointing someone to a position. If I am in a position to veto a motion and I do so, I need not intend to produce any effects on my audience, although, of course, I intend my veto to have certain consequences. But, this is not a perlocutionary intention. To summarize, many illocutionary acts have as their characteristic purpose the performance of a perlocutionary act which I have called the 'primary intention' of the illocutionary act. Such illocutionary acts must generally be performed with this intention, although on a given occasion they need not be. However, even then to perform the illocutionary act, the speaker must have some perlocutionary intention. In contrast, there are other illocutionary acts which require no perlocutionary intention for their successful performance.

What, then, of Reichenbach's 'instrumental usage'? That

is, using language to influence the listener for certain purposes intended by the speaker. Clearly, all perlocutionary acts fall within instrumental usage, as do many illocutionary acts. But there are other illocutionary acts, those requiring no perlocutionary intention, which do not. Hence, Reichenbach's instrumental usage does not include all the acts we can perform in or by using language. For this reason, we shall abandon it. We are left, then, with using language to perform perlocutionary and illocutionary acts.

These acts do not exhaust the different uses of language. There are many acts and activities we can perform in and by using language which do not fit either kind.[27] For example:

(32)   telling a joke
         telling a story
         acting in a play
         writing a poem
         reciting a poem
         hinting
         insinuating
         expressing emotions
         swearing (saying 'Damn!')
         deriding
         defending a client in a trial
         orating
         getting married
                  et cetera

These are a mixed bag. Some are speech activities which involve both illocutionary and perlocutionary acts. But they include much else besides. In addition, there are other uses of language which are more interesting philosophically and which are difficult to classify. For example:

(33)   predicating
         referring
         presupposing
         describing
         classifying

identifying
saying
   et cetera

'Saying' is perhaps the most interesting in light of our earlier discussion of illocutionary acts. Is it an act of this sort? The question is too complex to discuss here.[28] In fact more attention should be paid to 'saying' than 'stating'. As I have pointed out, in normal discourse we do not make statements, but we do say a good many things to one another. Only important people make statements and, then, only when speaking to the press or the public. When talking to one another, they too say things to one another, rather than state them.[29] However, in what follows I will adopt what has become common philosophical parlance and take it that when we talk to one another, we are making statements.

4 Linguistic Objects

Determining the different uses of language so far, though interesting in its own right, has not thrown much light on traditional philosophical problems. In what follows I will consider three questions which have philosophical import. First, what are the different sorts of things speaking a language commits us to? Second, of which of these things, if any, do we predicate truth and falsity? Third, is there a relationship between illocutionary acts and meaning? Let us begin with the first question and consider first illocutionary acts.

We can view illocutionary acts in two ways, either as *types* or *tokens*. Types of things can be general or specific. Consider a bird, which is a type of animal. In turn there are types of birds; for example, orioles and pigeons. We can be even more specific. For certain purposes we might want to talk about orioles living on the southern tip of Staten Island as a type of oriole. Tokens, on the other hand, are individual exemplifications of types. The bird on my front lawn, for example, is a token of the type of bird called a 'pigeon'. Notice that two different things can be tokens of the same type. The bird on your lawn as well as the one on mine can both be pigeons. Similarly, ordering someone to do something is a type of illocutionary act. And ordering Cohen to do something or ordering Cohen to get the milk are types of orders. Two people can perform illocutionary acts of the same type. Both you and I can order someone to do something. We can even perform an order of the same type; we can both order Cohen to get the milk. How can our individual acts of ordering Cohen to get the milk be distinguished? The difference can be drawn in several ways. You did your act and I did mine; you did yours in the corner and I did mine on the table; or you did yours three weeks ago and I did mine yesterday. In each case we perform an act of the same type, ordering Cohen to get the milk, but our act tokens are different.

The type-token distinction does not apply to illocutionary act contents. For it to apply, it must be possible to specify content types and to distinguish content tokens which are different instances of that type. Consider the following sentences:

(34) (i)   The president is Jack Armstrong.

       (ii) *What I stated, namely that the president is Jack Armstrong, occurred in Jake's at 4:00 P.M.

Let us suppose that you and I utter (34) (i), that in uttering it we are referring to the same person who is Jack Armstrong, that we mean the same thing by the words we utter, and that we intend our utterance to be a statement. If all these conditions are met, then in uttering (34) (i) we have made the same statement. One might suppose that our statements are different tokens of the same type. But for this to be true, it should be possible to distinguish different statement tokens, yours and mine. We saw that difference in person, place, and time are sufficient to distinguish between our acts of stating. None of these, however, apply to statement contents. It might be thought that our statements

can be distinguished because your statement is your statement and my statement is my statement. This does not cut
any butter. For, my car is my car and your car is your car,
but it does not follow from this that there are two cars.
Your car and my car can be the same car. Nor do differences
of place and time enable us to mark off different statement
tokens. It makes no difference whether you utter (34) (i) in
Jake's at 5:00 P.M. and I utter it in Harry's at 6:00 P.M.;
we have made the same statement. As the oddity of (34) (ii)
shows, statement contents do not occur in a place or at a
time. To put the matter grammatically, locative and temporal adverbs are predicated of verbs, not sentences. Of
course it does not follow from all this that there is no way
to distinguish what you state from what I state when we
utter (34) (i) under the conditions I have specified. But, it is
incumbent on anyone who maintains there is such a distinction to find a property which distinguishes the two.

It is possible for an illocutionary act we attempt to perform not to come off. An illocutionary act can misfire for
the sorts of reasons mentioned in Austin's doctrine of
infelicities. For example, we might think we are in a position to order Cohen around, but he politely informs us that
we are not. So, we cannot be said to have ordered him to
fetch the milk, but yet we did do something. For one, we
uttered a sentence. We can apply the type-token distinction
to our utterance acts. Both of us can perform the same
kind (type) of act of uttering a sentence. We can both utter
the same sentence. But your act (token) of uttering a sentence differs from my act of uttering the same sentence. Just
as a difference of person, place, or time enables us to distinguish your illocutionary act from mine, it enables us to
distinguish your utterance act from mine.

Let us suppose that in uttering (34) (i) I state that the
president is Jack Armstrong. Have I performed two different acts or only one act which can be described in two
different ways? Richard Cartwright argues that my utterance
act is identical to my illocutionary act, for I do not utter

(34) (i) *and then* state that the president is Jack Armstrong. Nor can it be such that I utter (34) (i) and *at the same time* state that the president is Jack Armstrong.[30] Although Cartwright's observations are correct, his claim that I have done only one act rather than two is not. If two things are identical, then whatever is a property of one is a property of the other. This principle, which will be employed again, is called the *indiscernibility of identicals*. There are properties which are true of my illocutionary act which are not true of my utterance act. For example, it is true of my act of stating that the president is Jack Armstrong that I have done it in uttering (34) (i). But it is not true of my uttering (34) (i) that I have done it in uttering (34) (i). Consequently, since my act of stating that the president is Jack Armstrong has a property that my act of uttering (34) (i) does not have, they are not identical.[31] It is easy to generalize this. That is, to find for any given illocutionary act and its corresponding utterance act a property true of one not true of the other. Hence illocutionary acts and utterance acts are not identical acts described in different ways.

Sentences are related to acts of uttering as illocutionary act contents are to illocutionary acts. What someone states is a statement (content) and what someone utters is a sentence. However, there is a difference. The type-token distinction applies to sentences, but not to illocutionary act contents. Consider the sentence within the quotation marks, 'However, there is a difference'. This sentence occurs twice on the page, once just now and once a few lines back. They are occurrences of the same sentence type, since they contain the same words in the same construction. But, they are different tokens, since they occur at different places on the page.

One might wonder whether sentence types or tokens can be identified with illocutionary act contents. They cannot. For if either are identical with illocutionary act contents, then whatever is true of either should be true of illocutionary act contents. But there are many things true of sentence

types or of sentence tokens not true of illocutionary act
contents. Suppose I say

(35)   The boy up the tree is an anarchist.

and in doing so make the statement that the boy up the
tree is an anarchist. What I utter is an English sentence,
but the statement I make is not English, but *in* English.
Moreover, the sentence I have uttered is present tense,
indicative, and active. But my statement is none of those,
though in uttering (35) I am talking about the present and
am saying something about the boy, rather than asking
something about him. The sentence token I have written
is composed of Roman letters in pica type and is approxi-
mately three inches long. But neither of these are true of
my statement. Moreover, what statement I make depends
upon what I mean by the words in (35) and to whom I am
referring in using the phrase 'The boy up the tree'. However, what sentence token I utter depends on neither of
these. Consequently, illocutionary act contents are not
identical to either sentence types or tokens.

Suppose you and I are talking about the same person, the
woman next door, who is a heart doctor and you utter (36)
(i) and I utter (36) (ii).

(36)   (i)   The woman next door is a cardiologist.

         (ii)   The woman next door is a heart doctor.

In uttering these sentences we make the same statement.
Moreover, the sentences we utter have the same meaning.
But the statement we make must be distinguished from the
meaning expressed by the sentences we utter, since there
are properties which our statement has which the meaning
of (36) (i) and (ii) does not have. For example, our statement can be affirmed, denied, substantiated, or disconfirmed, none of which are true of the meaning of (36) (i)
and (ii). Consequently, our statement and the meaning of
the sentences we utter are not identical. In general, then,
we must distinguish between the meanings of sentences and
illocutionary act contents. To accord with the usage of J. J.
Katz and W. V. O. Quine, who I shall discuss in the follow-

ing chapters, I shall call the meanings of sentences, *propositions*.

Suppose that I not only utter (36) (i) but also believe what I say. That is, I believe that the woman next door is a cardiologist. There are two things which must be distinguished in my belief. First, there is my state of believing and, second, what I believe. 'Belief', then, has an ambiguity similar to 'statement'. On the other hand it can be used to refer to the mental state of believing, and on the other to the object of the state. States of belief can be distinguished as to type and token. Suppose that you believe what you say in uttering (36) (ii). Both you and I, then, believe that the woman next door is a cardiologist. And, consequently, both of us are in the same sort of state. But, the particular state of belief that I am in is to be distinguished from the particular state of belief that you are in. That is, our states of belief exemplify different tokens of the same type. There is nothing, however, which distinguishes what you believe from what I believe and consequently the type-token distinction does not apply to the objects of our belief.

Russell calls mental states like believing, such as knowing, wishing, hoping, remembering, *propositional attitudes* and the objects of these attitudes *propositions*. That is, when someone believes something, what they believe is a proposition. To differentiate the two uses of 'proposition' we shall subscript it with an 'A' when it is used to refer to the objects of the propositional attitudes and with an 'M' when it is used to refer to the meanings of sentences.

Propositions$_A$ are to be distinguished from propositions$_M$, sentences, and illocutionary act contents, for it is possible that a child who knows no language has beliefs. And since to stand in some relation or other to a proposition$_M$, a sentence, or an illocutionary act content, one must know a language, a child who knows no language cannot stand in any relation to these things. Consequently, these cannot be identical to the object of the child's beliefs.

Sentences are used in performing illocutionary acts. But

ordinarily not any sentence can be used to perform a particular illocutionary act. Rather, there is a systematic relationship between the sentence we utter and the illocutionary act we intend to perform. For example, the sentence

(37)   I promise I will bring the poker chips.[32]

can be used to perform the illocutionary act of promising. The reason is that (37) contains the explicit performative verb phrase 'I promise'. However, it is not altogether clear what the relationship is between acts of promising and 'I promise' as it occurs in (37). One plausible explanation is that 'promise', when it occurs as a main verb in a first person, present tense, active, declarative sentence, has connected with its meaning a specification of the illocutionary act of promising. Here we are connecting the sentence type with an illocutionary act type by virtue of the meaning of a phrase in the sentence and the grammatical structure of the sentence. On the other hand, it might be a question of regularity that this phrase in a certain kind of construction is used to make promises. In this case the connection is between sentence tokens on particular occasions and particular acts. From these particular occasions a generalization is made connecting a sentence type with an illocutionary act type. Whichever of these is the case, we can say that the sentence type exemplified in (37) has the *illocutionary act potential* of a promise. That is, sentence tokens which are instances of (37) can be used to make a promise. In general the illocutionary act potential of a sentence type is the set of illocutionary acts which sentence tokens of that type standardly can be used to perform.

Many sentences do not bear their illocutionary act potential on their sleeve; they do not contain performative verbs. However, there are other aspects of a sentence which play a role in determining its illocutionary act potential—for example, tense, person and sentence type.[33]

(38)   John will be there.

is future tense, third person and indicative and for this

reason can be used to make a prediction. These sorts of features, however, can connect a sentence with more than one type of illocutionary act. For example,

(39)   I will be there.

can be used to make a promise or a prediction or to declare one's intention. We can conclude from this that what sentence is uttered on a particular occasion plays an important role in determining what illocutionary act, if any, a speaker intends to be performing or has been performed on that occasion.

But this does not mean that the context of utterance cannot play an overriding role in determining what illocutionary act is intended or has been performed.

(40)   Where are your shoes?

has the illocutionary act potential of a question. But a sergeant, seeing one of his men marching on the parade grounds in full dress uniform without his shoes, who utters (40), is not and should not be taken to be asking a question. Hence, it is not a necessary condition for the illocutionary act of x-ing to come off that a sentence with the illocutionary act potential of an x be uttered. But usually the sentence uttered and the illocutionary act performed are systematically related.

We have distinguished among the following:

(41)   (i)   utterance act tokens
       (ii)   utterance act types
       (iii)   illocutionary act tokens
       (iv)   illocutionary act types
       (v)   sentence types
       (vi)   sentence tokens
       (vii)   illocutionary act contents
       (viii)   illocutionary act potentials
       (ix)   propositions$_M$
       (x)   propositional attitude types
       (xi)   propositional attitude tokens
       (xii)   propositions$_A$

These distinctions are interesting in their own right, but also, hopefully they can help us answer some questions related to truth.

5   *Linguistic Objects and Truth*

Imagine the following conversation.
(42)   (i)   *A:* This country has fifty states.
         (ii)   *B:* That's true.
A has uttered a sentence and in doing so performed an illocutionary act. As a result, he has made a statement. Let us also suppose that *A* believes what he says. We have then:
(43)   (i)   *A*'s uttering 'This country has fifty states'
          (ii)   the uttering of 'This country has fifty states'
          (iii) *A*'s stating that this country has fifty states
          (iv)   stating that this country has fifty states
          (v)   the sentence type 'This country has fifty states'
          (vi)   the sentence token, (42) (i), which *A* utters
          (vii) the statement that this country has fifty states
          (viii) the illocutionary act potential of 'This country has fifty states'
          (ix)   the proposition$_M$ expressed by 'This country has fifty states'
          (x)   *A*'s believing that this country has fifty states
          (xi)   believing that this country has fifty states
          (xii) the proposition$_A$ that this country has fifty states

To which of these is *B* referring by using the demonstrative pronoun 'that'? And what property is *B* ascribing to it by saying that it is true? P. F. Strawson argues that these are bogus questions.[34] According to Strawson, 'is true' is never used ". . . to talk *about* something which is *what [A] said,* or the sentences [A] used in saying it."[35] If (42) (ii) is not about these, then what is it about? Strawson claims that it is not about anything, that ". . . the phrase 'is true' is not descriptive at all."[36] But, if it is not descriptive, in saying

(42) (ii), *B* cannot be ascribing a property to anything. What then is the point of *B*'s remark? Strawson's view is that in saying (42) (ii), *B* is confirming what *A* said, rather than making a statement about it.[37] In fact, he holds that 'That's true' can be replaced with 'I confirm it' without any important changes in meaning. Strawson compares the use of 'That's true' with the use of 'Ditto'.[38] Were *B* to say 'Ditto', he would not be referring to what *A* said, nor making a statement about it. Rather, he would be agreeing with what *A* said. Strawson contends that in order to understand 'Ditto' we must understand the illocutionary acts which it can be used to perform. Similarly, Strawson argues, to understand sentences which contain 'is true' we must understand their illocutionary act potential. And, according to Strawson, understanding this is to know all there is to know about truth.

It is true that in uttering (42) (ii), *B* is confirming what *A* said. But this does not establish Strawson's negative theses that in saying (42) (ii), *B* is not referring to anything nor predicating anything of it. There are two arguments against Strawson's negative theses. First, let us assume that there is no more to *B*'s remark than the illocutionary act he performs in making it. However, if that is all his utterance of (42) (ii) comes to, we can replace it with

(44)   I confirm it.

But then questions similar to the ones Strawson rejects can be applied to *B*'s uttering of (44). In uttering (44) to what is *B* referring by using the pronoun 'it'? And what property is *B* ascribing to it by confirming it? In fact to confirm something is to say that it is true. So, the second question is merely a variant of one of our old questions.

Strawson recognizes the first criticism and in reply argues that "anyone who says this is misled . . . by the fact that the verb 'confirm' takes a grammatical object; . . ."[39] Strawson's point is that not every occurrence of what is ostensibly a referring expression is used to refer. Consider, for example,

(45)   The average American family has 1.5 snooker tables.

In saying (45) I am not referring to some particular average American family who has 1.5 snooker tables. In fact I am not referring to anything, and no one who speaks English would be misled into thinking that I am. Suppose in a philosophical frame of mind we ask how one can tell whether someone who uses a definite description is using it to refer to anything? This is a difficult question which cannot be answered completely here. But, one way, which is surprisingly simple, is to ask. If I were to utter (45) and you were to ask me to which family I was referring or about which family I was talking, I would understand that you had misunderstood my remark. To explain it to you I would tell you about averages and how in this case I arrived at the 1.5 figure.

The question is whether 'it' in (44) functions as does 'the average American family' in (45). Suppose you overhear me say (44), but not the bit of conversation which has gone before. To find out what has gone on you might well ask me to what statement I am referring or what statement I am talking about. I would not think that you have misunderstood (44) and begin to explain to you what it is to confirm something. Rather, I would tell you to whose statement I was referring in saying (44). But, once it is established that in saying (44) a speaker is referring to something, we can go on to ask what property the speaker is ascribing to that thing in confirming it. And I think it will turn out that to confirm something is to say it is true. So Strawson's analysis of uttering (42) (ii) as confirming (42) (i) leads us back to the questions which Strawson rejects.

Secondly, Strawson's analysis is incomplete. Strawson draws our attention to the uses of sentences containing 'is true'. However, there are many other sentences which contain similar predicates. Consider the following conversations:

(46)   (i)   *A:* The president is soft on Eskimos.
        (ii)   *B:* That is a bit of an exaggeration.
or   (iii) *B:* That is an understatement.
or   (iv)   *B:* That fits the facts.

In uttering each of these sentences B is performing an illocutionary act. He is assessing what A said. In so doing he
is not only referring to what A said, but saying something
about it. The function of B's utterance of 'That's true'
seems to be like his utterance of (46) (ii)–(iv), rather than
like an utterance of 'Ditto'. Consequently, for Strawson to
make out his case he must show how in uttering (46) (ii)–(iv)
a speaker is doing no more than performing an illocutionary
act and in doing that he is not referring to anything nor
saying anything about it. But Strawson has not done so and
there is no reason to think that he could.

To what, then, is B referring in saying 'That's true', and
what property is he ascribing to it in saying it is true? It is
impossible to answer both questions here, and I will only
attempt an answer to the first. However, I want to answer
a generalization of this question: What are the sorts of
things we ordinarily take to be true or false? To put the
question in a more philosophical tone, what are *the bearers
of truth value?* Here we are not concerned with what things
could be the bearers of truth value in a reconstructed language, but rather with what things we take to be bearers
of truth value in speaking our ordinary non-technical language. It might well turn out that what we ordinarily take
to be true or false involves us in difficulties and that we
must diverge from our ordinary ways of talking in order to
have a coherent theory of truth. But to be in a position to
see that we should depart from our ordinary ways of talking, we must first know what we ordinarily take to be
bearers of truth value. Let us begin with Austin's view of
the matter.

Austin takes statements to be the bearer of truth value.[40]
As we have seen, 'statement' is ambiguous. It can be used
to refer either to an act of stating or to what is stated.
Which of these Austin has in mind is not clear, though he
talks of "stating truly" and in discussing statements as the
bearers of truth values, he says that 'statement' has ". . . the
merit of clearly referring to the historic use of a sentence

by an utterer."[41] The historic use of a sentence by an utterer is not what is stated, but is a particular act of stating. So Austin seems to take (43) (iii) to be the bearer of truth value. But can it be of A's act of stating that this country has fifty states that B is saying that it is true? I think not. For we can say things of acts of stating which we cannot say of the bearers of truth value. Compare:

(47)   (i) A's statement is hurried.

(ii) A's statement is true.

(iii)   *A's statement is hurried and true.[42]

In saying (47) (i) we are referring to A's act of stating. If in saying (47) (ii) we were referring to A's act of stating as well, then it should be possible to say (47) (iii) without oddity. But, it is not. Consequently, in saying (47) (ii) we are not referring to A's act of stating. And, thus, in saying (42) (ii) B is not saying of A's act of stating that it is true. Similar arguments can be used to show that (43) (i), (ii), (iv), (x), and (xi) cannot be the bearers of truth value. And since the illocutionary act potential of a sentence is the set of illocutionary act types which the sentence can be used to perform, it cannot be what is true or false.

In addition, the proposition$_M$ expressed by 'This country has fifty states' cannot be what is true or false. Let us suppose that in uttering (42) (i) A is referring to the United States and that on another occasion C utters (42) (i) referring to Mexico. Since A and C have uttered instances of the same sentence type, which is unambiguous, the meaning of the sentence A uttered is identical to the meaning of the sentence C uttered. But what A said is true and what C said is false. Let 'm' designate the meaning of the sentence A uttered and 'n' the meaning of the sentence C uttered. Thus, $m = n$. And on the hypothesis that the meaning of the sentence A uttered has the property of being true, m has the property of being true. It follows, then, that n has the property of being true. But, what C said is false and, hence, n, the meaning of the sentence C uttered, is false. Thus, the meaning of the sentence A and C utter is both true and false. Consequently, our hypothesis leads to inconsistency and hence, is false. That is, the proposition m expressed by the sentence A uttered is not what is true. This does not show, of course, that we can never take a proposition$_M$ to be the bearer of truth value, but only that in this case we cannot take it to be so.

In uttering 42 (ii) is B referring to the sentence type of which (42) (i) is an instance? An argument parallel to the one above shows that this is not the case. The only change we need make is to have 'm' designate the sentence type A utters and 'n' the sentence type C utters. Since they have uttered instances of the same sentence type, $m = n$. Moreover, by hypothesis m has the property of being true. It follows, then, that n has the property of being true. But what C said is false and hence, n, the sentence type C utters, is false. Thus, the sentence type A and C utter is both true and false. Consequently, our hypothesis leads to inconsistency and is false. That is, the sentence type A utters is not the bearer of truth value. As with proposition$_M$, this does not show that no sentence types are the bearers of truth value, only that the sentence type, (42) (i), is not.

This leaves us with (43) (vi), the sentence token which A utters, (43) (vii), the statement that this country has fifty states, and (43) (xii), the proposition$_A$ that this country has fifty states. To which of these is B referring? There is no doubt that we do say of someone's statement, what is stated, that it is true or false. In this case, then, B is referring to what A states. Without much change in what is meant B could have said 'What you state is true' or 'Your statement is true'. In this case, then, we can take B to be referring to what A states. As well, we could take B to be referring to the belief that this country has fifty states, for we do say of beliefs that they are true or false and without much change in what is meant B could have said 'The belief you express is true'. Thus, in saying 'That's true' the reference of *B*'s use of 'that' is ambiguous. It could be either to the statement *A* makes or to the belief *A* expresses to which *B* is referring and of which he is predicating truth.

There are other things of which truth and falsity are predicated which are not brought out by (42). We say of other illocutionary contents, such as what is claimed, maintained, or concluded, that they are true or false. However, not all illocutionary act contents can be true or false—for example, questions, promises, and motions. And there are other illocutionary acts, such as apologizing, welcoming, and appointing, which do not have any illocutionary act contents. As well, there are objects of propositional attitude, besides beliefs, to which we attribute truth and falsity, for example, thoughts, opinions, and doubts. However, not all objects of the propositional attitudes can be true or false. For instance, when I wonder about what the weather will be like tomorrow or wish that it will hail, what I wonder about or wish cannot be true or false. So, we do not ascribe truth and falsity to all illocutionary act contents or propositions$_A$, but only to some of them.

Are there any cases where we ordinarily take propositions$_M$, sentence types, or sentence tokens to be the bearers of truth value? The arguments I used above only show that in some cases we cannot take a proposition$_M$ or a sentence type to be what is true or false. This does not show that there are no cases in which they are bearers of truth value. I think, however, that there is a quite general, but simple argument which rules out propositions$_M$ from consideration. We never say that they are true or false. Notice the oddity of

(48) *The meaning of *A*'s sentence is true.

In contrast, there are cases, although a bit archaic, where we do seem to attribute truth or falsity to the sentence a speaker utters, rather than to the statement he makes.

(49) (i) *A*'s words are true.

(ii) Truer words were never spoken.

And there are cases where it appears that the only thing we can attribute truth and falsity to is the sentence a speaker utters. Let us reconsider the Israel atomic bomb case. I wander before television cameras set up for an interview with the Israeli ambassador. The reporters, taking me to be the ambassador, ask me how many atomic bombs Israel has. And thinking that this is the impromptu skit I am to be in, I say

(50) Israel has several bombs.

Of course, I have no idea whether they have any bombs and moreover, I do not know that I am being asked seriously how many they have. Let us even suppose that I do not know that Israel is a country. Consequently, I have not made a statement to the press or to anyone else. Hence it cannot be what I stated which is true. But in the example we are considering, what I said is true. What have I said? We must be careful how we put this. I have not said *that* Israel has several bombs. It would be misleading to report what I said using indirect quotation. For this would imply that I know what Israel is and I meant what I said to be taken seriously. Rather, I said 'Israel has several bombs'. And what I said is true. But, what is true in this case? It cannot be what I stated, for I did not make a statement.

And it cannot be the sentence type. Suppose that you, too, are an actor who is to be in a television skit. Just as I did, you pick the wrong studio. But you walk before the television cameras set up not for the Israeli ambassador, but for the police commissioner who is to report on Israel Schwartzkopf, an alleged mad bomber. Thinking that you are the police commissioner, the reporters ask you how many bombs Israel has. And believing this is the skit you are to be in, but having no idea who or what Israel is, you utter (50). You are immediately discovered. The police commissioner is then interviewed. When asked how many bombs Israel has, he says that Israel has no bombs. It turns out that what the police commissioner said is true, but what you said is false. Israel Schwartzkopf is not a mad bomber, but only a baker. Moreover, you did not make a statement to the press; you were in no position to do so.

Nor did you say that Israel has several bombs, since you had no idea who or what Israel was. Rather, you said, 'Israel has several bombs' and what you said is false. So in both examples you and I have uttered instances of the same sentence type. Let '*m*' designate this sentence type. But, what you said is false and what I said is true. To what does 'what you said' and 'what I said' refer? It cannot be our statements, since we did not make any. Let us suppose they refer to *m*. Consequently, we are attributing truth and falsity to *m*. It follows that *m* is both true and false, which is absurd. There is a way to avoid this undesirable consequence. We could take 'what you said' to refer to *m* and 'what I said' to refer to something else or vice-versa. But, then, in these exactly parallel examples we would be taking different things to be the bearers of truth value. I can see no good reason for doing so. We can avoid these difficulties altogether by giving up sentence types as the bearers of truth value in these examples. Instead, we can take the referent of 'what you said' to be the sentence token you uttered and of 'what I said' to be the sentence token I uttered. Since these are different, no absurdity arises. Consequently, there are cases in which we seem to take sentence tokens to be the bearers of truth value.

We have shown that there are contexts in which it appears that we ordinarily take propositions$_A$, sentence tokens, and illocutionary act contents to be the bearers of truth value. Perhaps parsimony should lead us to drop illocutionary act contents in favor of sentence tokens as the bearers of truth value, for whenever a speaker performs an illocutionary act and produces, thereby, a content of this act which can be a bearer of truth value, the speaker has, also, uttered a sentence token which could be the bearer of truth value. On this view, in saying 'That's true', *B* is not referring to *A*'s statement, but to the sentence token 'This country has fifty states'. In general, then, the thesis is that when speakers ascribe truth and falsity to something, they do not ascribe it to illocutionary act contents, but to sentence tokens. But against this, one should notice that B could, as well, have said

(51) (i) What you stated is true.

   (ii) Your statement is true.

And in using these sentences, B would be referring to A's statement, what A stated, which is an illocutionary act content. Anyone who argues that sentence tokens, rather than illocutionary act contents, are the bearers of truth value would have to show that, despite appearances to the contrary, in uttering (51) (i) or (ii), B would not be referring to an illocutionary act content. But it seems unlikely that this could be done. For, if B were to utter (51) (i) or (ii), there are contexts in which it would be appropriate to ask him to what statement he was referring. And most probably he would be able to tell us. So, the use of 'what you stated' and 'your statement' in (51) (i) and (ii) is quite different from the use of 'the average American family' in (45). They are referring expressions which are used to refer to what is stated. Consequently, illocutionary act contents are among the things to which speakers ascribe truth and falsity. And though frugality is a desirable virtue in determining what linguistic entities speakers take there to be, we cannot dispense with illocutionary act contents in favor of sentence tokens.

We have not exhausted the sorts of things to which we attribute truth and falsity. Suppose I say

(52) One billion years ago it was true that there was water on earth.

Now that there was water on earth was true before there were any languages or beliefs, God aside. And consequently, what was true cannot be identical to an illocutionary act content, sentence, or proposition$_A$. Moreover, there are truths which have yet to be discovered and thus which are neither believed nor stated. And consequently, such truths also cannot be identical to illocutionary act contents, sentences, or propositions$_A$. What, then, in these cases are the bearers of truth value? To fill this role philosophers have hypothesized as the bearers of truth value abstract entities which are called *propositions*. To distinguish this use of 'propositions' from the others I shall subscript it with a 'T'. There are many philosophers who regard propositions$_T$ to be the sole bearers of truth value. Thus, when someone makes a statement what is stated is held to be a proposition$_T$. And when someone has a belief what is believed is also taken to be a proposition$_T$. That is, those illocutionary contents and those objects of the propositional attitudes to which truth and falsity are attributed are really propositions$_T$. And hence, when we say that a statement or a belief is true or false what is true or false is actually a proposition$_T$. However, this does not cover the skit about the bomb in which we appear to ascribe truth and falsity to sentence tokens. Even in this case there are philosophers who would hold that the sentence tokens uttered express propositions$_T$ and that it is these propositions which are the bearers of truth value and not the sentences uttered. All this needs argument and raises questions about the interrelationship among the different sorts of entities discussed which goes well beyond the scope of this book. We shall leave open the questions whether propositions$_T$ are the sole bearers of truth value and whether the objects of propositional attitudes and the contents of illocutionary acts can be assimilated to propositions$_T$.

There are entities to which truth and falsity are attributed and entities to which they are not attributed. In the former fall illocutionary act contents, sentence tokens, propositions$_A$, and propositions$_T$, and in the latter illocutionary acts, utterance acts, illocutionary act potentials, propositional attitudes, and propositions$_M$. I have not shown that sentence types fall into either of these classes. In discussing W. V. O. Quine's views on language in Chapter V, I will again take up the question whether sentence types are the bearers of truth value. But, the spirit with which Quine approaches the question is quite different from the spirit of this chapter. He is not concerned with what linguistic entities our ordinary language commits us to, but with what linguistic entities our using language for scientific purposes commits us to. However, I shall postpone discussing whether sentence types can be the bearers of truth value until I consider Quine's theory of language.

6 Illocutionary Act Potential and Meaning

One of the philosophical payoffs in describing the uses of language has been its bearing on truth. Some philosophers hold that there is a close connection between the meaning of some words and the uses of language. There are those who connect the meaning of some words with illocutionary act types.[43] As we have seen, Strawson claims that in saying

(53) That's true.

in response to what someone else has said, what we are doing is confirming, underwriting, or agreeing with what has been said. Hence, in uttering the following sentences we are doing the same thing we are doing when we utter (53).

(54)   (i)   I confirm what you say.
        (ii) I agree with what you say.
        (iii) I admit what you say.
        (iv) I underwrite what you say.

All this is true enough. But it is a mistake to hold, as some do, that (52) means the same as (54) (i–iv). A further step toward error is taken when it is noticed that replacing 'true' with 'red' changes the illocutionary act potential of (53). It is incorrectly concluded that 'true' does not differ in meaning from the explicit verb phrases in (54). In fact Strawson argues that 'I confirm' can be substituted for phrases containing 'true' or 'is true' in a good many cases without any change of meaning.[44]

Were this view correct, one would think it would apply to other explicit performative verb phrases as well. When I say

(55) This is worth $5.

what I could be doing is assessing or evaluating something.

And if 'skinny' were substituted for 'worth $5', it would change the illocutionary act potential of (55).

But it certainly is not the case that 'worth $5' means the same as the explicit performative phrases in

(56)   (i)   I evaluate that to be worth $5.

      (ii)   I assess that at $5.

Nor would it make sense to substitute these phrases for 'worth $5' in (55).

J. R. Searle has a more direct argument against Strawson's position.[45] Consider the following two sentences

(57)   (i)   I believe that it is true that Sam sank the nine.

      (ii)   It is true that Sam sank the nine.

In both (57) (i) and (ii) 'true' means the same. The thesis we are considering maintains that we can replace 'it is true', in (56) (ii) with 'I confirm', without any change in meaning. But, then we should be able to do it in (57) (i). Obviously, we cannot.

(58)   I believe that I confirm that Sam sank the nine.

means something quite different from (57) (i). (57) (i) expresses a belief about Sam's sinking the nine whereas (58) expresses a belief about the person who utters (58). We can conclude that 'is true' or 'true' does not mean the same as 'I confirm' or any of the other explicit performative verb phrases in (54).

There is some truth in the above view which should not be overlooked.

(59)   What he said is true.

can be used to perform the same illocutionary act as

(60)   I confirm what he said.

If we replace 'true' with 'stupid' in (59), then the resulting sentence does not have the same illocutionary act potential as (60). Hence, 'true' does contribute to the illocutionary act potential of (59). As we have seen, difficulties arise when it is thought that (59) and (60) mean the same or when 'true' is thought to mean the same as 'I confirm'. The question which must be answered is how 'true' contributes to the illocutionary act potential of (58). We can generalize the point made here by example. If we cut up our descriptions of illocutionary act types fine enough, for almost every word, we can ask what contribution it makes to the illocutionary act potential of the sentence in which it is contained. For example,

(61)   (i)   Close the door.
       (ii)   Close the window.

can be used to make two different requests. Hence, 'door' and 'window' make different contributions to the illocutionary act potential of (61) (i) and (61) (ii).

A theory advanced by W. P. Alston provides an analysis of 'meaning' and 'illocutionary act potential' which attempts to show how they are related and which in addition is supposed to move us closer to a solution of the problem raised above.[46] Alston holds that two sentences mean the same if and only if they can be used to perform the same illocutionary acts. He puts it in the following way:

(62) S_1 means $S_2' = {}_{df}' S_1$ and S_2 have the same illocutionary act potential.[47]

Sameness of word meaning is also dependent on sameness of illocutionary act potential.

(63) W_1 means $W_2' = {}_{df}' W_1$ and W_2 can be substituted for each other in a wide range of sentences without altering the illocutionary act potentials of those sentences.[48]

As Alston admits, these two definitions cannot tell us what contribution the meaning of a word makes to the illocutionary act potential of a sentence. But, it is his hope that they begin to solve this problem and that at least they show the relationship between 'meaning' and 'illocutionary act potential'. I am afraid, though, that both these hopes must be dashed. Alston's definition of word meaning is circular. In order to show this it is necessary to discuss his treatment of illocutionary act potential, since his definition of 'meaning' depends upon this notion.

In our earlier discussion we have seen that the illocutionary act potential of a sentence is that set of illocutionary acts which a speaker standardly can perform using that sentence. Hence, the problem of determining the illocutionary act potential of a sentence is equivalent to determining what illocutionary acts a speaker standardly can perform in using the sentence. According to Alston, for a speaker to perform an illocutionary act in uttering an appropriate sentence the speaker must recognize that certain conditions apply to his uttering that sentence. For example, a speaker asks a hearer to close the door only if the speaker regards the following conditions as being relevant to what he says:

(64)　(i)　There is a door in the immediate vicinity.

　　　(ii)　The door is not closed.

　　　(iii)　It is possible for the hearer to close the door.

　　　(iv)　The speaker has an interest in getting the door closed.[49]

It should not be thought that these conditions must be true in order for the speaker to be asking the hearer to close the door. It is only that the speaker regards them as being relevant to what he is saying.

This can be more easily understood if we consider the negations of these conditions arising as criticisms of what the speaker said. Let us imagine that the person to whom the order is given says

(65)　The door is closed.

Now, I think we would take the speaker to be giving an order only if he recognizes that what his hearer said is relevant to what he said. Hence, this shows that in order for a speaker in uttering

(66)　Close the door.

to be giving an order the speaker must recognize that (66) is not to be uttered unless the conditions in (64) hold.

The above discussion relates to illocutionary act potential in the following way.

(67)　A sentence, S, can be used to perform the illocutionary acts, A, if and only if speakers in uttering s recognize a set of conditions, C, to apply to their utterance of S.

We can take it that

(68) Two sentences have the same illocutionary act potential if and only if the same conditions, *C,* apply to them.

We are now in a position to show that Alston's definition of word meaning is circular. Let us take as our example of a specification of meaning

(69) 'Bachelor' means 'unmarried male'.

According to (63), this is true if and only if 'bachelor' and 'unmarried male' can be substituted in a great many sentences without changing their illocutionary act potential. For example, in substituting in

(70) Tell the bachelor to come into the room.

we obtain

(71) Tell the unmarried male to come into the room.

Now for Alston's view to be correct we must be able to determine that (70) and (71) have the same illocutionary act potential. This amounts to determining that the same conditions must be recognized by a speaker to govern the utterance of both of these sentences. Moreover, and most importantly, we must be able to do this without relying on the truth of (69). For to do so would make the whole enterprise circular. But I hope to show that we must do so.

Using the analysis developed above, a condition which a speaker must recognize applies to his utterance of (70) is

(72) The bachelor is not in the room.

and a condition on (71) is

(73) The unmarried male is not in the room.

But these are two different sentences. The question is whether they express the same conditions. They do if

(74) 'Bachelor' means the same as 'unmarried male'.

This however, is tantamount to assuming the truth of (69). Perhaps, a way out is to apply Alston's definition of sentence meaning to (72) and (73). This would allow us to say that they are the same conditions. But this puts us back in the soup. In order for this definition to provide us with a criterion for the synonymy of (72) and (73) we must be able to determine that they have the same illocutionary act potential. However, difficulties arise similar to those above in determining this. A speaker in uttering (72) must recognize that this sentence is not to be uttered, unless

(75)   The speaker believes that the bachelor is not in the room.

Similarly, a speaker in uttering (73) must recognize that this sentence is not to be uttered unless

(76)   The speaker believes that the unmarried man is not in the room.

Once again these sentences are different and hence, we have no way of determining that (72) and (73) are synonymous. In turn, we cannot determine whether substituting 'bachelor' for 'unmarried male' changes the illocutionary act potential of (70). Consequently, we have no way of determining whether (69) is true. With a little bit of imagination we could find two conditions for (75) and (76), respectively, which differed only by virtue of the fact that one contained 'bachelor' and the other contained 'unmarried male'. We could, I suppose, continue to do this ad infinitum. But, this would not allow us to determine the truth of (69). It is possible, of course, anywhere along the way to assume this to be true in order to determine that two of our conditions were synonymous. But this would be circular. I am afraid that Alston's analysis of word meaning in terms of illocutionary act potential is not much help.

Alston's definition of sentence meaning is also open to criticism. It follows from Alston's definition that if two sentences have the same illocutionary act potential, then they have the same meaning. I take it that if two sentences are synonymous, then whatever follows from the proposition expressed by one would follow from the proposition expressed by the other. The following sentence

(77)   Schultz eats lox.

can be used to state that Schultz eats lox. Consequently, (77) has the same illocutionary act potential as

(78)   I state Schultz eats lox.

From (77) it trivially follows that Schultz eats lox. But no such thing follows from (78). Thus, (77) and (78) do not mean the same. Consequently, either the two sentences cannot be used to perform the same illocutionary act or Alston's definition is incorrect. Since the two sentences can be used to perform the same illocutionary act, we can conclude that Alston's definition of sentence meaning is inadequate. Consequently, the meaning of a word or a sentence cannot be specified in terms of the illocutionary act potential of sentences.

This chapter has been devoted to a discussion of Austin's theory of speech acts and its purported relationship with truth and meaning. There has been no discussion of the light an analysis of particular speech acts can have on philosophical problems. For example, Austin holds in "Other Minds" that 'I know' has a performatory aspect.[50] It would be of great value to the theory of knowledge to explore the similarity and dissimilarity between epistemic qualifiers like 'I know', 'I believe', 'I remember' and explicit performative verb phrases.[51] There are other branches of philosophy where illocutionary act types abound—for example, aesthetics and ethics. The hope is that analysis of speech act types in these fields will illuminate some long-standing philosophical problems.

III

Innate and Unconscious Linguistic Knowledge

Introduction

In Chapter II we discussed the different uses of language, in particular using the sentences of our language to perform illocutionary and perlocutionary acts. But in order to be able to perform these acts we must be able to understand the sentences of our language. What enables us to understand them? There is no obvious answer to this question. We do not learn them one by one; there are too many of them, in fact an infinite number. Many, and hopefully, if you are not to die of boredom, most of the sentences I have written and will write are sentences you have never read before. How are you able to understand these novel sentences? It is often said that we understand them by analogy. But saying this is saying precisely nothing, or almost nothing. Supposedly we understand novel sentences on the basis of their similarity with sentences which we have heard and understood before. However, this is part of the problem, not part of the solution. What is the similarity among

(1) Abigail believes that Benjamin loves her.
(2) It is believed by Abigail that Benjamin loves her.
(3) That Benjamin loves her is believed by Abigail.

These three sentences do not *look* similar, though they mean the same.

Noam Chomsky has devised a theory which purports to offer part of an explanation for our problem.[1] He claims that we are able to utter and understand the sentences of our language, because we have unconscious or tacit knowledge of the rules of our language.[2] According to Chomsky, when we hear or utter a sentence of our language, we use the rules of our language in understanding and uttering the sentence, of course without being aware that we are doing so.[3] There are two questions which arise here. First, what are the rules of which we are supposed to have unconscious or tacit knowledge? Second, how do we employ these rules in speaking our language? Chomsky maintains that the initial task of the linguist is to answer the first question, since an answer to the second question presupposes an answer to the first. On Chomsky's view a *generative grammar* of a language is the linguist's description of the rules which speakers of that language know unconsciously.

Children are not born knowing the rules of their language. How do they come to know these rules? There appears to be a simple answer. They hear a language spoken, attempt to imitate it, are corrected when they make mistakes, and, thereby, after a year or two learn the rules of their language. Chomsky argues that this answer is wrong on several counts. The simple story obscures some important details. The rub is in the 'thereby'. It suggests that experience, imitation, and correction are all that is required to learn a language. Chomsky claims that there is more to learning a language than meets the ear. According to Chomsky, our unconscious linguistic knowledge goes beyond what we hear as children at our mother's knee or any other joint. What more is there to the story? Chomsky holds that the gap between linguistic experience and acquired linguistic knowledge is bridged by the innate linguistic knowledge with which children are born.[4] Innate linguistic knowledge should not be confused with unconscious knowledge of linguistic rules. The former is what enables the latter to be learned. The linguistic rules of which we have unconscious knowledge are rules of particular languages. But, it is clear that a child is not born with knowledge about any particular language. Rather, Chomsky claims that children are born with knowledge about human languages in general, or to use a little linguistic jargon, knowledge about *linguistic universals*. Of course, such knowledge is unconscious. Children, at least the children I have met, are not aware that they know anything about language. Chomsky's second goal, then, is to describe our innate linguistic knowledge. The linguist's description of this knowledge is called *linguistic theory* or *universal grammar*.

This brief description raises many questions of interest to philosophers, linguists, and psychologists. Since it is impossible to discuss all of them, I shall concentrate my attention on three which are of special interest to philosophers: namely, that speakers of a language have unconscious knowledge of linguistic rules, that they use these rules in understanding and uttering sentences of their language, and lastly, that they have innate linguistic knowledge which in part enables them to learn these rules.

1 Linguistic Facts

Let us backtrack a bit. Since Abigail's love for Benjamin, like any love, is complicated, we will begin with a simpler example. Suppose that a speaker of English, S, believes that Dixon stopped the war and wants to communicate this belief to a hearer, H, also a native speaker of English. The most natural way for S to do this is to utter seriously

(4) Dixon stopped the war.

Here we are faced with the following questions:

(5) What enables S to express his belief by uttering (4)?

(6) What enables H to understand (4)?

Why are these questions important? Hopefully, by answering generalized versions of these questions we will be able to explain how speakers use and understand the sentences of their language. This in turn will be part of an explanation of how speakers communicate with one another. But we can begin with (5) and (6). In order for S to express his belief by uttering (4) and for H to understand (4), both must know a good deal about this sentence. For example, they must know what the sentence means and they know this by virtue of knowing the meaning and the grammatical relationships of the words in the sentence. That is, they must not believe that 'war' means *peace* and that 'the war' in (4) bears the same grammatical relationship to 'stopped' as it does in

(7)   The war stopped Dixon.

Moreover, they must know that (4) and

(8)   Hixon copped the door.

do not sound the same. The upshot of these examples is that S and H can speak and understand their language because they know certain semantical, syntactical, and phonological facts about sentences of their language.

Do speakers know these sorts of facts about the sentences of their language? Clearly, speakers do not know anything specific about sentences they have neither uttered nor heard before. What sense, then, can be made of the claim that speakers have knowledge about sentences of their language? I suppose it can be put conditionally. If a speaker is presented with a sentence of his language, then he will be able to determine certain facts about the sentence. And by doing so, he will come to know these facts. However, speakers are not normally 'presented' with sentences of their language, even when engaged in conversation. Rather, linguists present sentences to speakers and ask questions about them. It might be argued that even then most speakers, not being trained in linguistics, do not know the answers to the linguist's questions. This argument only has force if the linguist must phrase his question in technical vocabulary, but he need not do so. For example, most speakers do not know whether the grammatical relation between 'the war' and 'stopped' is the same in (4) and (7), for most speakers do not know what 'grammatical relation' means. However, the linguist can ask his informant whether he would be saying that it is the *war* which is stopped were he to utter (4) or (7). By asking questions of this sort he can find out what speakers know about sentences which he presents to them and, thereby, discover what they know in general about sentences of their language—on the assumption, of course, that the sentences he presents to them are a fair sample of the sentence types of the speaker's language. Obviously, there are difficult cases where speakers cannot determine these sorts of facts. But I imagine that for most sentences there are no problems.

There are many facts we are able to determine about sentences and about parts of sentences of English. In the above we have only scratched the surface. Let us begin with the syntactic facts. First, we know that (4) is grammatical in contrast to

(9)   *War the Dixon stopped.

Second, we recognize that (4) can be divided into constituents or parts in the following way:

(10)   [(Dixon)] [(stopped) (the war)]

rather than into

(11)   [(Dixon) (stopped) (the)] [(war)]

Third, we know that 'Dixon' and 'war' are of the same type, they are both nouns, and that 'stop' is of a different type, a verb. Of course, we might not know that 'Dixon' and 'war' are nouns and that 'stop' is a verb. What we do know is that the former two occur in different positions in sentences than does 'stop'. Fourth, we know that in (4) 'Dixon' is the subject and 'the war' is the object of the sentence. Fifth, we know that (4) can be paraphrased by

(12)   (a)   The war was stopped by Dixon.
         (b)   What Dixon stopped was the war.
         (c)   It was the war Dixon stopped.
         (d)   What was stopped by Dixon was the war.

Notice the reason that these sentences are paraphrases of one another is not because there are different but synonymous words in each of the sentences. Rather, the paraphrase relation rests upon the fact that in each of the sentences 'the war', 'Dixon', and 'stopped' bear the same grammatical relationship to one another. We shall call such paraphrases *structural paraphrases*.

There are additional facts we are able to determine about sentences of our language not illustrated by the examples above. For example, we know that

(13)   They are flying planes

is ambiguous. The ambiguity of (13) is due to the ambiguous structure of the sentence rather than its containing an ambiguous word. It is *structurally ambiguous* in two ways.

(14)   (a)   They [(are flying) planes]
(b)   They [are (flying planes)]

We know, then, the following *syntactic* facts about many of the sentences of our language. Specifying these facts in the linguist's technical vocabulary, we know:

(15)   (a)   whether the sentence is grammatical
(b)   what its constituent structure is
(c)   to what grammatical categories the words and phrases in the sentence belong
(d)   what grammatical relationship holds among the constituents of the sentence
(e)   whether another sentence is a structural paraphrase of the sentence
(f)   whether the sentence is structurally ambiguous.

We also know something about the *semantic* features of sentences in addition to their syntactic features. For example, we know that

(16)   Dixon halted the belligerency.

is synonymous with (4), that

(17)   The number five stopped the fact

is meaningless, and

(18)   Sam is warm

is ambiguous where the ambiguity turns on the meaning of 'warm', rather than on the structural characteristics of (18). In addition we can recognize the difference among:

(19) (a) Cohen is the vicar's cousin.
     (b) Cohen who is the vicar's cousin is the vicar's cousin.
     (c) Cohen who is the vicar's cousin is not the vicar's cousin.

Using traditional philosophical terminology, we are able to recognize *synthetic, analytic,* and *contradictory sentences.* It does not follow from our having this ability that we are able to recognize, and thereby, come to know, that (19) (a) is synthetic, (19) (b) analytic, and (19) (c) contradictory. For we might not know what 'analytic', 'synthetic', and 'contradictory' mean. Despite this we shall specify what we know about the semantic facts of our language using traditional linguistic and philosophical terminology. We know, then, whether a sentence is:

(20) (a) analytic
     (b) synthetic
     (c) contradictory
     (d) synonymous with another sentence
     (e) meaningless
     (f) ambiguous

This list contains many features which are of obvious interest to philosophers.

The last set of facts which speakers know about sentences of their language is *phonological.* We can recognize stress patterns within phrases:

(21) (a) [light] [house keeper]
     (b) [light house] [keeper]

and within words:

(22) (a) export (verb)
     (b) export (noun)
(23) (a) photograph
     (b) photographer

In addition we know that there is a sound difference between:

(24) (a) stab
     (b) stub
(25) (a) pat
     (b) pap

There are many other phonological facts we know about our language. However, phonological facts have only a marginal connection at present to philosophical problems. For this reason they will not be discussed further.

I said at the outset that linguistic knowledge enables us to speak and understand our language. Knowledge of some of the facts listed above clearly plays such a role. For example, were we not able to distinguish between 'stub' and 'stab', we would not be able to understand the difference in meaning between:

(26) (a) He stubbed his toe.
     (b) He stabbed his toe.

Similarly, our knowledge of grammatical relations enables us to understand the difference in meaning between:

(27) (a) Amos kissed Melinda.
     (b) Melinda kissed Amos.

Lastly, in order to understand the ambiguity of

(28) Hand me the pot.

we must know what 'pot' means. Not all our linguistic knowledge has such an obvious bearing on our linguistic ability. What role does our knowledge that a sentence is grammatical play in being able to speak and understand our language? Let us suppose that we want to express the belief that one and only one dog is crossing the street. If we said

(29) * The dog are crossing the street.

we would not be expressing our belief perspicuously. We might well be misunderstood. Our failure would arise because we uttered a string in which the subject and verb do not agree in number. It is unclear whether we are expressing a belief that one and only one dog is crossing the street or that many dogs are crossing the street. In general an inability to recognize such errors would greatly increase the difficulty of expressing ourselves accurately and would reduce the chances of our being understood.

The facts listed above have been presented as if they were unrelated to one another. But this is far from the truth. Our knowledge of both semantic and phonological facts depends upon our knowledge of syntactic facts. Proper stress, for example, cannot be assigned to (21) (a) or (b) unless we know the constituent structure of these phrases. And we would be unable to recognize that

(30) Hand me the pot which is made of copper.

is unambiguous, if we did not know the grammatical relationship between 'pot' and the following relative clause. Consequently, any theory which attempts to account for the facts enumerated above must explain the relationship among them.

2 Unconscious Linguistic Knowledge

I have listed many facts we know about some sentences in English. It might seem that all we need do in order to specify what we know about English is to complete the list of the facts we know about the sentences of our language. However, this is wrong for two reasons. First, a list of this sort cannot explain how we know these facts. For example, it cannot explain how we know that 'Dixon' bears the same relationship to all the sentences in (12), even though these sentences are structurally dissimilar. Second, and most importantly, it cannot in principle be completed. It will not do merely to list the sentences we have heard and the facts we know about them. Our ability to determine facts about the sentences of our language extends beyond this. For example, we are able to determine whether almost any string of English words is grammatical, even if we have never heard it before. We face two problems. First, how do we know what we do about the sentences of our language and second, how can we describe this knowledge?

Illumination can be cast on these problems by examining a similar case in another area of human knowledge. Let us suppose that we have a random list of fifty numbers. Pointing to each of the numbers in turn, we ask a child what number is the successor of the number indicated. In each case we obtain the correct answer; we could say that the child knows only what number is the successor of each of the numbers on our list. But, is is obvious that the child knows more than this; on the basis of his responses we can conclude that for any given number he knows what number follows it. How does he know this? He cannot have learned the successor of each number, for the set of numbers is infinite. What, then, does the child know which allows him to determine the successor of any given number? A plausible account of what the child knows is that he has learned the following rule

(31)   Where x and y are numbers to find the successor, y, of x add 1 to x.

On a given occasion, when asked for the successor of some number, the child applies this rule in order to obtain the correct result. We say, then, that the child knows the successor of each number on our list because he knows (31) and obtains the correct answers to our questions by using this rule. Hence, (31) specifies part of the child's arithmetical knowledge and explains how the child knows what he does on a particular occasion. Against this one might argue that the child does not know (31), because he cannot tell us what he knows. To meet this objection, we might say that the child has unconscious knowledge of (31).

According to Chomsky, a similar account can be given of our linguistic knowledge. As we have seen, we know a good many facts about the sentences of our language. Chomsky claims that we know them because we have ". . . mastered and internalized . . . a grammar that expresses our knowledge of our language."[5] That is, in learning a grammar what we learn are sets of syntactical, phonological, and semantical rules. To understand a sentence of our language, we use these rules to determine certain facts about the sentence. And our knowledge of these facts in turn enables us to understand it. All this goes on in those inner reaches inaccessible to eye or ear. We are neither conscious that these rules exist, nor that we employ them to determine linguistic facts, nor that our knowledge of these facts enables us to understand these sentences.[6] Although direct access is not available to these rules, Chomsky claims that the linguist can describe them. In Chomsky's view a grammar *is* a description of our unconscious knowledge of the rules of our language.

Much confusion has arisen about Chomsky's theory on this point. Many have supposed that grammars explain how speakers use and understand their language. Chomsky makes it quite clear that this is a misinterpretation of his views.

> [A grammar] attempts to characterize in the most neutral possible terms the knowledge of the language that provides the basis for actual use by a speaker-hearer.[7]

To avoid confusion Chomsky distinguishes between a speaker's unconscious knowledge of his language, *competence,* and a speaker's use of this knowledge in speaking his language, *performance.* This distinction can be brought out more clearly by considering our arithmetic example. (31) describes what the child knows which enables him to determine the successor of any given number, it does explain how he uses this knowledge on a given occasion to determine the successor of some number. That is, (31) describes what the child knows (competence), but does not explain how the child uses this knowledge (performance). Grammars, then, are models for speaker competence, not performance. They describe what a speaker unconsciously knows about his language, but they do not explain how he uses this knowledge in uttering and understanding sentences of his language. There is a clear relationship between theories which describe competence and which explain performance. A model of competence is a description of what a speaker unconsciously knows about his language which enables him to use and understand his language. Hence, any theory which purports to explain performance must include a description of what a speaker knows about his language. For, a theory of performance is supposed to explain how a speaker uses his competence in speaking his language. As a consequence, before a linguist can construct a theory of speaker performance he must construct theories of speaker competence. The transformational grammars which Chomsky and others have described are theories of the latter sort.

It should be noted that Chomsky uses 'grammar' with a systematic ambiguity. On the one hand he uses it to refer to a speaker's unconscious knowledge of the rules of his language, and on the other to refer to a linguist's description of these rules. To avoid confusion I will use *linguistic competence* for the former and *grammar* for the latter. In this use, 'competence' becomes a technical term in linguistic theory. It should not be taken to mean *ability*, but rather *unconscious knowledge*.

3 Innate Linguistic Knowledge

Since a child is not born knowing a language, we must explain how he learns it. From Chomsky's point of view a theory of language acquisition must explain how the child learns the rules of his language—that is, acquires linguistic competence—on the basis of his linguistic experience. According to Chomsky, the child's linguistic experience is highly fragmented.[8] Often the adult speech he hears contains false starts, ungrammatical sequences, abbreviated sentences, and so forth. Moreover, the ways adults speak vary. Some stutter; some have high voices; some have low voices; and others have accents. Moreover, linguistic experience is not the same for all children. Some children are corrected by their parents when they make mistakes; and a few, most notably children of academics, are taught small parts of their language, the color words, for example. In contrast other children, such as children of immigrants, are seldom corrected at home for their mistakes in speaking English. We see that the child in learning his language may have several sources of information: people speaking the language, instruction in this language, and corrections of his own speech. All this is called the child's *primary linguistic data*.

Primary linguistic data has two features. First, it differs from child to child within a speech community;[9] second, for any one child in a speech community it is highly fragmented information. Despite the first feature, most children in a speech community grow up speaking much the same language. There are regional, ethnic, and class differences, but on closer examination these differences turn out to be rather superficial. After all, 'ain't' and 'am not' are not so different. Consequently, any adequate theory of language acquisition must explain how children learn the same language on the basis of divergent primary linguistic data. Furthermore, even though children are confronted with linguistic data which is fragmented, they are able to learn sets of rules which are highly complex. So, for a theory of language learning to be adequate, it must also explain this fact.

We have focused our attention on one language community in establishing criteria for adequate language learning theories. We must broaden our view. Children of any ethnic group and cultural background can become native speakers of any natural human language in the world. A Maori child can become as fluent in English as any American child and vice versa. All it takes is adequate exposure to the respective languages at an early age. Lips, palate, tongue, and larynx are not designed for learning one language rather than another. This shows us that the human capacity to learn languages is the same for all children. Any adequate theory of language learning must take account of this.

On Chomsky's view, what the child hears while learning a langauge is highly fragmented, and the competence which a child acquires is extremely complex. Moreover, the child's primary linguistic data provide the child with insufficient information to construct the rules he learns. How, then, does a child learn a language? According to Chomsky, a child is born with innate linguistic knowledge which he uses in learning a language.

> As a precondition for language learning, he [the child] must possess . . . a linguistic theory that specifies the form of a grammar of a possible human language. . . .[10]

When the child hears snatches of a particular language, he formulates rules of the language on the basis of what he hears and in conformity to the linguistic theory with which he is born. Since children are born with the ability to learn any language, it is reasonable to suppose all children are born with the same innate linguistic knowledge.

The linguist's task is twofold. On the one hand, he must describe speaker competence and thereby provide a grammar for each language. On the other hand, he must describe a speaker's innate linguistic knowledge and in doing so specify features found in all languages—that is, a universal grammar. Just as grammars do not explain how speakers use their language, universal grammar does not explain how they acquire it. Rather, it describes the innate knowledge which enables a speaker to learn a language, but does not explain how he uses this knowledge. In order to explain language acquisition, then, the linguist must provide a theory of language acquisition which will include universal grammar as a part. The distinction between universal grammar and a theory of language acquisition is parallel to the distinction between a grammar and a theory of performance.[11]

How does a linguist decide which linguistic features are learned and which innate? That is, how does he determine which linguistic features are to be included within universal grammar and which described within the grammar of a particular language? There are two sorts of evidence which have a bearing on this question. First, it is reasonable to assume that all human beings have the same innate linguistic knowledge. Consequently, if some linguistic feature is discovered in the grammars of all languages, then we can suppose that this feature is innate. Of course, its universality cannot arise from universal properties of the world in which we live or of the cultures which we possess. For example, if we discovered a word for stone in every language, it would be unreasonable to suppose that having a word for stone is innate. Thus, with this proviso, finding a linguistic feature in all languages is grounds for describing it within universal grammar. The second sort of evidence for a linguistic feature's being innate is obtained by comparing grammars with primary linguistic data. As we have seen, grammars are descriptions of speaker competence—that is, of what a speaker knows when he knows a language. Hence, if a feature is described in a grammar, then what is described is part of a speaker's competence. If this feature is not found in or could not be learned from primary linguistic data, then it must be contributed to the speaker's competence by his innate linguistic endowment or, as Chomsky puts it, his innate linguistic knowledge. And as a consequence, it should be described within universal grammar. In actual linguistic practice the former sort of evidence is much more widely employed than the latter, since so little is known about the relationship between primary linguistic data and speaker competence.

4   A Critical Appraisal of Innate and Unconscious Linguistic Knowledge

There are many philosophical issues raised by various aspects of Chomsky's view. It is impossible to consider all the issues, but in the following we will critically evaluate three of them:

(32)   Speakers have *tacit or unconscious knowledge* of the rules of their language.

(33)   Speakers *make use* of these rules in speaking and understanding their language and in determining certain facts about the sentences of their languages.

(34)   Speakers have *innate knowledge* of linguistic universals which enable them to learn their language.

In order to evaluate the first claim we must distinguish between knowing how to do something and knowing that something is the case. For certain human activities it is neither necessary nor sufficient for someone's knowing how to do such an activity that he know anything about that activity. Our knowing how to walk does not depend upon our knowing anything about the mechanics or physiology of walking or knowing any other fact. It is equally true that knowledge about an activity is not sufficient for knowing how to do that activity. A paraplegic might know all there is to know about the mechanics, physiology, and skill rules of skiing without knowing how to ski. But there are other human activities which do involve rules which one knows how to do if and only if one knows the rules governing them. And in turn one knows the rules of such activities only if one is able to say, indicate, or show to someone what the rules are. Chess, checkers, and other games are paradigmatic examples of activities of this sort.

Is knowing how to speak a language more like knowing how to walk or how to play chess? Chomsky thinks it is like playing chess, but with the proviso that a speaker cannot tell or show anyone else what the rules are, for his knowledge of the rules is unconscious. Gilbert Harman, on the other hand, thinks it is more like walking. He claims that

> . . . Chomsky's use of the phrase 'tacit competence' betrays a confusion between the two sorts of knowledge of a language. Competence is knowledge in the sense of knowing how to do something; it is ability. It is not the sort of knowledge that can properly be described as "tacit." Tacit knowledge must be knowledge that something is the case. . . . [Chomsky] confuses knowing how with knowing that.[12]

In the above quotation Harman takes 'competence' to mean 'knowing how to do something' and 'tacit knowledge' to mean 'knowing that something is the case'. Since Chomsky claims that a speaker's competence in a language is his tacit knowledge of the grammar of that language, Harman concludes that Chomsky is confusing knowing how with knowing that. In addition to this criticism, Harman also maintains that Chomsky confuses a speaker's intuitive knowledge of his language with knowing the rules of the language.

> . . . Speakers can be brought to judge that certain sentences are ambiguous, that certain sentences are paraphrases of each other, or that certain strings of words are not grammatically acceptable. Such judgments are often taken as representing a speaker-learner's "linguistic intuition"; . . . Notice that this sort of intuitive or unconscious knowledge is not the knowledge of particular rules of a transformational grammar. . . . [Chomsky] confuses knowing that certain sentences are grammatically unacceptable, ambiguous, etc., with knowing the rules of the grammar by virtue of which sentences are unacceptable, ambiguous, etc.[13]

Harman claims that Chomsky has not shown the need for "linguistic competence" (tacit linguistic knowledge) in explaining how people talk.[14]

There is much that is confused in Harman's criticisms. First, Chomsky does not use 'competence' to mean 'ability' but uses it as a technical term to mean 'unconscious knowledge of the rules of a language'. Consequently, when Chomsky says that our linguistic competence is our tacit knowledge of linguistic rules, he is not confusing knowing how with knowing that. Rather, given his special use of 'competence', he is saying something tautological. Second, Chomsky does not confuse the linguistic intuitions we have about our language with our unconscious knowledge of the rules of our language. He clearly distinguishes the two. In fact, he proposes the latter to explain how we know the former. He claims we know, for example, what the subject and object of a sentence are because we have tacit knowledge of a rule which determines which constituents of a sentence bear these relations to the sentence. I suppose Harman's confusion arises because speakers are often unaware of what they know about their language and are made aware by the linguist's questions. So, there is a sense in which a speaker's knowledge about the facts of a language is unconscious, but there is a fundamental difference between this kind of knowledge and tacit knowledge of linguistic rules. The latter sort of knowledge cannot be elicited from speakers, even by the most subtle questioning. The upshot if this is that Harman's criticisms of Chomsky fall wide of the mark.

There is a criticism which can be raised against (32). Chomsky holds that a speaker's ability to make judgments about sentences of his language can be explained in part by supposing that the speaker has unconscious knowledge of linguistic rules which he uses in making such judgments. Why should we think this to be true? One of the judgments speakers are able to make is whether a string of words in their language is grammatical or not. And one of the goals of transformational linguists is to devise rules for a particular language which generate all and only the sentences of that language. Let us suppose that there is a language for which linguists have constructed a set of rules of this sort. On this supposition what the rules generate and what speakers of this language know to be grammatical are identical. Let us further suppose that the grammar is able to account for all the linguistic knowledge these speakers have about their language.

(35) The speakers of L know that the sentences of L have properties a . . . . . z.

(36) Linguists can devise a set of rules, 'R', which attribute to the sentences of L the properties a . . . . . z.

It follows from (35) and (36) that

(37) What the rules specify and what the speakers know are identical, namely, that the sentences of L have properties a . . . . . z.

However, it does not follow that the speakers know that R attributes a . . . . . z to the sentences of L or even that the members of R are the rules of L. Furthermore, there is reason to suppose that speakers do not have knowledge of such rules. On the basis of our chess example, a necessary condition for someone to know the rules which govern some activity is that he must be able to say or show us what the rules are. Most speakers of a language, not being linguists, cannot do either. Consequently, against Chomsky, speakers do not know the rules of their language.

We have been assuming with Harman that 'knowing how' and 'knowing that' exhaust the categories of knowledge. In replying to Harman Chomsky remarks that ". . . it does not seem to me to be true that the concepts 'knowing how' and 'knowing that' constitute exhaustive categories for the analysis of knowledge."[15] However, if 'tacit knowledge' is neither an instance of 'knowing how' nor 'knowing that', then it must be shown that it falls under another ordinary concept of knowledge or that it is an extension of one of our ordinary concepts. Chomsky has done neither and it is unclear how either would be accomplished. Until Chomsky has shown how his technical use of 'knowledge' connects in some way with our ordinary uses, he should avoid using the word.

Let us turn to a discussion of Chomsky's claim in (33). To evaluate this claim we must distinguish between one's action being in accordance with a rule and following a rule. The distinction can best be brought out by an example. Let us contrast a non-chess player with a chess player, both of whom move a bishop along the diagonal of a chess board. We would say, I think, that what the non-chess player is doing is in accordance with the bishop rule, but, not knowing chess, he is not following the rule. The chess player, on the other hand, is following the rule. What distinguishes the chess player from the non-chess player? Obviously, the chess player knows what the bishop rule is and can tell us what it is, more or less, while the non-player neither knows nor can tell us what the rule is. Generalizing from this, we can say that someone follows a rule only if he knows what the rule is and can tell us what it is. Speakers of a language cannot tell us what the rules of their language are and, hence, if the above analysis of 'following a rule' is correct, cannot be said to follow rules in making judgments about their language or in speaking and understanding it. The most that can be said is that their judging, speaking, and understanding are in accordance with the rules of their language.[16]

In the chess example we have drawn a sharp distinction between 'following a rule' and 'one's action being in accordance with a rule'. The distinction between the two depends upon the chess player's knowing what the bishop rule is and being able to tell us what it is and the non-player not knowing and not being able to tell us what it is. The distinction can be blurred. Suppose there is a rather inarticulate chess player who cannot tell us what the bishop rule is, but can show us how it moves. Moreover, he can teach us how to move the piece. In doing so, he is able to recognize whether a move of the bishop is correct and to correct mistaken bishop moves. In addition he knows how the bishop move fits in with the other chess moves; he knows that it cannot jump over other pieces and he knows some of the strategy employed in using the piece. A player of this sort is not just acting in accordance with the rules of chess. Rather he is following these rules even though he cannot say what they are. Speakers of languages seem to be more like inarticulate chess players than non-chess players. They can teach others how to speak their language. In doing this they correct mistakes in pronunciation, syntax, and word usage. Moreover, they can recognize or be brought to recognize these sorts of mistakes in their own speech. Just as the inarticulate chess player cannot tell us what the rules of chess are, speakers of a language cannot tell us the rules of the language they speak. On the basis of the similarities between our inarticulate chess player and speakers of a language, we might want to say that in speaking their language speakers are following rules and not that their speaking is just in accordance with them.

There is a dissimilarity, however, between our inarticulate chess player and a speaker of a language. Even though the inarticulate chess player cannot say what the bishop rule is, he would realize if he were told, that what he had been doing falls under some specification of the rule. It is not clear what we would say if he were unable to do so. It is doubtful that we would consider him to be a chess player and to be following the bishop rule, rather than acting in accordance with it. Speakers, on the other hand, are unable to recognize most linguistic rules as rules of their language no matter how they are specified. It is highly unlikely that any speaker, when told, recognizes that the language he has been speaking is governed by transformational rules. If we take this dissimilarity between the inarticulate chess player and speaker seriously, we would be forced to say that the chess player follows the rules of chess while the speaker only acts in accordance with linguistic rules. Consequently, Chomsky cannot claim that speakers use rules in determining facts about sentences of their language or in speaking and understanding sentences of their language.

Chomsky's most contentious claim is that children in learning their language have innate linguistic knowledge.

It is clear that humans and other animals are born with certain kinds of knowledge. Children, for example, are born knowing how to suckle and to grasp, and chicks are born knowing how to peck and to walk. To put this another way, children and chicks are born with the ability to do certain things. Clearly, knowledge in this sense does not apply to our ability to speak a language, for no one is born with the ability to speak a language. However, we are born with the ability to learn a language. Perhaps what we can say is that we are born knowing how to learn a language. Even this way of putting the point is stretching language a bit, but not deforming it.

However, this is not Chomsky's view. He holds that we are born with knowledge that certain facts about human language are the case; for example, we are born with the knowledge that the grammars of all languages contain transformational rules. Accordingly, when a child is confronted with the problem of constructing a grammar of a language on the basis of primary linguistic data, he will construct one which conforms to his innate knowledge of the form of all human languages. And, if Chomsky is right, any grammar he constructs will contain transformational rules.

Chomsky's primary evidence for the innateness hypothesis is the disparity between the grammars children learn and information children have available to construct such grammars. On Chomsky's view the latter underdetermines the former. That is, the child cannot construct an adequate grammar for his language by simple inductive procedures applied to what he hears. Chomsky argues that since linguistic information given to a child in experience is not sufficient for him to construct grammars of his language, this information must be available to him from another source. In order to explain how children learn languages, then, Chomsky supposes that they are born with innate knowledge about the form of human languages.

The sticking point for many is Chomsky's claim that

infants who speak no language have innate knowledge of rules which specify the form of any human language. An objection, similar to one raised against Chomsky's contention that we have unconscious knowledge of linguistic rules, can be made against this claim. In criticizing the former we took as a necessary condition for someone's knowing and following a rule that he could tell us, indicate to us, or show us what the rules are. I would think the same holds for rule schemata as well. We would seriously doubt that a student of logic knows or is able to use the rules of inference, if he were not able to tell us what the rules of inference are. It is obvious that an infant who speaks no language cannot tell us what the form of human languages is and, consequently, cannot be said to have such knowledge, innate or otherwise.

We have rejected Chomsky's thesis that speakers have tacit and innate linguistic knowledge. What, then, can we say about people and languages? It is quite obvious that people have the ability to learn them and in learning a language most people acquire the ability to speak and understand it. In fact it is not possible for someone to have learned a language without having one of these abilities, though both are not necessary. There are some people who are able to speak a language without being able to understand it, and there are others who are able to understand a language without being able to speak it, but these sorts of cases, luckily, are very rare. In addition to these abilities many speakers have the ability to recognize many facts about the sentences of their language. We can then attribute linguistic abilities and capacities to people, though if we say no more than this we would have explained nothing. For, to say merely that our innate linguistic capacity is what enables us to learn languages explains no more than saying that the dormative powers of opium are what enable opium to put people to sleep. To have any explanatory content, not only must we attribute linguistic abilities to speakers, but we must also describe them. And if Chomsky is right about the nature of language, our descriptions in part would be the same as Chomsky's description of tacit and innate linguistic knowledge. Consequently, the goals linguists have set for themselves, describing grammars of particular languages and a universal grammar, are not changed. What is changed is that they should not be considered to be theories of, respectively, tacit and innate linguistic knowledge.

Replacing 'knowledge' with 'ability' removes some philosophical problems from Chomsky's view, but by no means all of them. J. J. Katz, one of the leading exponents of the position being explored in this chapter, characterizes it as a theory committed to explaining our linguistic ability in terms of ". . . *mental* events, capacities and processes. . . ."[17] Among the mental objects Katz supposes speakers and hearers have are grammars of their language and procedures to produce and recognize sentences of their language. Given these, Katz describes communication in the following way:

> The speaker . . . chooses some message he wants to convey to the hearer. He selects some thought he wishes to express to him. . . . This message is . . . in whatever form the semantic component of his linguistic description uses to represent the meaning content of thoughts. . . . The speaker then uses the sentence producing procedure to obtain an abstract syntactic structure having the proper conceptualization of his thought as its semantic interpretation. . . . After he has suitable syntactic structure, the speaker utilizes the phonological component of his linguistic description to produce a phonetic shape for it. This phonetic shape is encoded into a signal that causes the speaker's articulatory system to vocalize an utterance of the sentence. The sound waves of which these utterances consist are transmitted through the air and, after they reach the hearer's auditory system, are converted into a signal which is decoded into a phonetic shape. On the basis of that shape the hearer's sentence recognition procedure then produces a syntactic structure. . . . Once the hearer is in possession of this syntactic structure, he employs the semantic component of his linguistic

description to obtain its semantic interpretation. He thus represents to himself the same message that the speaker wished to convey to him, and communication has taken place.[18]

The picture we get in brief is that there is some message, M, which the speaker chooses to convey to a hearer. What the speaker wants to convey, M, has the same form as the semantic representation, R, of an equivalent class of sentences. The speaker uses his sentence producing mechanism to produce a phonetic representation, P, of one of these sentences, S. P, encoded into a signal, causes the speaker to utter S. When received, this utterance produces in the hearer a series of events which are the temporal reverse of those occurring in the speaker ending in the hearer's representing M to himself. Katz claims that when this occurs the speaker has communicated with the hearer.

Even if what Katz holds is acceptable, and there is good reason to believe that it is not, it is an insufficient analysis of communication. Suppose that you want to tell me that you are hungry, and being a direct sort of person, you say

(38)   I am hungry.

Now I might well understand (38), that is what the sentence means, without understanding that you meant to be *telling* me something or what *you meant* to tell me. That is, for communication to take place a hearer must not only understand the meaning of the sentence uttered, but also, the illocutionary act performed and the speaker's meaning, the latter of which could be different from what the sentence means.

I do not want to suggest that Katz's account of communication is merely incomplete. It seems to me that there are difficulties with it. He advances the thesis that before we know what we are going to say, we 'choose' or 'select' a message or a thought which we then represent phonetically. But, this appears to suppose that there is a stock of messages or thoughts which we thumb through, so to speak, until we come to the appropriate one for our purposes.

Now this denies one of the basic assumptions of transformational linguistic theory, namely that our conversing is essentially creative. That is, when we talk to one another, we do not draw on a stock of messages and thoughts which we have learned by prior experience. Rather, most of the time our thoughts and the sentences we utter to express them are novel, never before having been uttered or heard by us at least. Suppose, then, that our messages and thoughts, rather than being chosen, are created. There is still a problem. The form of the message, in Katz's view, is the same as the form of the semantic representation of an equivalent class of sentences. As we shall see in the next chapter, semantic representations have rather complex structures. And since our thoughts have the same structure, they too are complex. On the rather contentious assumption that our thoughts are constructed, the question is, how do we go about constructing our thoughts? Do we need a grammar of thoughts and a procedure for constructing them apart from the grammar of our language and a procedure for constructing sentences? These rather complicated questions go well beyond the scope of this book.

But there are two further questions I would like to consider here. First, in what sense are the events, capacities, and processes which the linguist attributes to a speaker to explain his ability to speak and understand a language mental? And second, what is the relationship between these mental 'objects' and the physical movement of the tongue, lips, and larynx? This is, of course, the traditional and hoary mind-body problem. In the last chapter, I shall consider Katz's answer to this question, but before doing so, we should have before us the sorts of mental 'objects', acquired and innate, which transformational linguistic theory attributes to speakers. And it is to this I turn my attention in the next chapter.

IV

Transformational Linguistic Theory

1 The Goals of Transformational Linguistic Theory

It is very difficult to understand the force of the philosophical problems raised in the last chapter without understanding some of the details of transformational linguistic theory. In this chapter I shall set aside the criticisms raised in the previous chapter and present the theory of transformational grammar which appears in Chomsky's *Aspects of the Theory of Syntax* and in Katz and Fodor's "The Structure of a Semantic Theory."[1] Recently, Chomsky, Dougherty, Jackendoff, and others have presented arguments for revising this theory.[2] At the end of this chapter, I consider one of Jackendoff's arguments for doing so and the revision he thinks necessary for meeting his argument. At present within transformational linguistic theory there is an opposing view to the above theory, called *generative semantics,* represented primarily by the work of Lakoff, McCawley, Postal, and Ross.[3] It is impossible to present both theories fully in this chapter. Because the philosophical issues in the last chapter are those raised by Chomsky, I will describe his theory of transformational grammars. However, I shall consider one aspect of generative semantics, Ross's performative thesis, which shows one way in which part of Austin's work described in Chapter II might be integrated within linguistic theory. Before proceeding, it will do us well to reiterate the goals set by Chomsky for transformational grammarians.

As we have seen, a speaker knows a good many things about his language. He knows, for example, whether a given string of words is a sentence of his language, and if it is, whether it is a paraphrase of another sentence, whether it is analytic, and so forth. How does he know these facts? Chomsky's hypothesis is that a speaker has such knowledge of these facts because he has tacit or unconscious knowledge of a set of rules which constitutes the grammar of his language. On a particular occasion when a speaker makes a linguistic judgment about his language, he uses his grammar. Further, Chomsky holds that when a speaker speaks and understands his language, he also uses his grammar without being aware that he is doing so. The linguist's first task is to describe a speaker's unconscious or tacit linguistic knowledge—that is, to specify the grammar of the speaker's language. To be descriptively adequate the linguist's grammar must predict what a speaker consciously knows about his language. For example, if a speaker knows that a certain sentence of his language is grammatical, then the linguist's grammar must also mark this sentence as being grammatical. In general, a grammar of a language is descriptively adequate if and only if it accounts for the facts which speakers know about their language. Since a linguist's adequate grammar and a speaker's tacit linguistic knowledge determine the same facts about a language, Chomsky claims that an adequate grammar is a theory of a speaker's unconscious linguistic knowledge (competence).

The second and more important goal Chomsky sets for the linguist is to describe a speaker's innate linguistic knowledge. According to Chomsky, the linguistic data a child has available in learning his language provides insufficient information for the child to construct a grammar of his language. To bridge the gap between data and grammar Chomsky supposes that the child is born with innate knowledge of the form of grammatical rules, of the vocabulary of these rules, and of their organization. Adopting linguistic terminology, we shall call these *linguistic universals* and the set of such universals, *a universal grammar.* We shall use these terms ambiguously to refer both to a speaker's innate linguistic knowledge and also to the linguist's description of such knowledge.

The child's innate linguistic knowledge provides him with the apparatus to construct the grammar of any human language. Analogously, a universal grammar provides the linguist with devices which enable him to describe the grammars of any possible human language. Accordingly, Chomsky holds that a universal grammar which enables the linguist to accomplish this task is an adequate theory of a speaker's innate linguistic knowledge.

To fully understand what linguistic universals are it is necessary to see them applied to a particular language. We shall apply them to a fragment of English and in doing so describe part of its grammar. To test the adequacy of our grammar we shall see whether it gives an account of the facts listed in the previous chapter. The bit of English grammar we present should not be taken to be universal, for languages, as we all know, have idiosyncratic features which are reflected in their grammars. Rather, the descriptive apparatus used in describing a grammar is universal to all languages. There are three types of linguistic universals to which we shall pay special attention: *formal universals, substantive universals,* and *organizational universals.* The first specify the form of the rules used in a grammar, the second, the vocabulary items for these rules, and the third, the different parts of the grammar and the relationship among these parts.

2   *Transformational Syntactic Theory*

A grammar of a language is divided into three parts or *components: a syntax, a semantics,* and *a phonology.* The syntactic component which is the central part of a grammar has two functions: to generate all and only the sentences of a language and to assign to each sentence its linguistic structure(s). If a syntax fulfills the former function, then it accounts for a speaker's intuitions about what are and are not sentences of his language. And a syntax's ability to assign structural descriptions to sentences accounts for a speaker's intuitions about grammatical relations, constituent structure, syntactic ambiguity, paraphrase relationships among sentences, and so forth.[4] The output of the syntactic component provides the input to the semantic and phonological components of the grammar. These components, operating in part on syntactic information, assign, respectively, a meaning and a sound pattern to sentences. That the semantics depends for its operation on syntactic information can be seen from this example:

(1)   (a)   Josephine hugged Edward.
     (b)   Edward hugged Josephine.

It is obvious that these sentences differ in meaning and this difference turns on the fact that in (1) (a) 'Josephine' is the subject and 'Edward' is the object of 'hugged', while in (1) (b) the reverse is true. So, for the semantics to mark the difference in meaning between (1) (a) and (b) it must make use of information about the grammatical relations of these sentences which is determined by the syntax. Similarly, the phonology operates on syntactic information. In order to assign the correct intonation contour to questions in English we must know whether they are yes-no questions or wh-questions. And this is determined by the syntax. In what follows, I shall first discuss the syntax and then the semantics. Along the way I shall account for many of the facts for which these components must give an explanation, if they are to be adequate. Since phonological facts are peripheral to philosophy, the phonological component will not be considered.

An initial condition is placed on the adequacy of a grammar of any human language by virtue of the fact that the set of sentences of a particular human language is infinite. That it is infinite can easily be shown. Consider the following sentence.

(2)   John ran down the street.

Another English sentence can be produced from (2) merely by modifying 'street' with a relative clause.

(3)   John ran down the street which was in New York.

In turn another English sentence can be obtained by adding a relative clause after 'New York'. Since this process can be repeated *ad infinitum,* the number of English sentences is infinite. There are other ways in English of compounding sentences which have the same effect. For example, two indicative sentences conjoined with 'and' form another sentence. Similar phenomena are found in all human languages. In order to account for this fact an adequate grammar of a language must consist of a finite set of rules capable of generating an infinite set of sentences containing all and only the sentences of the language in question. The reason the set of rules must be finite is that it is supposed to be a theory of a speaker's tacit linguistic knowledge. Since this knowledge is stored in the speaker's brain, which has a limited number of brain cells and, thus, a finite storage capacity, it too must be finite. Consequently, an adequate theory of tacit linguistic knowledge cannot be infinite.

There are many different kinds of rules capable of generating infinite languages. We shall begin by considering two of them: *context-free* and *context-sensitive phrase structure rules.* Both of these rules can be represented by one schemata:

(4) $A \rightarrow Z/X\_\_Y$

'$\_\_\rightarrow\_\_$' is to be read as '$\_\_$ is rewritten as $\_\_$'. The vocabulary items of rules formed from (4) consist of two types: *terminal symbols* and *non-terminal symbols.* A non-terminal symbol is one which can be rewritten as another symbol or set of symbols, while a terminal symbol cannot be so rewritten. There are restrictions on the range of the variables, *A, Z, X,* and *Y*. *A* ranges over non-terminal symbols and *Z, X, Y* range over terminal and non-terminal symbols. Furthermore, only one non-terminal symbol can be substituted for *A*. More than one vocabulary item can be substituted for *Z, X,* and *Y,* but *Z* cannot be null, whereas *X* and *Y* can be. The material after the slash in the rule specifies the conditions under which a substitution instance of *A* can be rewritten as a substitution instance of *Z*. That is, given a rule which is a substitution instance of (4), any string of symbols which has the form *XAY* can be rewritten as the string of symbols which is the substitution instance of *XZY*. The difference between context-free and context-sensitive phrase structure rules is that the former do not contain any context conditions. That is, *X* and *Y* are null. To see how these rules operate let us suppose we have a language, ABA, in which the sentences consist of the letter '*b*' flanked on either side by an equal number of '*a*'s, for example, '*aba*', '*aabaa*', '*aaabaaa*', et cetera. Two simple context-free phrase structure rules allow us to generate all and only the sentences of ABA and because of this constitute its grammar:

(5) (i) $S \rightarrow aSa$
     (ii) $S \rightarrow b$

Our grammar contains the non-terminal symbol '*S*' and the terminal symbols '*a*' and '*b*'. The rules in (5) are used in *derivations* to generate the sentences of our language. A derivation consists of the initial symbol *S* and subsequent lines which result from application of grammatical rules. For example, the rules in (5) can be used to construct the following derivation:

(6)   *S*
       aSa   (5) (i)
       aaSaa (5) (i)
       aabaa (5) (ii)

In using the schemata in (4) to construct rules which describe human language, the non-terminal symbols are *grammatical categories* and the terminal symbols *lexical* and *grammatical formatives.* The grammatical categories, contained within universal grammar, are noun, 'N', noun phrase, 'NP'; verb, 'V'; auxiliary, 'Aux', and so on. Grammatical categories should not be confused with grammatical relations, such as 'subject', 'object', and 'main verb', which will be discussed shortly. Most lexical formatives in contrast to grammatical categories are not linguistic universals, but belong to the grammars of individual languages. For example, the lexical formatives of English include 'boy', 'run', 'the', '-ing', '-ed', and so on. But it is an open question whether grammatical formatives such as 'present', 'passive', 'progressive', and 'negative' are linguistic universals.

To see how (4) operates when applied to a natural language let us consider the following rules of English which are substitution instances of it.[5] In these rules X and Y are null and so no substitution instances of them appear.

(7) (a)   S→(PreS)NP-Aux-VP(Adv)[6]

(b)   Pre S→ $\left\{ \begin{matrix} Q \\ Imp \end{matrix} \right\}$ (Neg)(Emp)

(c)   VP→ $\left\{ \begin{matrix} V\text{-(Prt)-(NP)-}(\left\{ \begin{matrix} NP \\ S \end{matrix} \right\}) \\ Adj\ (\left\{ \begin{matrix} NP \\ S \end{matrix} \right\}) \\ be\text{-}\quad NP \\ Adv \end{matrix} \right\}$

(d)   NP→ $\left\{ \begin{matrix} P\quad \text{-}\ NP \\ NP\ \text{-}\ S \\ (Det)\text{-}N\text{-}(S) \end{matrix} \right\}$

(e)   Aux→Tns(M)(Perf)(Prog)(Pass)

(f)   Adv→ $\left\{ \begin{matrix} NP \\ here \\ possibly \\ \quad etc. \end{matrix} \right\}$

(g)   Perf→*have en*

(h)   Prog→*be-ing*

(i)   Pass→*be-en*

(j)   Tns→ $\left\{ \begin{matrix} Pres \\ Pst \end{matrix} \right\}$

(k) M→*can, may, must, shall, will,* etc.

(l) N→*boy, idea, water, girl,* etc.

(m) *Det→the, this, these, a,* etc.

(n) V→*run, resemble, know, eat, love,* etc.

(o) Adj→*blue, big, new, clear,* etc.[7]

Parentheses mean that the enclosed elements can be optionally selected; brackets mean that only one of the elements may be selected. Lexical items arranged horizontally, as in (7) (k), should actually be arranged vertically within brackets.

To derive a sentence we begin with an initial symbol, ##S##, apply (7) (a), and then any rule which applies to the result.[8] We shall derive

(8) The boy may love the girl.

(a) ## S ##

(b) ## NP-Aux-VP ## (7) (a)

(c) ## Det-N-Tns-M-VP ## (7) (d) and (7) (e)

(d) ## Det-N-Tns-M-V-NP ## (7) (c)

(e) ## The-boy-present-may-love-the-girl ##
        (7) (j)-(n)[9]

Obviously, (e) does not match (8); we need a rule which rewrites 'present may' as 'may'. With the addition of this rule (7) (a)–(o) can be used to derive a sentence which speakers of English intuit to be grammatical. And thus on the hypothesis that speakers of English have unconscious knowledge of these rules we can give an account of the intuition that (8) is grammatical. One should not think that if we were to utter (8), we would unconsciously go through the derivation in (a)–(e). Such derivations are part of a theory of competence, not performance. Clearly, the set of rules is not complete. It cannot generate, for example, questions, imperatives, and negatives. Let us suppose for the moment that we can add to (7) phrase structure rules which can be used to generate all and only the sentences of English.[10] We would then be able to explain how speakers of English know what the grammatical sentences of their languages are by ascribing to them unconscious knowledge of these rules. Still, this would leave unexplained many facts given in the previous chapter that speakers of English know about their language.

Some of these facts can be explained by a sentence's structural description which is mechanically provided by the derivation of the sentence. Starting with the first rule used in the derivation, the symbol on the left of the arrow is written as a topmost node in a tree diagram from which branch the symbols on the right of the arrow. Next, each symbol branching from the initial symbol is treated as a node from which branch other symbols depending upon what rule has been applied to this symbol. Branches are attached to nodes until we reach the last line of the derivation the parts of which serve as bottom nodes of the lowermost branches. This procedure can be used to construct a tree diagram or *phrase marker* (P-marker) for (8).

(9)

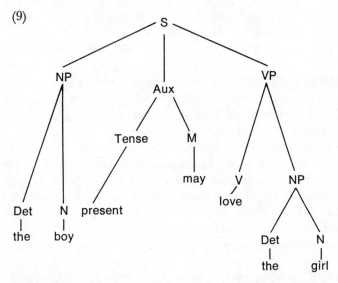

The P-marker for (8) constitutes the structural description for this sentence.

P-markers provide an account for many facts speakers know about sentences of their language. Taking (8) as an example, we shall show how P-markers account for

(10)   (a)   constituent structure

         (b)   categorization of formatives

         (c)   grammatical relations

Let us begin with (10) (a). There are many ways English speakers would divide (8) into parts or constituents when asked. For example,

(11)   'The', 'boy', 'may', 'love', 'the', 'girl', 'The boy',

        'love the girl', 'the girl'

However, they would not regard the following as proper divisions of the sentence:

(12)   'boy may', 'love the', 'the boy may love the', 'boy

        may love the girl'

That speakers of English regard (11), and not (12), as correct ways of dividing up (8) is reflected in (9). A set of formatives is a constituent of a sentence, if it can be traced back to a node in a tree. For example, 'love the girl' can be traced back to VP in (9). Hence, 'love the girl' is a constituent of (8). Consequently, the P-marker predicts that a speaker of English regards

(13)   'The', 'boy', 'present', 'may', 'love', 'the', 'girl',

        'The boy', 'present may', 'love the girl', 'the girl'

as constituents of (8). Since (11) and (13) match, we can say that the P-marker gives an account of the speaker's intuitions about the constituent structure of (8).[11]

Not only do speakers have conscious knowledge of the constituents of a sentence, but they know as well that the constituents are of different types. For example, they know that 'love' and 'boy' belong to different grammatical categories while 'boy' and 'girl' belong to the same grammatical category. The P-marker of (8) accounts for these facts. We said that if we can trace a set of formatives back to a node in a tree, then that set is a constituent. Since the nodes are labeled, tracing a set of formatives back to a node also tells us what type of constituent that set of formatives is. (9) tells us that:

(14)   (a)   'love' is a V

         (b)   'boy' is an N

         (c)   'the boy' is an NP

   (d)   'love the girl' is a VP
   (e)   'girl' is an N
   (f)   'the girl' is an NP

Consequently, the prediction the P-marker makes about
constituent types matches the conscious knowledge of speakers and thereby gives us an account of this knowledge. It
should not be thought that speakers have conscious knowledge of linguistic nomenclature and thus know what V, NP,
and N mean. All they know is that constituents are of the
same or different types. This is reflected in (14) (b) and (e)
and (14) (c) and (f) by N appearing in the former and NP
in the latter. The same end could be achieved by replacing
these letters with numbers or even shapes.

   In addition to knowing the constituents and their type,
speakers know what function the constituents play in the
sentence. They know that 'the boy' is the subject, 'the girl'
the object, and 'love' the main verb of (8). The P-marker can
also account for this knowledge. To see this we must first
define *dominates* and *immediately dominates*. A symbol *A*
dominates a symbol *B*, if *B* is derived from *A* by rules of the
grammar. Hence, in the derivation of (8), VP dominates V
and 'love', since both are derived from VP. A symbol *A*
immediately dominates a symbol *B*, if *B* is derived from *A*
using only one rule. Consequently, VP immediately dominates V in the derivation of (8). We will define *subject of a
sentence* as 'the set of formatives dominated by the NP
which is immediately dominated by S', *object of a sentence*
as 'the set of formatives dominated by NP which is immediately dominated by VP', and *main verb* as the 'formative
dominated by V immediately dominated by VP'. The subject of a sentence is symbolized by [NP, S], the object of
sentence by [NP, VP], and the main verb by [V, VP]. [NP,
S] is to be read as 'the set of formatives dominated by NP
which is immediately dominated by S' and the others are to
be read in a similar fashion. Using these definitions of
'subject', 'object', 'main verb', 'dominates', and 'immediately
dominates', we can determine the subject, object, and main
verb of (8). 'The boy' is the set of formatives dominated by

NP which is immediately dominated by S; 'the girl' is the set of formatives dominated by NP which is immediately dominated by VP; and 'love' is the formative dominated by V which is immediately dominated by VP. From this we can conclude that 'the boy' is the subject, 'the girl' the object, and 'love' the main verb of (8). Once again our rules can explain facts speakers of English know about (8).[12]

In the previous chapter we noticed that

(15)   They are flying planes.

is ambiguous and that the ambiguity is not due to there being an ambiguous word in the sentence. Rather, it depends upon the structure of the sentence. We are now in a position to account for this fact. (15) has two derivations employing different rules and, consequently, two structural descriptions associated with it.

(16) (a)

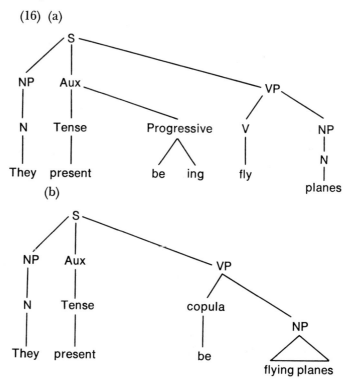

(b)

A rule must be applied to (16) (a) and (b) which hops 'present' over 'be' and 'ing' over 'fly' giving us (15) in both cases. The P-markers in (16) explain the ambiguity of (15); in (16) (a), but not in (16) (b), 'planes' is the object of 'fly'.

We see then that phrase structure rules enable us to explain a good deal of the conscious knowledge speakers have about English. It might seem that all we need to do in order to finish the task of describing English is to complete our list of phrase structure rules. However, there are several reasons why this is inadequate. First, a set of phrase structure rules which would generate all and only the sentences of English would be enormously complex. Second, for many English sentences such a set of rules would give an incorrect explanation for the sorts of facts discussed above. Third, there are many facts speakers of English know about their language for which it could not give an account. However, it should be stressed that it is theoretically possible for a set of phrase structure rules to generate all and only the sentences of any human language.[13] But we want much more from a grammar. We require it to explain the conscious linguistic knowledge speakers have about their language. Phrase structure grammars do not reach this level of adequacy, and to achieve this goal we must introduce rules called *transformations* into our grammar.

Consider the following sentences:

(17)   (a)   John gave a book and Sam a candle.
         (b)   John talked about war and Sam about peace.
         (c)   John wants the war to continue and Sam the
                war to end.

To generate these sentences with phrase structure rules requires us to have the following rules in our grammar:

(18)   (a)   S→NP-Aux-VP-*and*-NP-NP
         (b)   S→NP-Aux-VP-*and*-NP-PP
         (c)   S→NP-Aux-VP-*and*-NP-NP-V

(17) represents only a sample of the kinds of conjoined sentences which have missing constituents in their second con-

junct. For each of these different kinds we would need a different phrase structure rule similar to those in (18). Clearly, generating these sentences in this way is unnecessarily complex. What they fail to take into account is the obvious fact that the material missing in the second conjunct is identical to material in the first conjunct. It would simplify the grammar enormously if we generated these sentences by a rule which could delete items in a string of formatives under conditions of identity. As we shall see, transformations can do just that.

In addition to being overly complex, phrase structure grammars cannot account for some of the facts English speakers know about their language. The following sentences are paraphrases of one another:

(19) (a) It is obvious that John who rejected Mary corrupted Jane.

    (b) It is obvious that John whom Mary was rejected by corrupted Jane.

    (c) It is obvious that Jane was corrupted by John who rejected Mary.

    (d) It is obvious that Jane was corrupted by John whom Mary was rejected by.

    (e) That John who rejected Mary corrupted Jane is obvious.

That these sentences are paraphrases of one another does not depend upon there being synonymous morphemes in the different sentences, but rather upon there being different structural rearrangements of the morphemes, which do not affect meaning. Since in a phrase structure grammar each of these sentences is generated separately, they are syntactically unrelated. It is of course possible to add a semantics to a phrase structure grammar which marks these sentences as synonymous, but this would not explain our intuition that these sentences are structurally related to one another. As we shall see, our problem can be solved by deriving all these sentences transformationally from the same underlying P-marker which is generated by phrase structure rules.

Not only are phrase structure grammars overly complex and unable to explain certain facts, but they also give incorrect accounts for certain facts. Consider the following English sentences:

(20) (a) What book did you think that Sam gave Alice?
      (b) There will be a bird in the bush.

We know the following about these sentences:

(21) (a) 'What book' is the object of the embedded sentence containing 'gave'.
      (b) 'You' is the subject of the sentence which has 'think' as the main verb.
      (c) 'Gave what book to Alice' is a VP.
      (d) 'A bird' is the subject of (20) (b).
      (e) 'Will be a bird in the bush', does not constitute a constituent of (20) (b).
      (f) 'Be in the bush' is a VP.

Phrase structure rules similar to those in (7) can generate these sentences, but will assign P-markers to both in which 'what book' and 'there' are NP's immediately dominated by S. The definition previously given for 'subject' will incorrectly mark these NP's as subjects of (20) (a) and (b), respectively, and 'you' and 'a bird' will not be so marked. Furthermore, there is no way to determine 'what book', as the object of the sentence containing 'gave', from the P-marker of (20) (a). Lastly, the P-markers of these two sentences will not give us their correct constituent analysis and will thereby not be able to account for the facts in (21) (c), (e), and (f). Hence, generating these sentences by phrase structure rules provides an incorrect account for some of the facts in (21). In what follows I hope to show that by adding transformations to our grammar it can account for these facts.

When we add transformational rules to our grammar, we do not dispense with phrase structure rules. They are grouped together in what is called the *phrase structure component* of the grammar. However, the function of phrase structure rules is changed. The output of the phrase structure component is no longer a sentence, but rather an abstract string with an associated P-marker called the *deep structure* of a sentence. The deep structure of a sentence provides the input to the *transformational component* of the grammar which contains a partially ordered set of transformations. Since the function of transformations is to alter P-markers, the input to and output of both an individual transformation and the transformational component are P-markers. The output of the transformational component is a sentence with its associated P-marker called the *surface structure* of that sentence. The deep structure of a sentence is the input, not only to the transformational component, but also to the *semantic component* which assigns a meaning to the sentence. This places a heavy constraint on the phrase structure and transformational components. The output of the former, the deep structure of a sentence, must provide all the syntactic information necessary for assigning a meaning to the sentence. And in transforming a deep structure into a surface structure the transformational component must not produce changes in the structure of a sentence which affect meaning. These constraints will be examined at the end of the chapter. The surface structure of a sentence is the input to the *phonological component* which assigns a sound pattern to the sentence and consequently the surface structure must contain all the necessary syntactic information for assigning such sound patterns. The relationship among the various components in a grammar can be represented in the following manner:

(22)

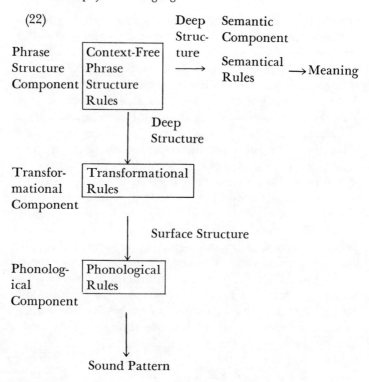

The phrase structure and transformational components constitute the syntax of a grammar.

A transformation is divided into two parts: a *structural description* (SD) and a *structural change* (SC). The structural description indicates the P-markers to which the transformation can apply, and the structural change the change which the P-marker undergoes. Consider the following transformation called *There Insertion*.

(23)

$$\text{SD:} \quad \#\#\underbrace{\text{NP}}_{1} - \underbrace{\text{Tense (Modal) (Perfect)}}_{2} - \underbrace{\begin{Bmatrix} be \\ V \end{Bmatrix}}_{3} - \underbrace{X}_{4}\#\#$$

$$\text{SC:} \quad \text{There} \qquad\qquad 2 \qquad\qquad\qquad 3+1 \quad 4$$

Parentheses indicate optional selection of an element, and

braces indicate alternative selection. For this transformation to apply to a P-marker it must contain nodes labeled NP, Tense, and either 'be' or V in that order, and optionally it can contain Modal or Perfect between Tense and 'be' or V. X indicates that any string of elements can follow 'be' or V. (23) can apply to

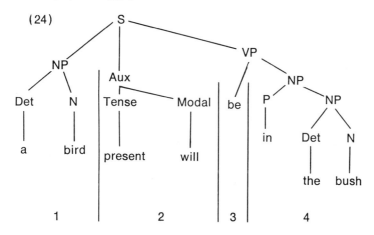

(24)

resulting in

(25)

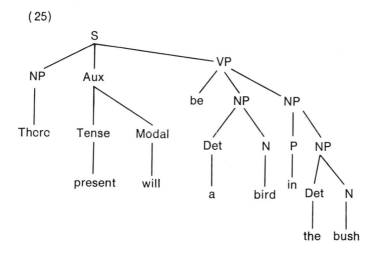

The terminal nodes of (25) do not constitute a sentence. In addition we need a transformation which hops 'present' over 'will' and a morphophonemic rule which realizes 'will + present' as 'will'. Adding these transformations and morphophonemic rules to our grammar allows us then to derive (20) (b). However, as (23) stands, it produces undesirable results. We could apply it to P-markers underlying:

> (26)   (a)   *There are some swans black.
>
> (b)   *There is a man an animal.
>
> (c)   *There has been everybody loved by somebody.

To prevent derivation of the strings in (26) we must add restrictions to (23). First, X cannot be an adjective phrase. Second, if X is an NP, it must be a prepositional phrase. And lastly, the initial NP must be indefinite.

Deriving (20) (b) transformationally explains many facts which are either left unexplained or explained incorrectly by a phrase structure derivation. We account for these facts on the basis of (24), the deep structure of (20) (b). First, we can correctly determine the constituent structure of (20) (b). In (24), 'be in the bush' is a constituent, whereas 'will be a bird in the bush', not dominated by a single node, is not a constituent. Second, 'a bird' is the subject of (20) (b), since in (24) it is dominated by NP which is immediately dominated by S. Lastly, (20) (b) and

> (27)   A bird will be in the bush.

are paraphrases of one another since both are derived from the same deep structure, (24). We see that the addition of transformations to a grammar greatly simplifies linguistic description and enables us to account for facts which phrase structure grammars cannot explain.

Of course many more transformations are needed to describe English. However, the power of transformations which universal grammar makes available for describing languages must be limited. If transformations could perform any type of operation, they would not fail to generate all and only the sentences of every possible language. But then we would have a theory about the form of possible human languages for which there could not be any possible disconfirming evidence. And thus we would not have a scientific theory. To ensure that our theory is not vacuous in this way, we must constrain the operations of transformations. In current linguistic theory there are three different kinds of operations performed by transformations. The first, illustrated by There Insertion, is *substitution* which introduces into a P-marker lexical formatives which do not affect meaning. 'There' introduced by (23) does not affect the meaning of (24). The second kind of operation, *deletion,* eliminates formatives in a P-marker just in case the formatives deleted are identical to other formatives in the P-marker. The conditions placed on this operation are still unclear and are a point of controversy in contemporary linguistic theory. It is a transformation containing this operation which enables us to derive the sentences in (17). The last kind of operation, *adjunction,* moves elements from one place to another in a P-marker. Some transformations contain more than one of these operations. For example, There Insertion both substitutes and moves formatives. Other transformations contain only one of these operations. *Question Formation,* for example, which enables us to derive (20) (a) and to explain some of the facts about the sentence listed in (21), only moves formatives.[14]

(28)   SD: $Q - X - NP - X$[15]

             1   2   3   4

         SC: 3   2   0   4

     Condition: 3 must contain wh + some.

This transformation applies to producing

(29)

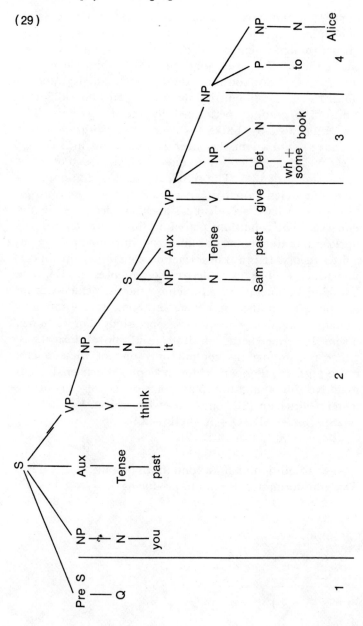

$(30)^{16}$

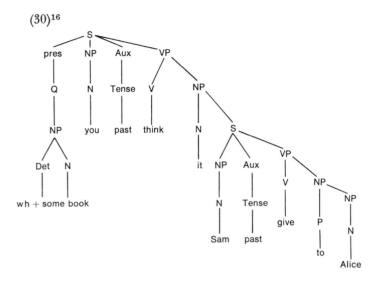

Many other transformations must apply to (30) in order to produce an English sentence. 'You' and 'past' must be inverted; 'do' must be added to support 'past'; 'it' must be deleted; and 'past' must be hopped over 'give'. Finally, rules must be applied to the result of these transformations rewriting 'which' for 'wh + some', 'did' for 'do + past', and 'gave' for 'give + past'.

We are now in a position to explain the facts in (21) on the basis of (29), which is the deep structure of (20) (a). First, since 'you' is dominated by NP which is immediately dominated by S, it is the subject of (20) (a). Second, 'wh + some book' is the object of the embedded S, since it is dominated by VP which is immediately dominated by the embedded S.[17] Lastly, 'Give what book to Alice' is a VP, because it is dominated by VP in (29). We see again that transformations enable us to derive an English sentence, (20) (a), more simply than phrase structure rules and also allow the grammar to account for many facts about this sentence for which phrase structure grammars cannot give an account.

There are two essential differences between phrase structure rules and transformations. First, phrase structure rules operate on one category symbol, rewriting it as a string of symbols. As a consequence, in a derivation a phrase structure rule can apply only to one line at a time; it does not have access to previous lines in the derivation. Addition of context conditions does not change this factor. Context conditions indicate only the context in a line in a derivation in which a symbol must occur for a phrase structure rule to apply. Transformations, on the other hand, can make use of information from any line in a derivation. This can be easily seen. Transformations can refer to and change any node in a P-marker. Since P-markers are essentially maps of phrase structure derivations, transformations, in being able to operate on any node in a P-marker, are in effect able to operate on any line in a derivation. Thus, transformations can make use of more information in their operation than phrase structure rules. Second, transformations can contain variables ranging over strings of terminal symbols which do not have to be constituents of a sentence and which do not have to be similar to one another. For example, the first X in (28), the Question Transformation, must range over quite disparate strings of symbols to derive

(31) (a) Who did it?
     (b) Whom did Alice know?
     (c) Whom did Alice know that Sam loved?

Yet, there are limits on the sorts of strings over which such variables may range. The Question Transformation cannot be allowed to derive

(32) (a) *Who did the boy who hit love the girl
     (b) *What did Sam ate apples and Harry ate

To prevent the derivation of the strings in (32) the initial variable of the Question Transformation must be restricted.[18] Even with such restriction on variable reference, transformations have available a device which greatly increases their derivational power and differentiates them from phrase structure rules which do not contain variables.

Our fragment of English grammar has made use of organizational, formal, and substantive universals. The organizational universal specifies the relationships among the syntactical, phonological, and semantical components of our grammar. The syntax is further divided into a phrase structure and a transformational component. The syntax generates sentences of the language and provides input to the semantical and phonological components. More specifically, the phrase structure component generates a P-marker, the deep structure of a sentence, which is the input to the semantical and transformational components. In turn, the transformational component produces a P-marker, the surface structure of a sentence, which is the input to the phonological component. The semantical component assigns a meaning to a sentence, while the phonological component assigns to it a sound pattern. The formal universals we have considered describe the form of two types of rules: phrase structure and transformational rules. The former are further subdivided into context-sensitive and context-free phrase structure rules. However, in our fragment of English we used only context-free phrase structure rules. At present it is not thought to be necessary to use context-sensitive phrase structure rules. We shall add as a constraint to our linguistic theory that the phrase structure components of any grammar can contain only context-free phrase structure rules. Substantive universals specify the symbols employed in the different sorts of rules. For phrase structure rules we have symbols such as 'NP', 'N', 'V', 'VP', '( )', '{ }', and for transformations in addition we have $X, Y, \ldots ,$ $1, 2, 3, \ldots ,$ et cetera.

Even though by adding transformations we have increased the power of our universal grammar and also the range of our description of English, neither our universal grammar nor our description of English is descriptively adequate. The fragment of English grammar above allows us to generate the deviant strings

(33) (a) *The man was sleeping the bed.

> (b) *The boy kicked that Sam was late.
> (c) *The woman hoped the door.

These strings are deviant because the verbs in each sentence occur in incorrect categorical frames. 'Sleep' can be followed by an NP only if it is a prepositional phrase; 'kick' cannot take a sentential complement; and 'hope' must take a sentential complement. In the universal grammar outlined above there is no rule schema for constructing rules of English grammar to prevent the generation of these strings. It might be thought that context-sensitive phrase structure rules can do the job. However, as we shall see, the rules which we must introduce to prevent derivation of the strings in (33) are transformations, rather than context-sensitive phrase structure rules.

In order to block the derivation of the strings in (33) we must prevent V in the derivation of each string from being rewritten as 'sleep', 'kick', and 'hope', respectively. To do this we must add to the grammar three devices: first, a *lexicon* which lists the lexical items of the language with an accompanying specification of the categorical frames in which they can occur; second, a rule, called a *strict subcategorizational rule,* which rewrites V in terms of the categorical frames in which it occurs in a P-marker; and third a *lexical insertion rule* which allows insertion of a verb under V just in case the categorical frames in the lexical entry for the verb match the categorical frames in which V occurs.

The lexical entry for each verb in a language consists of a *complex symbol* which specifies the categorical context into which the verb can be inserted. In addition, to facilitate the operation of the semantical and phonological components, each lexical entry contains a set of *semantical markers* and *phonological features* which specify, respectively, the meaning and sound pattern of the lexical item. We shall not discuss these features here. The complex symbol for 'sleep' is

(34) [+ V, [+_____]   ]
           [+_____ P NP]
           [+_____ Adverb]

This complex symbol specifies that 'sleep' can be attached to a node labeled V which is followed by nothing, by a prepositional phrase, or by an adverb. Attachment to any other node is disallowed.

Let us consider the following P-marker as an output of a set of phrase structure rules.

(35)

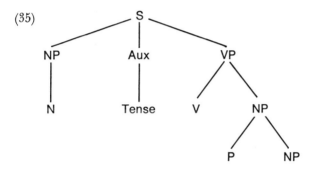

Can 'sleep' be attached to V? It can only if the complex symbol under V matches the complex symbol in the lexical entry for the verb. However, in (35) V does not dominate a complex symbol. In order to rewrite V as a complex symbol we introduce into the grammar a strict subcategorizational rule which inspects the nodes following V in (35) and rewrites V as [+ _____ P NP]. The strict subcategorizational rule in English for verbs is

(36) V→CS / ⎧ ____NP   ⎫
              ⎪ ____   ⎪
              ⎨ ____P NP   ⎬
              ⎪ ____Adverb ⎪
              ⎪ ____S   ⎪
              ⎩ etc.   ⎭

'CS', which means 'complex symbol', is a variable which is a function of the context in which V occurs. For example if

V occurs in the context '_____NP' in a P-marker, then CS is written as [+_____NP]. The list in the braces is to be completed by all the contexts in which verbs can occur in English.

Applying (36) to (35) gives us

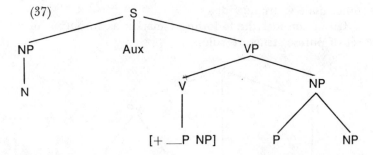

(37)

Since in (37) the complex symbol which V dominates matches the lexical entry for 'sleep', we can insert 'sleep' below V. In addition, we can block the derivation of the strings in (33). For example, in the P-marker underlying (33) (a), V would dominate [+_____NP]. Since this does not match the lexical entry for 'sleep', we are prevented from inserting it below V, thereby blocking the derivation of (33) (a).

The rule in (36) appears to be an abbreviated context-sensitive phrase structure rule. However, there is a general condition which must be placed on strict subcategoriza-tional rules for verbs which makes (36) a transformation. The material in the braces must be dominated by VP. This universal constraint greatly restricts the kinds of subcate-gorizational rules for verbs which can appear in grammars and greatly increases the empirical content of universal grammar. It makes the claim that verbs are only categori-cally subclassified in terms of categorical material which appears in verb phrases. Adding this constraint to universal grammars means that (36) must take into account more than one line in a derivation. For example, it applies to

(38) NP Aux V Adverb

rewriting V as [+_____Adverb] only if Adverb is dominated by VP. In effect (36) is applied to a P-marker rather than to a line in a derivation. Since this is what distinguishes phrase structure rules from transformations, (36) is a transformation.

Strict subcategorizational rules are added to a grammar to account for certain facts about verbs. As well, rules of this sort are needed for nouns and adjectives.

(39) (a) *Horace is yellow that Sally took the milk.
      (b) *Sam was fat about the cake.
      (c) *Nancy's resemblance by Bill surprised everyone.
      (d) *Harry's love of Mary to Fred was obvious.

To block derivation of these constructions we must add complex symbols to the lexical entries for adjectives and nouns and strict subcategorizational rules to the syntax which rewrite N and Adj in a P-marker as complex symbols. There are, however, lexical items, prepositions, auxilliaries, and determiners, for example, for which no strict subcategorizational rules are necessary. In order to introduce lexical items into a derivation in a uniform way, we will allow a lexical item to be attached to one of the lowest nodes in a tree if and only if its complex symbol matches the complex symbol attached to the node. But it is possible for a lexical item to have only the category to which it belongs as a complex symbol. For example, determiners such as 'the' have only Det as their complex symbol. Accordingly, determiners can be attached to a lowest node in a tree if and only if that node is immediately dominated by Det. By adding a lexicon, strict subcategorizational rules, and a lexical substitution rule to a grammar, we can dispense with phrase structure rules which introduce lexical items. This alters our conception of a syntax. It no longer consists of a phrase structure and a transformational component, but of a base component and a transformational component. The base component contains context-free phrase structure rules, strict subcategorizational rules, and a lexicon. The lexical substitution rule need not appear in each grammar, but can be stated once in universal grammar. As before, the transformational component contains a set of transformational rules. The base component has as its output a P-marker, the deep structure of a sentence, which has attached to its lowest nodes lexical items with their accompanying sets of syntactical, phonological, and semantical features. Since this P-marker is the input to the semantic component, it must contain sufficient syntactic information upon which the semantics can operate. In particular it must contain information which allows the determination of the grammatical relations among the lexical items on the lowest nodes. The semantics, operating on this information, assigns semantic properties to the string appearing at the bottom of the P-marker. Since abstract structures generated by the base component are paired with sentences by the transformational component, the semantics in effect assigns meanings to sentences. Of course, this is on the condition, mentioned earlier, that transformations do not affect meaning.

3 Transformational Semantic Theory

What function does the semantic component have? According to J. J. Katz, for a semantic component to be adequate it must be able to account for all the semantic properties which are possessed by sentences of a language.[19] It must determine whether a sentence is:

(40) (a) semantically anomalous
      (b) semantically ambiguous
      (c) synonymous with another sentence
      (d) analytic
      (e) contradictory

The list can be extended by adding any property of a sentence which is determined by virtue of its meaning. However, we shall not attempt to account for all the semantic properties which can be assigned to sentences. Rather, our main task is to outline the central apparatus which enables a semantics to provide an account for these properties. But, since analyticity has loomed so large in philosophy, we shall describe how a semantic theory accounts for it. The success of our task will be determined by whether the semantics matches the intuitions of native speakers. A semantic component of a grammar is adequate if and only if for every semantic property, P, which speakers ascribe to a sentence, S, the semantical component ascribes P to S. For example, if speakers of English take

(41) (a) Alberto is a bachelor
      (b) Alberto is an unmarried male

to be synonymous, then the semantical component for English must, also, predict that they are.

The central insight in the theory of semantics devised by J. J. Katz and J. A. Fodor is that the meanings of a sentence are determined on the basis of the meanings of its parts and the grammatical relations these parts bear to one another.[20] In order for the semantic component to carry out its task it must contain two features: first, a lexicon which assigns meanings to individual formatives and second, a set of rules, called *projection rules,* which join together or *amalgamate* the meanings of the formatives to form meanings for sentences. Once we have determined the meaning or meanings of a sentence, we can determine its semantic properties by applying to its meanings the definitions of these properties, contained within *universal semantics* which is a part of universal grammar.[21]

Since the syntax includes a lexicon which contains lexical entries with semantic information, it is unnecessary to introduce a separate lexicon containing the same information for the semantic component. The function of the semantic part of a lexical entry is to specify the meanings for a lexical item. Clearly, if the lexical item is ambiguous, then the semantic entry must contain more than one sense for the lexical item. The meaning of a lexical item is the total set of senses associated with it in its lexical entry. Here we are using 'meaning' somewhat technically to refer to the whole set of meanings which a lexical item can have. 'Sense' is used to refer to individual members of the set. The basic theoretical constructs in terms of which senses are represented are called *semantic markers,* and the representation of a sense is called a *reading.*[22] For example, one of the senses for 'man' can be represented as

(42)   (Object) (Physical) (Animate) (Animal) (Human) (Male) (Adult)

The concatenation of semantic markers should be read as 'conjunction' and this conjunction constitutes one of the readings of 'man'. The semantic markers appear in English, but they should not be thought of as English expressions. Rather, according to Katz, semantic markers are linguistic universals on a par with syntactic category symbols. There is, however, a difficulty with this conception of semantic markers which we shall discuss at the end of the chapter.

Not all semantic lexical entries consist only of a set of semantic markers. The lexical entries for adjectives and verbs must contain *selectional restrictions* which determine the readings with which the readings of these kinds of lexical items can be amalgamated. 'Addled', for example, can only be said of eggs and brains and 'chase' of animals. In a lexical entry selectional restrictions are represented by semantic markers in angles. The function of selection restriction is to determine whether a reading, S_1, which has a selectional restriction, SM_1 can be compounded with another reading S_2. In general

(43) S_1 which contains $<(SM_i)>$ can be amalgamated with S_2 if and only if S_2 contains (SM_i) within its set of semantic markers, $(SM_1 \ldots SM_n)$

By placing a condition on amalgamation, selection restrictions do two things. First, they prevent assignment of meanings to semantically anomolous sentences. For instance, since 'chase' has a selection restriction on its subject $<(Animal)>$,

(44)   The chair chased the car.

is not assigned a meaning. In addition they provide a method for selecting among senses of expressions. The adjective 'light' predicated of physical objects has one sense and predicated of colors another. The first reading of 'light' has the selection restriction $<$(physical object)$>$ and the second $<$(color)$>$. Since 'red' has (color) as part of its reading in the phrase 'light red', 'light' in this phrase will have associated with it the reading which contains $<$(color)$>$.

Lexical items for verbs are more complex than those for nouns and many adjectives. Consider one of the readings for the verb 'chase' as used in

(45) The man chased the woman.

(46) $(\hat{x})\ (\hat{y})\ (Fxy \cdot R_F \cdot A_F \cdot P_F \cdot M_F)$ $F = $ (Follow)
     $\hat{x} = $ [NP, S] $R = $ (Rapid)
     (Intention: x catches y by Fxy) $A = $ (Activity)
            $<$(Animal)$>$ $M = $ (Movement)
     $\hat{y} = $ [NP, VP] $P = $ (Physical)
        $<$(Object)$>$
       (moving away from x)

The material in parentheses and $F,R,A,M,$ and P are semantic markers. '$\hat{x}$' and '$\hat{y}$' are quantifiers such that readings of lexical items are substituted for the variables which these quantifiers bind. '$\hat{x} = $ [NP, S]' indicates that we substitute for 'x' the reading of the subject, and '$\hat{y} = $ [NP, VP] indicates that we substitute for '$\hat{y}$' the reading of the object of the sentence of which 'chase' is the main verb. As indicated before, selection restrictions are represented by material in angles. Hence, the semantic markers we substitute for '$\hat{x}$' must contain (Animal) and those for '$\hat{y}$' (Object). (Intention: x catches y by Fxy) and (Moving away from x) represent the presuppositions of a sentence containing 'chase'. The referent of the subject expression is presupposed to have the intention of catching the referent of the object expression by following it, and the referent of the object expression is presupposed to be moving away from the referent of the subject expression. In forming the reading for a sentence these semantic markers are added to the semantic markers substituted for x and y, respectively. We shall see shortly how (46) functions in forming the reading for a sentence.

The lexical entries we have considered can be abbreviated by having *lexical redundancy rules* in universal semantics. Obviously, if (Human) occurs in a lexical entry, (Object), (Physical), (Animate), and (Animal) are redundant, since humans are animate physical objects which are animals. Consequently, we can dispense with the latter semantic markers in (42) and retain (Human), (Male) and (Adult). We can as well simplify the lexical entry for 'chase'. If we take 'follow' in the sense of a physical activity, then we can dispense with (Movement).

In order to determine the reading(s) of a sentence we apply projection rules to the readings accompanying lexical items affixed to the lowest node of a P-marker. The function of projection rules is to amalgamate readings of lexical items to form readings of phrases and then to amalgamate these until a reading for a sentence is obtained. There are essentially two projection rules: the one amalgamates two readings, neither of which contains quantifiers, resulting in a union of the readings, and the other operates on readings which contain quantifiers, and substitutes the readings over which the quantifiers range for the variables bound by the quantifiers. Consider the following P-marker for (45), an output of the base component.

(47)[23]

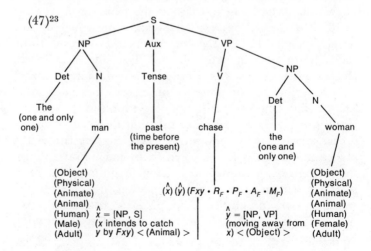

We first compound the readings for the subject and object with their determiners, neither of which have variables.

(48) (a) (one and only one) (Object) (Physical) (Animate) (Human) (Male) (Adult)

(b) (one and only one) (Object) (Physical) (Animate) (Human) (Female) (Adult)

Since the readings of the subject and object in (47) accord with the selection restrictions for the subject and object of 'chase', we can substitute these readings within the reading for 'chase'. Simplifying the reading by employing semantic redundancy rules, we obtain

(49) (one and only one) (Human) (Male) (Adult) (who intends to catch
(one and only one) (Human) (Female) (Adult) by following her)
(Follows) (one and only one) (Human) (Moving) (Female)
(Adult) (Moving away from (one and only one) (Human) (Male) (Adult))
(The following is rapid physical activity) (The following is during a time before the present)[24]

In order to simplify presentation of the material we have only presented one reading for (45). However, in order to specify the meaning of (45) fully we would have to operate on the full set of readings associated with the lexical items in the sentence.

There are many problems in the semantic representation in (49). First, the semantic representation for 'the' must be unpacked. Second, there is no distinction made between what a speaker uttering (45) normally presupposes on the one hand and asserts on the other. In using (45) one would assert that the person referred to by 'the man' followed one and only one human, moving, female, adult, and one would presuppose that the person referred to by 'the man' is human, male, and an adult. Third, the intention of the referent of the subject is not to catch the referent of the object by following her, but by chasing her. That is, the supposed intention of the person to which the subject expression refers is a function of the act he is purported to perform. This must be represented. Fourth, the reading (Rapid) and the reading of the tense are not properly related to the reading of the verb. 'The following' is a cover up for a problem. There is nothing which relates 'The following' to (Follows). Lastly, the whole representation cannot be read as a conjunction of semantic markers, for that would make no sense. (Follows) expresses a relation and obviously plays a different role from the other semantic markers. Moreover, variable binding is necessary to capture the fact that both occurrences of '(one and only one) (Human) (Male) (Adult)' refer to the same individual. And it is probably necessary for readings of sentences to have structural descriptions associated with them which are quite similar to the structural descriptions associated with sentences.[25] These problems arise in the reading of a relatively simple sentence. The difficulties increase enormously when we consider the readings for negation, quantifiers, intensional verbs, modal operators, logical connectives, performative verbs, etc., and their relationship to the readings of other expressions in the sentences in which they occur.

Once we have obtained the reading(s) for a sentence we must determine its semantic properties on the basis of its reading(s). In order to do so, it is necessary to have definitions for these properties stated in universal semantics. We shall say that a sentence on one of its syntactic derivations[26] is:

(50) (a) meaningful if and only if it has at least one reading assigned to it.

(b) semantically anomalous if and only if it has no reading assigned to it.

(c) semantically ambiguous n ways where $n \geq 2$ if and only if it has n readings assigned to it.

Two sentences are:

(d) synonymous if and only if they are assigned the same reading.

(e) fully synonymous if and only if they are assigned exactly the same reading.[27]

Applying these definitions to the reading of (45), we see that it is meaningful, since it has a reading assigned to it.

Analyticity has played an important role in philosophy since Locke and Leibniz introduced the notion. Kant defines analytical judgments as those which

> . . . express nothing in the predicate but what has been already thought in the concept of the subject, though not so distinctly or with the same full consciousness.[28]

Translating this into a modern idiom, we would say that an analytic sentence is one in which the meaning of the predicate expression is contained within the meaning of the subject expression. For example, in

(51)   A man is an animal.

the meaning of 'animal' is contained within the meaning of 'man', since this latter word means 'a male human animal which is an animate physical object'. Analytic sentences contrast with synthetic sentences in which the meaning of the predicate is not contained within the subject; for example

(52)   All bachelors are lonely.

The reason philosophers are interested in distinguishing between analytic and synthetic sentences is that the statements each of these sorts of sentences can be used to make play a different role in our knowledge. For example, we know the analytic statement

(53)   All the pianos in the room are musical instruments.

by knowing

(54)   (a)   that there are pianos in the room.[29]

   (b)   what the words mean.

but knowing (54)(a) and (b) is insufficient for knowing the synthetic statement

(55)   All the pianos in the room are out of tune.

In order to know (55) we must know not only that there are pianos in the room, but also that they are out of tune.

How can we distinguish between analytic and synthetic sentences? According to Katz,

(56)   A sentence is analytic on one of its readings, R_1, R_2, if and only if every semantic marker in R_2 occurs in R_1.[30]

R_1 and R_2 are readings associated, respectively, with the subject and predicate of a sentence. We can see that Katz's notion of analyticity is a direct descendant of Kant's notion. Katz's notion makes precise what is meant by "the meaning of the predicate is contained with the meaning of the subject." Let us consider (57), the semantic representation of (51). After the relevant application of the lexical substitution rule to (57), we see that the reading of the predicate, 'animal', R_2, occurs in the reading of the subject, 'man', R_1. Hence (57) is analytic.

(57)

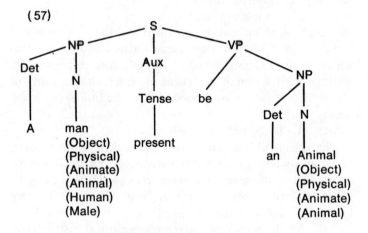

4   Ross's Performative Thesis

One of the facts speakers know about sentences of their language is the range of illocutionary acts for which the sentences can be used. That is, they know the illocutionary act potential of the sentences of their language. They know, for example, that

(58)   I will meet you at Harry's.

can be used to make a promise or a prediction or to declare one's intention. No account of these facts has been given in the above discussion of transformational linguistics. There is, however, a proposal of J. R. Ross which connects certain sentences with part of their illocutionary act potential.[31] This hypothesis, called the *performative thesis*, claims that the underlying form of all declarative sentences, such as,

(59) Prices slumped.

is

(60)

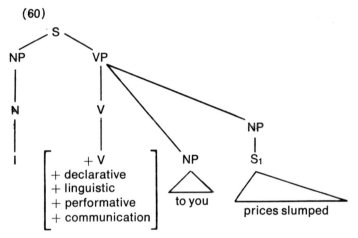

The features under the main V indicate that the highest verb in the sentence is something like 'say', 'state', or 'declare'. In what follows, I shall refer to this verb as a verb of 'saying', but it should be understood that Ross's hypothesis is committed only to the feature analysis. The fact that (59) can be used to make a statement or declaration is explained by its having as an underlying structure (60). The highest S in (60), that is S_0, is deleted by what Ross calls the *Performative Deletion Transformation* yielding (59). The hypothesis, of course, does not account for the illocutionary act potential of all sentences. However, we shall postpone considering this problem until the end of the section.

Ross provides a good deal of evidence for his hypotheses; some of it I shall present here. I will consider one argument apiece for an underlying *I,* for an underlying verb of saying, and for an underlying *you.* The argument for an underlying *I* depends upon the source of reflexives in *like*-phrases. Consider

(61) *Salesmen like himself make many sales.

(61) shows that reflexives cannot occur freely in *like*-phrases. There are conditions, however, under which 'himself' can appear in such phrases. For example,

(62) It surprised Sam that salesmen like himself made so many sales.

But not any reflexive can occur in the *like*-phrase in (62).

(63) *It surprised Sam that salesmen like herself made many sales.

The condition on the occurrence of the reflexive is that it stand in an anaphoric relationship with another noun phrase in the sentence. Since 'herself' cannot stand in such a relationship to either 'Sam' or 'salesmen', (63) is ungrammatical.

There are restrictions on the relationship between the anaphoric noun phrase and the reflexive in the *like*-phrase. The former must command the latter. *A* commands *B* if neither dominates the other and if the S which dominates *A* also dominates *B.* Consider the ungrammatical string

(64)

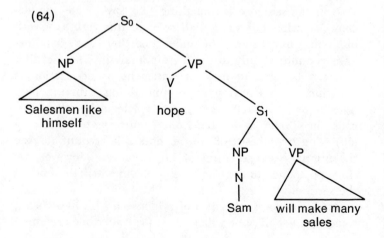

Since S_1 which dominates 'Sam' does not dominate 'himself', 'Sam' does not command 'himself' and thus the string in (64) is ungrammatical. The above facts lead us to propose the following hypothesis about the occurrence of reflexives in *like*-phrases.

(65)   A reflexive can occur in a *like*-phrase in a sentence if and only if there is an anaphoric noun phrase in the sentence which commands the reflexive.

But, there are sentences which appear to violate (65).

(66)   Salesmen, like myself, hoped to make many sales.

Obviously, there is no noun phrase in (66) to which 'myself' stands in an anaphoric relationship. Its occurrence, however, can be explained consistently with (65) by supposing that (66) has an underlying anaphoric 'I' in a higher S similar to (60) which dominates 'myself' and that this 'I' is deleted after 'myself' is introduced into the *like*-phrase in (66).[32]

The next of Ross's arguments, due to Robin Lakoff, purports to show that there is an underlying verb of saying in a higher S dominating declarative sentences. Compare (67) (a) and (b):

(67)   (a)   *Rachel hoped that Harry was there, but no one believed her

       (b)   Rachel$_i$ told the guards that Harry was there, but no one believed $\begin{Bmatrix} \text{*them} \\ \text{*him} \\ \text{her}_i \end{Bmatrix}$

Ross's hypothesis is that the object of clauses containing 'believe' must be anaphoric with the subject of a higher verb of saying which includes the verbs in (68) (a), but not in (68) (b) or (c).

(68)   (a)

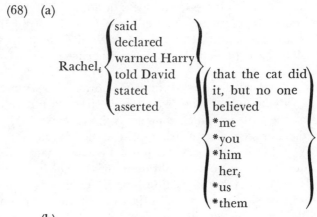

Rachel_i
{ said / declared / warned Harry / told David / stated / asserted }
{ that the cat did it, but no one believed / *me / *you / *him / her_i / *us / *them }

(b)

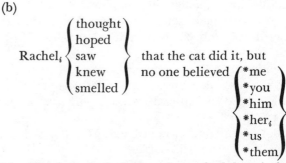

Rachel_i
{ thought / hoped / saw / knew / smelled }
that the cat did it, but no one believed
{ *me / *you / *him / *her_i / *us / *them }

(c)   *Rachel asked whether the cat had done it, but no one believed her.

The only sentences in (68) which are grammatical are those in (68) (a) where the object of 'believe' is anaphoric to 'Rachel', the subject of a verb of saying in a higher S than 'believe'.

However, there are sentences which contain *believe—* clauses which do not contain a higher verb of saying.

(69)

The cat did it; but if you don't believe
{ me / *you / *him / *her / *us / *them }, just smell.

We can explain the grammatical occurrence of 'me' in (69) by supposing that (69) has in its underlying structure a higher verb of saying with a first person subject, both of which are deleted by Ross's performative deletion transformation.

The last argument we shall consider shows that there is an underlying *you* as the indirect object of the higher verb of saying. Consider the following sentences:

(70)

(a) I told Larry that I wanted $\begin{Bmatrix} *my \\ his \end{Bmatrix}$ breath to be held for a minute.

(b) Sally warned me that she wanted $\begin{Bmatrix} my \\ *her \end{Bmatrix}$ breath to be held for a minute.

(c) They reminded us that they wanted $\begin{Bmatrix} *their \\ our \end{Bmatrix}$ breath to be held for a minute.

The restriction on the possessive pronouns in the phrase '_____ breath to be held' is that it must be identical to the object of the verb in the next highest S. However, there are sentences in which this phrase occurs where there is no higher S.

(71) Sarah wants $\begin{Bmatrix} *my \\ your \\ *his \\ *her \\ *our \\ *their \end{Bmatrix}$ breath to be held for a minute.

We can explain the occurrence of 'your' in (71) and the nonoccurrence of the other possessive by supposing that in the underlying structure of (71) there is a higher S which has a second person indirect object. On this supposition the distribution of possessives in (70) and (71) can be explained uniformly. And this assumption is quite neatly incorporated in Ross's performative analysis, since the indirect object of the underlying verb of saying is *you*.

Ross and others have generalized the performative thesis to apply to interrogative and imperative sentences, but the expanded hypothesis still does not account for the full range of illocutionary acts with which sentences of natural languages can be associated. The problem is not a simple one. Consider

(72) Janice is obese.

which cannot be used to give an estimate of Janice's weight or size. Notice that

(73) *I estimate that Janice is obese.

is ungrammatical. One would think that the same hypothesis which explains the ungrammaticality of (73) should, also, explain the fact that (72) cannot be used to give an estimate. A generalized version of the performative thesis could account for these facts.

(74) If S_1 has illocutionary act potential $IAP_1 \ldots . IAP_n$ and it does not contain a performative verb as its main verb, then it has n underlying structures of the form

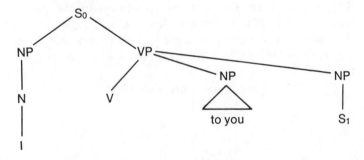

where for each IAP_i there is material dominated by V which is systematically related to that IAP_i.[33]

Of course, for each proposed underlying structure we need evidence of the sort Ross offers for his more modest proposal.

I would now like to consider an argument against Ross's performative thesis. On Ross's view of generative grammars, called *generative semantics,* the underlying structure of a sentence constitutes its logical form upon which rules of inference operate.[34] On this view, the underlying structure of a sentence is not a P-marker which has lexical items at its lowest nodes, as does the theory considered in this chapter, but rather is a P-marker which has representations of senses at its lowest nodes. Thus, on the generative semanticists' proposal the logical form of (59) is something like (60). But the underlying structure of

(75)   I say to you prices slumped.

should also be something like (60). However, (59) and (75) enter into different logical relations. (59) logically implies (59), but (75) does not. Consequently, either (59) or (75) does not have (60) as its logical form. Since one would suppose (75) has (60) as its logical form if any sentence has it, it follows that (59) does not have (60) as its logical form. A way out of this difficulty, proposed by Lakoff, is that rules of inference operate on the S_1 node of the underlying form of (59), but do not so operate on the underlying form of (75). This would save the performative thesis and the hypothesis that something like (60) is the logical form of both (59) and (75). There is a difficulty, I believe, with this way out. It is ad hoc. There is nothing to motivate drawing the distinction between the underlying structures of (59) and (75) which on this view are formally identical.

Notice that my criticism applies to the standard theory as well. For on that theory if we accept the performative thesis, (60) is the deep structure of both (59) and (75). But, if two sentences have the same deep structure, then they have the same meaning. And I take it that a necessary condition for sameness of meaning is identity of implications. But (59) and (75) do not imply the same things. Consequently, they cannot have the same deep structure. And since there is every reason to suppose (75) rather than (59) has (60) as its deep structure, (59) does not have (60) as its deep structure.

If we reject Ross's performative thesis, we are still left with the task of explaining the facts he adduces to support it. And even if we accept his thesis, we have not solved the more general problem of how to describe within a grammar the systematic relationship between a sentence and its illocutionary act potential.

5 A Critical Appraisal of Transformational Semantic Theory

Does the Katz-Fodor semantic theory accomplish what it sets out to accomplish? According to Katz and Fodor,

> A semantic theory describes and explains the interpretative ability of speakers by accounting for their performance in determining semantic anomalies, by deciding upon paraphrase relations between sentences, and by marking every other semantic property or relation that plays a role in this ability.[35]

By "interpretative ability" Katz and Fodor mean the ability to understand and use sentences of a language. However, at this stage of linguistic inquiry we cannot hope to explain linguistic ability. Rather, Chomsky's view is that we are in a position to specify the tacit knowledge speakers have which enables them to understand and use their language. So, strictly speaking, the Katz-Fodor semantics is part of a competence model rather than a performance model. Its purpose is to describe that part of a speaker's linguistic knowledge which enables him to speak and understand his language, which is not described by the syntax. In the quotation above Katz and Fodor seem to claim that this can be accomplished by describing the knowledge which enables a speaker to recognize anomaly, synonymity, analyticity, and so on. The question I want to raise is whether describing the knowledge which enables speakers to recognize semantic properties of sentences is sufficient for describing the knowledge which enables speakers to understand and use sentences of their language. There are reasons to think that it is not. However, the objection I will raise here is not a fatal one; I hope to provide a way of overcoming it.

In order to determine what data a semantics must ac-

count for to be descriptively adequate, Katz and Fodor
ask us to imagine a non-speaker and a speaker of English,
both presented with an English sentence, *S*. The non-
speaker has available a complete syntax and phonology of
English. The question is what does the English speaker
know about *S* that the non-speaker, equipped with a syntax
and a phonology, does not know? As we have seen, the
English speaker knows whether *S* is ambiguous, anomalous,
analytic, synonymous with another sentence, and so forth.
The non-speaker, on the other hand, is not in a position to
judge whether *S* has any of these properties, though he is able
to judge whether it has various syntactic and phonological
properties. On this basis, we can say that a semantics, to be
descriptively adequate, must account for those properties
of a sentence for which the syntax and phonology give no
account. And we test the adequacy of a semantics of a language by comparing the properties which it assigns to sentences with those assigned by speakers of the language. For
example, if a speaker of English judges *S* to be ambiguous,
then the semantics of English must predict that it is ambiguous.

Let us now turn to our criticism of the Katz-Fodor semantic theory. Suppose our non-speaker is a German who understands no English. He is given a universal grammar
which contains the definitions of linguistic properties and
a syntax and phonology of English which are written in
German. In addition, he has available a monolingual lexicon, the lexical entries of which are in English, and a set
of projection rules with a description of their use in German. Moreover, the syntax contains correct structural descriptions of many English sentences. The German speaker,
so equipped, would know all that the Katz-Fodor semantic
theory can tell us about these English sentences. He would
know, for example, whether one of these sentences is ambiguous. He could determine this by observing whether
there is a lexical item in the sentence which has two readings which are not excluded by a selection restriction else-

where in the sentence. But even with a syntax, phonology, lexicon, and projection rules, our German speaker is not able to understand the English sentences presented to him. The reason for this is that he cannot understand the entries in the dictionary, since they are written in English. Consequently, though he knows enough about English to know the properties of English sentences, he does not know enough to enable him to understand these English sentences. So, a theory which describes the knowledge which enables a speaker to detect ambiguity, anomaly, and so on, does not necessarily describe the knowledge which enables a speaker to understand the sentence. Hence, it seems that the Katz-Fodor theory which describes the former is insufficient for describing the latter.

The same point can be made in terms of semantic markers. Semantic markers are the basic theoretical terms of the Katz-Fodor semantic theory. They are used to represent senses of lexical items and selectional restrictions; projection rules operate on them to form readings of phrases and sentences; and the definitions of semantic properties operate on these readings to determine the semantic properties of sentences. Moreover,

> Semantic markers are the elements in terms of which semantic relations are expressed in a theory. . . . The semantic markers assigned to a lexical item in a dictionary are intended to reflect whatever systematic relations hold between that item and the rest of the vocabulary.[36]

Semantic markers, then, are the basic building blocks of the Katz-Fodor semantic theory. On Katz's view the theoretical vocabulary of semantics is on a par with the theoretical vocabulary of syntax, such as N, VP, NP.[37] The latter are used in representing the syntactical structure of sentences whereas the former are used in representing their semantical structure.

How do we understand semantic markers? Since they are supposed to be theoretical terms within universal semantics, we cannot equate them with the English words with which they are orthographically identical. Rather, we must understand them by observing the role they play in the semantic component and lexicon and by understanding the observation statements which are a consequence of the semantic component's assignment of readings to sentences. However, neither of these will enable us to understand the meaning of individual semantic markers. This can be demonstrated quite easily. Let us replace each distinct semantic marker in the Katz-Fodor semantic theory by a different number. These numbers are to be thought of as shapes which contribute no semantic content to lexical entries. Our revised theory can state exactly the same internal relationship among lexical items and can define the same semantic properties for sentences as the Katz-Fodor semantic theory. For example,

(76) (a) two sentences are synonymous if and only if the string of numbers associated with one sentence is identical to the string of numbers associated with the other.

(b) two readings are related if and only if they share one number in common.

However, sets of numbers do not represent senses for expressions, and since there is no way of assigning a meaning to these numbers, our theory does not provide a semantics for any natural language. The Katz-Fodor theory is confronted with precisely the same problem. Since their theory provides no more internal relations and observation statements than the revised theory, it imparts no more meaning to semantic markers than the revised theory imparts to numbers. The upshot is that the Katz-Fodor semantic theory does not represent senses for lexical items—it only associates uninterpreted shapes with them—and does not, thereby, describe the semantics for any natural language.

I think that there is an easy but incorrect answer to the problem. We could construe semantic markers not as theoretical terms, but as English words. This is not as paradoxical as it first seems. We can use English words to express the meaning of non-English words, for example, 'mann' means *human male*. The English words, 'human male', are used to express the sense of 'mann', and it is in using them in this way that we should construe the semantic markers in the Katz-Fodor semantic theory. They are English words being used to express the senses of expressions.

This might be thought to run contrary to the Katz-Fodor theory's goal to provide a description of what a speaker knows about his language. Let us suppose we are describing Norwegian. One might argue that since the semantic markers are in English—and there is no reason to suppose Norwegian speakers know English—we cannot take lexical entries written in terms of them to be a description of a Norwegian speaker's linguistic knowledge. What our critic has failed to notice is how meaning specifications function. We can say truly about Jan, a Norwegian speaker who speaks no English, that he knows that 'mann' means *human male*. What this means is that he can represent to himself the sense of the Norwegian word 'mann' and that sense is, also, the sense of 'human male'. In representing this sense to himself he would represent it in Norwegian words which mean the same as 'human male'. Consequently, we can describe what a speaker knows about the meaning of his language, any language, in English.

Since our semantics is now presented in English, in order for our German speaker to understand it, we must translate the semantic markers into German. He would, then, be able to understand the English sentences presented to him. That the semantic markers must be translated distinguishes them from the substantive universals of syntactic and phonological theory. For these universals need not be translated for our German speaker to understand and use them; their meaning is entirely determined by the role they play in grammatical theory.

There are four objections which can be raised against this way of construing semantic markers. First, by specifying the meanings of all words in every language in English, we are imposing on speakers of alien languages and cultures our own conceptual scheme. Second, many languages have words for particular cultural phenomena which we do not have. Consequently, there are no words in English to represent the senses of these words. Third, a theory is vacuous to the extent it leaves open the interpretation of any terms of the theory. Since no meanings are provided for semantic markers, semantic theory does not fully explicate the senses of expressions. Lastly, if semantic markers are English expressions, then they cannot be linguistic universals.

These four objections raise difficult problems which cannot be answered easily. In fact, the first objection will be considered more fully in the next chapter. There is, however, a first approximation to an answer. English can be used to talk about many different conceptual schemes. If our native thinks of men as manifestations of manhood, then that, too, can be represented in the semantics of his language using English words. After all, the works of Plato and Aristotle, two philosophers who have different conceptual schemes, have been translated into English. This gives us an answer to the second objection. Not only can English express a variety of conceptual schemes, but also it can express concepts for which it has no words. It can do this by introducing new words into its vocabulary or by defining the alien words in terms of sets of English words. The history of English is replete with the introduction of loan words into the language. Moreover, anthropologists have described in English cultural phenomena markedly dissimilar from our own. Often the cultures they describe use one word or a short phrase to talk about these cultural features. In some cases the anthropologist must describe them at length to give us an understanding of them. To reverse the situation, how would we explain to a Kurd in his language the meaning of 'baseball'? Though it would not be easy, the important point is that it is not impossible. The third objection is more difficult to answer. The most direct answer is that every theory makes use of terms which are not defined in the theory. Physics, for example, cannot get by without mathematical and logical terms, and taxonomic biology employs descriptive terms taken from our ordinary, non-technical vocabulary. This is not to say that the terms not defined in a theory will not be defined in some other theory, rather only that such terms need not be defined in the theory in which they occur.

The last objection requires a revision in our view that semantic markers are English terms. English is a language which began to be spoken roughly in the twelfth century and might not be spoken in the twenty-first. Moreover, it is just an accident of history that there is such a language. Let us suppose that English never existed. Even if English did not exist, it is perfectly possible that other languages exist. It would, then, be impossible to express the semantics of these languages by using English expressions, since by hypothesis they do not exist. Consequently such expressions cannot be linguistic universals, for linguistic features are universal if and only if they occur in the grammar of every possible language. A way around the impasse is to say that the English expressions in the theory represent concepts which are universal to all languages and it is these concepts which are part of universal semantics. In fact we can use any language to express the semantic markers. So, our German speaker does not understand our semantics of English, because he does not understand the terms which represent the semantic markers. In order for him to understand the theory, then, it must be translated into German. There are many difficulties with this way out, some of which will be raised in the next chapter.

6 Jackendoff's Revision of Transformational Linguistic Theory

In the foregoing we have assumed that transformations do not affect meaning and, consequently, no surface structure information need be supplied to the semantic component, in order for it correctly to assign meanings to sentences. I now will examine this assumption. R. S. Jackendoff noticed that the application of the Passive transformation to an underlying P-marker which contains sentence negation and quantifiers in the subject or object changes the meaning of the underlying form.[38] The Passive transformation exchanges the subject of a sentence with its object and places the subject in a noun phrase headed by 'by'. For example, (77) (a) is derived from an underlying form similar to (77) (b).

(77) (a) The woman is loved by the man
    (b) The man present passive love the woman

In the theory in Chomsky's *Aspects of the Theory of Syntax,* the semantics operates on (77) (b), disregarding 'passive', giving us a meaning which is synonymous with

(78) The man loves the woman.

Notice however, the effect that the Passive transformation has on the form underlying (79) (a)

(79) (a) Many men passive don't love Gertrude.
    (b) Gertrude isn't loved by many men.

(79) (a) and (b) are not synonymous. (79) (b) means the same as either

(80) (a) Not many men love Gertrude.
    (b) It is not the case that many men love Gertrude.

The reason the Passive transformation has changed the meaning of (79) (a) in deriving (79) (b) is that it has changed the scope of negation. In (79) (b), (80) (a), and (80) (b) the quantifier is within the scope of the negation, but not in (79 (a). Logical notation can express the difference. Let $M =$ many, $N =$ men, $g =$ Gertrude, and $L =$ love. (79) (a) is symbolized by (81) (a) and (79) (b) by (81) (b).

(81) (a) $(Mx) (Nx \cdot \sim Lxy)$
    (b) $\sim (Mx) (Nx \cdot Lxy)$

It might seem that we can avoid this undesirable result by deriving (79) (b) from a form containing 'passive' which underlies (80) (a) instead of deriving it from a form underlying (79) (a). We would first apply the passive transformation yielding

(82)   Not Gertrude is loved by many men.

Then we apply a rule called *Negative Incorporation* giving us

(83)   Gertrude is not loved by many men.

However, there are two difficulties with this solution. First, Negative Incorporation must be blocked from applying to a form underlying (80) (a) which does not contain 'passive'. For, it would produce

(84)   Many men don't love Gertrude.

which is not synonymous with (80) (a). Second, the analysis gives us no way of generating

(85)   Many women are not envied by Alice

We cannot derive it from a form containing 'passive' underlying

(86)   It is not the case that Alice envies many women.

(85) and (86) are not synonymous. That they are not synonymous can be seen by comparing

(87)   Many women are not envied by Alice, but many are.

(88)   It is not the case that Alice envies many women, but many are.

(88), but not (87) is a contradiction. Once again it is the scope of negation which produces the non-synonymity of (85) and (86). In (85) the quantifier is not within the scope of 'not', but in (86) it is.

To solve these problems Jackendoff proposes that sentences like (79 (b) and (85) be derived from deep structures underlying (79) (a) and (86), respectively. The result is that the deep and surface structures of these sentences are not synonymous. Consequently, in order to provide a semantic interpretation for (79) (b) and (85) we must provide the semantics with information about the scope of negation in their surface structure. On Jackendoff's analysis, then, we allow transformations to alter the meaning of deep structures in deriving surface structures, and, thus, we abandon the thesis that all transformations are meaning preserving.

Of course Jackendoff's argument does not show that all transformations change meaning. Deep structures still serve as input to the semantics, but in addition we must allow some surface structure information as input to the semantics. Schematically, with the revision of the theory in *Aspects* proposed by Jackendoff, a grammar of any language can be represented as consisting of the following components:

(89)

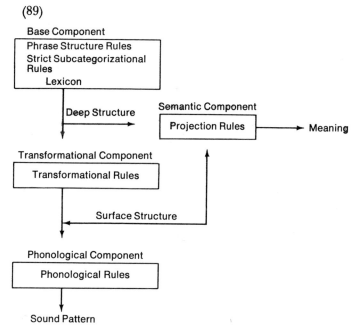

The lexical substitution rule is the same for all languages and, thus, can be stated once within universal grammar. It might turn out that the same set of projection rules or strict subcategorizational rules are linguistic universals. These, too, would be stated only within universal grammar, but it is still an open question which parts of a grammar are language specific and which parts are linguistic universals.

In this chapter I have presented with certain modifications the theory of linguistic description developed by Chomsky, Katz, Fodor, Postal, Jackendoff and others. Given the state of linguistics, however, it is uncertain whether any of the details of the theory presented here will be part of linguistic theory within the next five years. As I indicated in the beginning of the chapter, there are other theories falling under the general rubric of 'transformational linguistic theory' which call into question practically every part of the theory. Even if none of the details remain, the distinction between universal grammar and specific grammars will be maintained. Hopefully, this chapter has illustrated this distinction and thereby clarified some of the philosophical problems raised in Chapter III.

V

Behaviorism, Inscrutability of Reference, and Translational Indeterminacy

1 Quine's Behaviorism

Mentalism, the view we considered in the last two chapters, holds that language acquisition and use are to be explained in part by innate and acquired unconscious mental abilities, by the mental events and states to which these abilities give rise, and by the objects of these mental events and states. In this chapter we shall consider W. V. O. Quine's brand of behaviorism, which in places contrasts sharply with Chomsky's and Katz's mentalism.[1] The term *behaviorism* covers many sins and some virtues. Quine's variety appears in two forms: hard core and soft core. His hard core behaviorism is a version of Skinnerian theory, though Quine does not buy Skinner wholesale. He partly adopts Skinner with important modifications in formulating his own theories of language acquisition and use. Quine's soft core behaviorism is independent of but related to his hard core variety. A preliminary and much-simplified statement of this brand of behaviorism is that Quine holds that all the evidence a child has in learning his language and a linguist has in constructing his grammars is contained in the behavior of the people from whom they learn their respective languages and in the forces impinging upon the surfaces of these people.[2] This, of course, needs more than a bit of explanation.

According to Quine, the philosophical consequence of what I have dubbed his soft core behaviorism is that in explaining linguistic behavior the available evidence does not warrant the positing of the objects to which the mentalism of Katz and Chomsky commits them. However, as we shall see Quine does not criticize their views directly. Rather, he takes propositional attitudes and their propositional objects as paradigms of mental entities. Quine's arguments against these, which we will take up at the end of this chapter, can be applied, as well, to Chomsky's and Katz's mentalism. This we shall do in the final chapter.

2 Language Acquisition and Use

In this chapter we shall begin with Quine's theories of language acquisition and use. This in turn will lead into a rather extensive discussion of his views on translation and in particular of his theses of indeterminacy of translation and inscrutability of reference. Lastly, we shall consider Quine's arguments against the propositional attitudes and their propositional objects which Quine claims are a consequence of translational indeterminacy.

Let us start, then, with Quine's theories of language acquisition and use. As I pointed out above, Quine adopts a good deal of Skinner in constructing these theories, though there are important differences. I shall concentrate my attention on Quine's views and only bring in Skinnerian behaviorism where it clarifies my discussion. It would be an interesting and important task to compare the two and to discover the reasons for Quine's divergence from Skinner, but I shall not attempt it here.

For Quine there are two steps in a child's learning a

language. The first is a conditioning of the child's verbal responses to non-verbal stimuli; the second to verbal stimuli. The untutored child innocent of any language babbles unprovoked by his parents. Quine, following Skinner, calls this babbling *operant behavior* which is the natural behavior of an organism unshaped and unconditioned by experience or training. Again following Skinner, Quine claims that the child's babbling is shaped and conditioned into speech resembling mainly that of his parents. Suppose the child utters something like 'Mama' in the presence of his mother.

> The mother, pleased at being named, rewards the random act, and so in the future the approach of the mother's face succeeds as a stimulus for further utterances of 'Mama'.[3]

What Quine describes is a classic case of *operant conditioning.* The child babbles 'Mama', the *operant response,* in the presence of its mother who rewards the child's behavior with a smile, the *reinforcing stimulus.* The repeated reinforcement of the response in the presence of the mother tends not only to increase the probability of the response, but brings it under the control of the presence of the mother. That is, the mother becomes a *discriminative stimulus* in whose presence the child will tend to utter 'Mama'. If the control of the discriminative stimulus is firmly enough established, the child will continue to utter 'Mama' in the mother's presence, although his doing so is no longer reinforced. Notice that operant conditioning supposedly explains both the child's learning 'Mama' and his subsequent use of it. The child learns the one-word sentence because he is rewarded when uttering it appropriately. And his future use of it is occasioned by his mother's presence.

Operant conditioning can be much more complicated than the simple case described above. The schedule of rewards can be varied; reinforcing stimuli can be used to shape behavior as well as increase its probability; chains of stimulus and response can be established in which a stimulus which is reinforcing for earlier behavior becomes a discriminative stimulus for subsequent behavior.[4] But Quine does not make use of any more than the bare bones I have outlined.

Not all language learning is, on Quine's view, due to the conditioning of operants. The child's natural predilection for mimicry plays an important role in the acquisition of language.

> Mimicry . . . develops to the point where any new utterance from someone else becomes a direct stimulus for a duplicate. Once the child reaches this stage his further learning becomes independent of operant behavior. . . .[5]

However, even when the child's initial verbal response is due to mimicry, he learns the response because he is reinforced to do so.

> It remains clear in any event that the child's early learning of a verbal response depends on society's reinforcement of the response in association with the stimulations that merit the response. . . . This is true whatever the cause of the child's first venturing of the response. . . .[6]

That is, whether the child's initial response is due to babbling or mimicry Quine holds that his learning the response is due to reinforcement. However, one of the difficulties of such a view is to determine the reinforcements. Surely, when a child starts acquiring language hand over fist, neither parents nor passing strangers reward him for his efforts with a smile. But, Quine finds rewards in the most unlikely places. A reinforcing stimulus might be ". . . no more than corroborative usage, whose resemblance to the child's effort is the sole reward."[7] Why should we take such corroborative usage to be a reinforcing stimulus? It does make some sense to apply the notion of 'reinforcing stimuli' to the very early stages of child language learning and use.

Much beyond that it does not seem to have application. For an event is a reinforcing stimulus with respect to some piece of behavior only if the event increases the probability of the behavior. After a few months when the child has got onto learning his language, even if we know the past history of the child, we cannot assign a probability to the child's uttering any one sentence rather than another. And until we can assign such probabilities we have no grounds for attributing the child's language learning and use to reinforcing stimuli. Though this criticism has full weight against Skinner, it is difficult to know whether it applies to Quine.[8] In the above quotation, Quine qualifies his endorsement of reinforcement by saying that it is clear that it applies to "the child's *early* learning of a verbal response." But he does not say when this period begins or ends.

According to Quine, after a short time, a child goes beyond learning his language by being conditioned to non-verbal stimulations. He stops responding to presented stimulations with one-word sentences and begins to engage in limited conversation. To account for this Quine holds that the child is conditioned to associate sentence with sentence.

> Association of sentences is wanted not just with non-verbal stimulation, but with other sentences. . . . The most obvious case of the verbal stimulation of verbal response is interrogation. . . . 'Red' as a one-word sentence usually needs a question for its elicitation. . . . The question may be 'What color will you have?' or 'What color did it use to be?' In such a case the stimulus eliciting 'Red' is the verbal one unaccompanied by red light. . . .[9]

But how are sentences associated with one another? According to Quine, ". . . any such interconnection of sentences must finally be due to the conditioning of sentences as responses to sentences as stimuli." Quine's position here is not altogether clear. His use of 'stimulus' and 'response' suggests that the conditioning between sentences is Skinnerian. 'What color did it used to be?' is the discriminative stimulus which occasions the verbal response 'Red'. Now for these two sentences to be related in this way, the person to whom the question is asked must have heard the question before, responded with 'Red', and been reinforced for his response. Only in this way is it possible for 'Red' to be brought under the stimulus control of the question. But this is highly unlikely to occur very frequently, for most of the sentences in our conversations are sentences we have neither heard nor uttered before. Even if the speaker did hear the question before and responded with 'Red', what would be the reinforcing stimulus? Quine does not say. It seems that there is little reason for holding that speakers learn very many of the sentences of their language by their being conditioned to other sentences. And in fact there is reason against it, since most of the sentences a speaker utters or hears are novel and, thus, could not have been learned by past conditioning.

Linguistic novelty, or creativity, as Chomsky calls it, plays havoc with operant conditioning. We have abilities which enable us to project beyond our past verbal experience, without which we would say nothing new, a dreary prospect. Quine recognizes this.

> Not that all or most sentences are learned as wholes. Most sentences are built up rather from learned parts, by analogy with the way in which those parts have previously been seen to occur in other sentences which may or may not have been learned as wholes.
>
> It is evident how new sentences may be built from old materials and volunteered on appropriate occasions simply by virtue of the analogies. Having been directly conditioned to the appropriate use of 'Foot' . . . as a sentence, and 'Hand' likewise, and 'my foot hurts' as a whole, the child might conceivably utter 'my hand hurts' on an appropriate occasion though unaided by previous experience with that actual sentence.[10]

However, it is not at all evident what the "analogies" are which enable a child to project from what he has learned to novel sentences. As I indicated in Chapter III, 'analogy' is a cover term for a problem, not a solution to it. Consider the following set of sentences;

(1) John was certain that Bill saw whom?

(2) Whom was John certain that Bill saw?

(3) John was certain of the fact that Bill saw whom?

One would expect that on the basis of the similarity between (1) and (3) that

(4) *Whom was John certain of the fact that Bill saw?

which is analogous to (2) would be grammatical. But it is not. There are many cases of this sort which, I believe, can only be treated adequately by transformational grammar. Not that Quine rejects transformational grammar, but his endorsement is less than wholehearted, the reason for which we shall take up in the last chapter.[11]

Quine seems to suggest that the early stages of language acquisition and use can be explained by a theory of operant conditioning and the later stages by a theory of analogies. But the two theories are not about the same sort of thing. Chomsky's distinction between performance and competence is useful here. A theory of operant conditioning is a theory of verbal performance. That is, it is supposed to enable us, when equipped with knowledge of a speaker's past conditioning and present stimulations, to predict his future verbal response. Not so with analogy. Even if we did know what the analogies were which speakers draw among sentences, we would not be able to predict what a speaker would utter on any occasion. All we would know, had we a complete grammar, is whether what he uttered was grammatical. So, Quine's analogy does not enable us to explain speaker performance. Rather, it would be part of what Chomsky calls a competence model. Consequently, it will not do to attempt to explain part of speaker performance by a theory of operant conditioning and, then, shift to analogy to explain the rest, as Quine seems to do.

To be amenable to conditioning and to draw analogies, Quine recognizes that a child must have a tendency to group stimulations together and to consider some stimulations more similar to one another than to other stimulations.

> Otherwise a dozen reinforcements of his response 'Red' on occasions where red things were presented, would no more encourage the same responses to a thirteenth red thing rather than to a blue one . . .[12]

Moreover, Quine maintains that this tendency is innate rather than acquired.

> Language aptitude is innate; language learning, on the other hand, in which that aptitude is put to work, turns on inter-subjectively observable features of human behavior and its environing circumstances, there being no innate language and no telepathy.[13]

Both Chomsky and Quine, then, attribute innate characteristics to the language learner. There are, however, differences between their views. The first, which I take to be really terminological, is that Chomsky attributes to children innate linguistic knowledge while Quine endows them with innate abilities. We have seen, however, that it is possible to restate Chomsky's innateness hypothesis in terms of abilities, rather than knowledge without any loss in explanatory power.

The second difference is much more substantial. As we have seen, Chomsky claims that a child is born with a highly structured linguistic ability to learn languages containing formal, substantive, and organizational universals.[14] Quine, on the other hand, is much more parsimonious in his attributions. He maintains that children are born with what he calls *innate quality spaces*. Suppose a child has learned 'Red' in the presence of red things. If he would say 'Red' pointing to something pink, but not to something orange, we could conclude that pink is closer to red than is orange in his innate quality space.[15] Quine endows the child with a separate quality space for each of the senses. Moreover, he considers the possibility that each sense requires more than one quality space apiece, for there is no reason to think that one quality space applies to colors as well as shapes.[16] Quine's quality spaces can be used to explain more than just the acquisition of verbal behavior. The innate abilities Chomsky attributes to the child are particularly linguistic. Thus, Quine and Chomsky differ not only in the quantity, but, also, in the kind of innate abilities they attribute to the child to explain language acquisition.

To summarize Quine's theory of language acquisition and use, in the early stages a child learns sentences of his language by being conditioned to non-verbal stimuli. Once some sentences are learned in this way, new sentences are added to the child's repertoire by the conditioned association of sentence with sentence. Conditioning limits the child's verbal behavior to sentences he has heard in the past. To use and understand sentences beyond these, the child constructs sentences out of learned parts by analogy. Furthermore, Quine holds that for conditioning and analogizing to be possible the child must be born with innate quality spaces which enable him to group stimulations together.

Nothing has been said about how the child learns the meanings of the expressions of his language. One would think that precious little linguistic behavior could be explained without making use of the notion of 'meaning'. It is ordinarily held that communication proceeds in the following way. A speaker wishes to express a thought to a hearer. To do so he constructs a sentence which expresses his thought and utters it in the presence of his hearer. In turn the hearer recovers the speaker's thought by decoding the sentence. Of course, for the hearer to understand the speaker the thought in his mind must be the same as the thought in the speaker's. And on this model, in order for a child to communicate he must learn the meanings of the words and the grammar of his language. Using these, he too can encode and decode thoughts. This model of linguistic communication and acquisition is quite similar to Chomsky's and Katz's views, though much simpler. However, in Quine's theories of language acquisition and use, the meanings of sentences play no role. An utterance is a response to verbal or non-verbal stimulations. No meanings intervene. Hence, there is no reason to give an account of how children learn the meanings of sentences.

The most important aspect of Quine's views on language, I believe, is his criticism of the simple model of communication given above. What Quine tries to show is that there are no grounds on the basis of available evidence to say whether the meaning the speaker expresses is the same as the meaning the hearer decodes. And if there is no way to determine this, meaning can play no role in explaining linguistic behavior. This is what I have called Quine's soft core behaviorism.

3 Radical Translation and Behavioristic Semantics

To support his attack on meaning Quine switches to translation. Let us suppose we have the following: a native informant and a linguist whose language we will take to be English. The linguist's task is to construct what Quine calls a *translation manual,* consisting of a syntax and a lexicon. Using this manual, supposedly, we can translate any native sentence into an English sentence with the same meaning. Now there is a parallel between native and linguist, parent and child, and speaker and hearer. In all three, one member of the pair utters a sentence which expresses his meaning and the other, to understand the sentence uttered, must grasp this meaning. Quine's claim about meaning applied to translation is that

> . . . manuals for translating one language into another can be set up in divergent ways, all compatible with the totality of speech dispositions, yet incompatible with one another. In countless places they will diverge in giving, as their respective translations of a sentence of the one language, sentences of

the other language which stand to each other in no plausible sort of equivalence however loose.[17]

Quine's thesis is that on the evidence available to the linguist it is possible for him to construct different translation manuals which yield in English divergent translations. If this is correct, then to suppose that there is some one meaning expressed by both native and English sentences in these cases is to suppose something for which there is no evidence. Of course, all this needs argument. And more importantly, it must be shown how it can be applied to a speaker and hearer of the same language.

There is an obvious analogy between our linguist and a child learning his first language. To put them on a par, the task we shall set for the linguist is to translate a language totally unrelated to English spoken by people whose culture is quite different from his. Moreover, at the initial stages of translation the linguist will be unaided by an interpreter or bilingual. After all, the child, not knowing any language, is in a similar position. The linguist does have some obvious advantages over the child. He speaks a language and presumably has studied some linguistics. And both of these help him in describing the native's language, because he knows what features of the native's language to look for. But they do not necessarily enable him to learn the native's language more quickly than the child can learn his. And more importantly, they do not increase or alter the linguist's available evidence for his translation manuals. All that either linguist or child has to go on is what they obtain through their senses, including the verbal and non-verbal behavior of native and parent respectively. Precisely what this evidence is will become clearer in our exposition of Quine's views.

How does the linguist translate a language totally alien from his own without the aid of a bilingual interpreter? The ordinary paths are not open to him; there are no cognates and no loan words. The obvious way of beginning is observing the native's use of language and its accompanying behavior. One imagines that the native at some point will gesture toward an object, while uttering its name. But, the linguist should be wary about endowing native behavior with the same significance as his own, for a furrowed forehead might mean something quite different in the native's culture than it does in the linguist's. However, translation must start somewhere. And one would suppose that the best place to begin is with pointing. Imagine a rabbit flashes across the native's visual field. The native notices the creature and, pointing to it, cries 'Gavagai'. Can the linguist tentatively conclude from this that the one-word sentence 'Gavagai' is to be translated as 'Rabbit'? Hardly. 'Animal', 'Rodent', 'Furry creature', 'Four-footed animal', all qualify on the basis of the native's extended arm and his utterance. The linguist needs some way of narrowing down the field. To do this he must take matters into his own mouth and query the native about this and that. For example, the linguist could strike 'Animal' off his list, if he asked 'Gavagai?' pointing to a gnu or a gnat and the native in response dissented to the question. Conversely, the linguist would gain confirming evidence for translating 'Gavagai' as 'Rabbit' if he pointed to a rabbit, asked 'Gavagai?' and the native assented.

This assumes that the linguist is able to ask questions in the native's language and to recognize native assent and dissent. According to Quine, in order to recognize the latter responses,

> What [the linguist] must do is guess from observation and then see how well his guesses work. Thus suppose that in asking 'Gavagai?' and the like in the conspicuous presence of rabbits and the like, he had elicited the responses 'Evet' and 'Yok' often enough to surmise that they may correspond to 'Yes' and 'No', but has no notion which is which. Then he tries the experiment of echoing the native's own volunteered pronouncements. If, thereby, he pretty regularly elicits 'Evet' rather than 'Yok', he is encouraged to take 'Evet' as 'Yes'. Also he tries responding with 'Evet' and 'Yok' to the native's

remarks; the one that is more serene in its effects is the better candidate for 'Yes'. However inconclusive these methods, they generate a working hypothesis.[18]

But do they? What the linguist must avoid at this point and at every point in translation is projecting his own culture and beliefs about the world onto the behavior of the native. For the linguist wants to discover what native words and sentences mean, unclouded by the linguist's culture and beliefs. However, the procedure Quine proposes in the above quotation does not accomplish this goal. He suggests that the linguist begins to learn the native language by "asking 'Gavagai?'." But how does the linguist know how questions are asked in that language? In English there is a complex linguistic apparatus for asking questions, including the interrogative pronouns, inverted word order, falling intonation with wh-questions, and rising intonation with yes-no questions.[19] Features corresponding to these must be translated from an alien language into our own just as much as the words and the sentences of the language. Moreover, there is no reason to suppose that the response elicited by echoing the native's utterance corresponds to 'Yes' rather than to 'The gods willing' or that serenity indicates agreement rather than resignation to the stupidity of field linguists. But if we do not allow the linguist assumptions about the common significance of some human behavior, translation could not get off the ground. In order for the enterprise to begin let us assume that the linguist is able to ask the native questions and to recognize native assent and dissent. Later on in the chapter we shall examine these assumptions.

We have armed the linguist with some assumptions about native behavior that enable him to begin his translation. Let us return to our rabbit example. After some assiduous questioning, the linguist settles on 'Rabbit' as a plausible translation of 'Gavagai'. Underlying the linguist's translation, we can imagine the following rather simple procedure. The linguist attempts to isolate the set of things which prompt the native's utterance of 'Gavagai'. He then assays his own language, discovering that the same things, rabbits, prompt his utterance of 'Rabbit'. Because utterances of both are prompted by rabbits, the linguist's 'Rabbit' serves as a translation for the native's 'Gavagai'.

Plausible as this procedure seems, Quine argues that there are difficulties with it. Suppose that there is a fake rabbit in the bush. Not knowing this, both native and linguist might well assent respectively to 'Gavagai' and 'Rabbit'. Or suppose that a rabbit flashes by at an angle at which the native can get an eye full, but the linguist only gets a glimpse. The native would assent to 'Gavagai' but the linguist might dissent from 'Rabbit'. In the first case it is not a rabbit but a fake rabbit which prompts assent and in the second a rabbit prompts native, but not linguist assent. It cannot be rabbits, then, which prompt assent to both 'Gavagai' and 'Rabbit' which provide the basis for translation. To avoid these difficulties, Quine argues that in translation we must not take the native's and linguist's utterances to be prompted by rabbits, but by what Quine calls *stimulations*. And a native sentence can be translated by a linguist's sentence if and only if their utterances would be prompted by the same stimulations.

> It is important to think of what prompts the native's assent to 'Gavagai?' as stimulations and not rabbits. Stimulations can remain the same though the rabbit be supplanted by a counterfeit. Conversely, stimulation can vary in its power to prompt assent to 'Gavagai' because of variations in angle, lighting, and color contrast, though the rabbit remains the same. In experimentally equating the uses of 'Gavagai' and 'Rabbit' it is stimulations which must match, not animals.[20]

What then, does Quine take stimulations to be? On his view visual stimulations are to be equated ". . . with the pattern of chromatic irradiation of the eye" which appear on the native's and linguist's retinas.[21]

Quine's cure for the problem is on the face of it much too extreme. Translation does not proceed eyeball to eyeball. No field linguist I know of examines the native's retina. And informants already vexed by the linguist's interminable questions would, I think, find such examination intolerable. There are much better ways to overcome difficulties created by counterfeit rabbits and by variations in angle, lighting, and color contrast than focusing on the retina. We could take both linguist and native out of the field and put them in a more controlled environment, say a laboratory. It would be easy enough to determine that counterfeit rabbits do not prompt the native's 'Gavagai' and linguist's 'Rabbit'. Moreover, any effect lighting, angle, and color contrast have on the native's or linguist's response can be eliminated. Despite these obvious suggestions, Quine has a further, deeper reason for switching from objects to stimulations. He argues that identifying rabbits as prompting the native's utterance is to foist off onto the native the linguist's view of what there is in the world. To see this we must wait until we come to Quine's discussion of the translation of native terms. For the moment we shall accept Quine's "stimulations."

Let us more closely examine the linguist's translation technique. Suppose the linguist hears the native utter S while pointing to A's. As a working hypothesis, the linguist supposes that A-stimulations prompt the native's utterance of S. To check his hypothesis the linguist asks the native 'S?' under different stimulus conditions, determining the stimulations to which the native assents and those from which he dissents. These sets of stimulations serve in a definition of what Quine calls the *stimulus meaning* of a sentence. The *affirmative stimulus meaning* of S is the set of stimulations to which a speaker would assent, when asked 'S?' And the *negative stimulus meaning* of S is the set of stimulations to which a speaker would dissent, when asked 'S?' If the stimulations to which the speaker would assent are α and those to which he dissents, β then the ordered pair, $<\alpha, \beta>$, constitutes the stimulus meaning of S for that speaker.[22] Stimulus meaning in turn enables us to define *stimulus synonymy*. Two sentences are stimulus synonymous if and only if they have the same stimulus meaning. In translating from the native language to his own, the linguist's procedure, then, is to match up sentences from the two languages which are stimulus synonymous. On Quine's view of translation, 'Rabbit' serves as a translation for 'Gavagai' because the two sentences have the same stimulus meaning.

As Quine recognizes, stimulus meaning and stimulus synonymy do not do justice to our ordinary notions of meaning and synonymy. First, Quine's criterion for stimulus synonymy marks sentences as not being stimulus synonymous which would ordinarily be taken as synonymous. Second, the criterion marks sentences as stimulus synonymous which would be considered non-synonymous and, thirdly, the criterion blurs the distinction between empirical discoveries and changes in meaning. Let us begin with the first point. Suppose that known to the native, but not to the linguist there is a local rabbit fly which always accompanies rabbits. Imagine now that a rabbit fly goes whipping across the native's visual field. Even though the native is not stimulated rabbitly, he assents to 'Gavagai?' The linguist on the other hand, because he is ignorant of the constant conjunction between rabbits and rabbit flies, would dissent from 'Rabbit?' if he were asked. Consequently, the stimulus meaning of 'Gavagai' and 'Rabbit' differ for the native and the linguist. Rabbit fly stimulations belong to the affirmative stimulus meaning of 'Gavagai' for the native, but not to the affirmative stimulus meaning of 'Rabbit' for the linguist. But we in our wisdom know that the difficulty is the native's belief about the constant conjunction of rabbit flies and rabbits and that the native's 'Gavagai' and the linguist's 'Rabbit' *really* have the same meaning. The apparent difficulty is that Quine's criterion is not able to make the proper distinction between the native's response due to belief and to meaning and so it marks the two sentences as non-synonymous.

Let us turn to the second difficulty. Consider the two sentences, 'There is an animal which had a heart', and 'There is an animal which had a kidney'. For most English speakers with a little knowledge of biology these two sentences are stimulus synonymous. But these speakers, I suppose, would not take them to mean the same in the sense in which they would take 'There are bachelors' and 'There are unmarried males' to mean the same. Consequently, Quine's criterion marks sentences as stimulus synonymous for speakers who do not take them to be synonymous. The last difficulty with stimulus synonymy is that it blurs the distinction between empirical discoveries and changes in meaning. Suppose someone believes Venus and the evening star not to be identical. For that person, 'There's Venus' and 'There's the evening star' are not stimulus synonymous. But after discovering their identity, the two sentences would become stimulus synonymous for him. Now we would ordinarily take it that the speaker has changed his belief about whether the evening star and Venus are identical, and not that he has changed what he means by the sentences. However, Quine's behavioral tests for stimulus meaning and synonymy make no such distinction. Obviously, then, stimulus meaning and stimulus synonymy do not give an adequate account of our intuitive notions of meaning and synonymy. As Quine points out himself, his behavioral criteria ". . . are still not behavioristic reconstructions of intuitive semantics but only a behavioristic *ersatz*."[23]

One would think these criticisms show that stimulus meaning and stimulus synonymy do not give an adequate account of our intuitions about meaning and synonymy and so should be discarded along with Quine's behavioristic semantics. To do so is to assume that our intuitive notions of meaning and synonymy are the measures of a semantic theory. Quine rejects this. His measure is the evidence that the linguist has available; and for Quine, as we have seen, "all the objective data he [the linguist] has to go on are the forces that he sees impinging on the native's surface and the observable behavior vocal and otherwise of the native."[24] Any imputation of meaning or synonymy which goes beyond this evidence is, according to Quine, unwarranted.

In light of this let us reconsider the first criticism I raised against stimulus synonymy. The criticism turned on the linguist's inability to distinguish between affirmative responses to 'Gavagai' due to the native's belief about rabbit flies and rabbits and those due to what he means by the sentence. Because of this, rabbit-fly stimulations are included within the stimulus meaning of 'Gavagai' marking it as non-stimulus synonymous to the linguist's 'Rabbit'. It would seem easy enough for the linguist to weed out the effects of the native's belief and to determine those stimulations which are really part of the "meaning" of 'Gavagai'. Conceivably, the linguist would be able to capture some rabbit flies to present to the native in a place obviously uncontaminated by rabbits. One would suppose that the native would now dissent from the linguist's 'Gavagai?', since there are clearly no rabbits present. But clear to whom? To the native? It is possible that his belief that rabbit flies are always accompanied by rabbits is so deeply entrenched that he would assent to 'Gavagai?' when stimulated by rabbit flies no matter what the circumstances were. So we would not be able to screen out the intruding rabbit flies from the stimulus meaning of 'Gavagai'. On Quine's view then there is no way to distinguish between the native's responses to 'Gavagai' due to what he believes and those due to what he means.[25]

There are two philosophical theses underlying the criticisms of Quine's stimulus meaning and stimulus synonymy. It is held by many philosophers that a distinction can be made between a speaker's linguistic and factual knowledge and between the analytic and synthetic sentences of a speaker's language. These two theses are related. Consider an English speaker who knows that 'bachelor' means *an adult unmarried male who is not a widower*. Supposedly, he knows this by virtue of knowing his language. In contrast he knows that most bachelors do not live as long as spinsters, because he knows something about the world. Correspondingly, he knows the analytic sentence, 'All bachelors are adult unmarried males who are not widowers', to be true, because he knows the meaning of the words it contains, whereas he knows the synthetic sentence, 'Most bachelors do not live as long as spinsters' is true by knowing some facts about bachelors and spinsters. We can encapsulate the distinction between analytic and synthetic sentences, adding contradictory sentences for completeness, in the following criteria:

(5) S is *analytic* if and only if substituting synonyms for synonyms in S we can obtain a logical truth.

(6) S is *contradictory* if and only if substituting synonyms for synonyms in S we can obtain a logical falsehood.

(7) S is *synthetic* if and only if S is neither analytic nor contradictory.

Applying (5) to 'All bachelors are adult unmarried males who are not widowers', we obtain 'All adult unmarried males who are not widowers are adult unmarried males who are not widowers', which is a logical truth. Thus, the former sentence is analytic.

Let us restate the first criticisms against Quine's stimulus meaning and stimulus synonymy using these distinctions. The native assents to 'Gavagai', when having a rabbit fly stimulation. Thus according to Quine's criterion, rabbit fly stimulations are included within the stimulus meaning of 'Gavagai' making it non-synonymous with 'Rabbit'. However, a critic of Quine might argue that these stimulations should not be included, since they are due to the native's factual belief that rabbit flies are always accompanied by rabbits. But how does the linguist know this? He would be able to determine this if he could tell whether the native sentence corresponding to 'All rabbit flies are always accompanied by rabbits' were analytic or synthetic.

Quine, however, thinks that this is impossible. To determine that the native sentence is analytic, the linguist must be able to tell that the native expressions corresponding to 'rabbit fly' and 'insect which is always accompanied by rabbits' are synonymous. But, Quine regards 'synonymous' as much in need of clarification as 'analytic', or 'synthetic'.[26] And he claims that all definitions of 'synonymous' which have been proposed either turn ultimately on 'analytic' and thus are circular or contain an undefined term. We shall return to this later in the chapter. This aside, Quine maintains that

> . . . For all its a priori reasonableness, a boundary between analytic and synthetic statements simply has not been drawn. That there is such a distinction to be drawn at all is an unempirical dogma of empiricists, a metaphysical article of faith.[27]

Consequently, the linguist cannot tell whether the native sentence is analytic or synthetic and, thus, whether rabbit fly stimulations really belong to the meaning of 'Gavagai'. In fact, Quine thinks that there is nothing to determine, that there is no distinction to be drawn between linguistic knowledge and factual knowledge, and, correspondingly, between analytic and synthetic sentences. At heart, the other criticisms raised against stimulus meaning and stimulus synonymy assume that there are such distinctions. And because Quine thinks that there are not, he does not regard these criticisms as grounds for rejecting his behavioral criteria in favor of our intuitive notions of synonymy and meaning. Quine believes, however, that there is a bit which can be salvaged from (5). The questions corresponding to the sentences that (5) supposedly picks out are questions to which a speaker would assent no matter what stimulation we presented him. And for Quine this is the kernel of sense in 'analyticity'. A sentence is

> *stimulus analytic* for a subject if he would assent to it, or nothing, after every stimulation.[28]

But, this definition does not enable us to resurrect the distinction between linguistic and empirical knowledge. The linguist will still be unable to tell whether the native assents to 'Gavagai' when stimulated rabbit flyly because of what he firmly believes about the world or because of what he means by the sentence.

Let us pursue further Quine's theory of translation. We have examined the application of stimulus synonymy and stimulus meaning to only one sentence, 'Gavagai'. Can they be applied to other native sentences? Quine draws a distinction among four different kinds of sentences, between *occasion* and *standing sentences* and between *observation* and *non-observation sentences*. These sentential categories are not mutually exclusive. All observation sentences are occasion sentences. Let us begin with the first distinction.

> . . . Standing sentences contrast with occasion sentences in that the subject may repeat his old assent or dissent unprompted by current stimulation when we ask him again on later occasions, whereas an occasion sentence commands assent or dissent only as prompted all over again by current stimulation.[29]

We can ferret out of this quotation a necessary condition for occasion sentences.

(8)   *S* is an *occasion sentence* only if assent to or dissent from *S*? would occur after a current prompting stimulation.

By *current prompting stimulation,* Quine means something other than '*S*?' For instance, assent to 'Gavagai?' is prompted by a present rabbit stimulation. Quine gives as examples of occasion sentences, 'Gavagai', 'Red', 'It hurts', and 'His face is dirty', and of standing sentences, 'The crocuses are out' and 'The Times has come'. However, (8) excludes the former examples. None of them requires current prompting stimulations to elicit assent or dissent. Take 'It hurts'. Suppose my aunt and I are talking about my cousin's broken leg and I ask solicitously, 'It hurts?' Clearly, my aunt can respond without the prompting presence of my cousin's injured leg. It is easy enough to embed Quine's other occasion sentences in conversations where, when used as questions, they would command assent or dissent unprompted by current stimulation.

The underlying motivation for Quine's distinction is that the truth value of some sentences depends on the occasion of their use—Quine's occasion sentences, while the truth value of others remains fairly fixed from occasion to occasion—Quine's standing sentences. The former tend to have indexicals, the latter do not, though 'It's raining', an occasion sentence, contains no indexicals. There is no hard and fast line between standing and occasion sentences. The truth of 'The president of the U.S.A. wears glasses' might vary every four years, whereas the truth of 'It's raining' could change from day to day. I think the following criterion captures these features somewhat better than Quine's.

(9) A sentence, *S,* is an *occasion sentence* for a speaker if and only if

(a) on being asked *S* and presented with an α stimulation the speaker would assent (dissent)

(b) on being asked *S* again immediately, and presented with a β stimulation the speaker would dissent (assent)

(c) (a) is repeated.

The degree of occasionality depends upon how long it takes for (b) and (c) to be done successfully. The less the time the more the occasionality. The step between (b) and (c) is necessary to prevent 'The Times has come' from being on the occasion end of the scale, for before the delivery of the *Times* a speaker would dissent to the sentence and immediately after delivery switch to assent.

Supposedly, if we know the meaning of a sentence, we are able to understand and use it. Stimulus meaning does not account for our ability to do either. The sorts of prediction we can make about a speaker's behavior, given the stimulus meaning of a sentence S, is that if a speaker were asked S while stimulated with α, and α was part of the affirmative (negative) stimulus meaning of S, then the speaker would assent (dissent). This, of course, tells us nothing about when a speaker will say or ask S or perform any other illocutionary act in uttering S. For this reason we should not take Quine's stimulus meaning as an attempt to give a general behaviorist account of language, as I think some have done.

But there is some connection between stimulus meaning and our preanalytic notion of meaning. If the linguist knew the stimulus meaning of the native sentence corresponding to 'Red', he would know some of the situations in which it was appropriate to use it and would understand on some occasions what the native meant by using it. But the stimulations impinging on the native's surface when he utters a standing sentence give the linguist no clue about how to use or to understand the standing sentence. We can imagine the native assenting to his equivalent of 'The crocuses are out?' while having a linguist-stimulation, or a blue sky-stimulation or a house-stimulation. If the linguist were to attempt to determine the stimulus meaning of this sentence, these stimulations would belong to its affirmative stimulus meaning. But, knowledge of these and other stimulations which would belong to the stimulus meaning of this sentence would not enable the linguist to understand it. Similar problems affect other standing sentences and consequently the notion of 'stimulus meaning' does not apply to them.

Though the linguist can associate stimulus meaning with occasion sentences, not all occasion sentences can be translated. Consider the native sentence corresponding to 'He's a bachelor', the stimulus meaning of which might well capture all the bachelor stimulations in town. But, since being a bachelor does not go by face value, the linguist's knowledge of the sentence's stimulus meaning will not enable him to use the sentence, nor to translate it. Consequently, the linguist cannot translate standing sentences and many occasion sentences using Quine's behavioral criteria.

Stimulus meaning more closely approximates our ordinary meaning intuitions for what Quine calls *observation sentences*. An observation sentence is one

> . . . on which all speakers of the language give the same verdict when given the same concurrent stimulation. To put the point negatively, an observation sentence is one that is not sensitive to differences in past experience within the speech community.[30]

'Red' is an observation sentence, since most English speakers who are asked 'Red?' and stimulated similarly would respond in the same way.[31] 'Bachelor' is not, since undoubtedly there are English speakers, who if asked 'Bachelor?' and given the same stimulation, would respond differently. Stimulus meaning comes closer to our ordinary notions of the meaning of 'Red' than the meaning of 'Bachelor'. In most cases we can tell whether something is red by looking, but the looks of a person in many cultures tell us nothing about his marital state. To know whether someone is a bachelor, we must know something about his past history. Consequently, we can explain the meaning of 'Red' by pointing to red things. The information gained by eyeballing is enough to catch on to the use of the sentence. But pointing to any number of bachelors will not help in explaining the meaning of 'Bachelor'. The pointing must be accompanied by a little history. Now the stimulus meaning of 'Red' does contain red things—that is, red stimulations—but the stimulus meaning of 'Bachelor' can tell us nothing about the history of bachelor stimulations. Because stimulus meaning does a better job in approximating the meaning of observation sentences, stimulus synonymy can be used to translate them. There should be little difference in the stimulus meaning of 'Red' and of the corresponding native sentence, though for the reasons given above, stimulus synonymy cannot be used to translate the native equivalent of 'Bachelor'. However, not all sentences which turn out to be observation sentences on Quine's criterion can be translated. We can well imagine a speech community in which everyone knew who were the bachelors. To their 'Bachelor' sentence the linguist would receive community-wide agreement under the same stimulations. This sentence, then, would be marked as an observation sentence, but the linguist could not translate it.

Observation sentences play an important role in Quine's theory of language acquisition. Except for cases of the above sort, observation sentences wear their meaning on their sleeve. The linguist can understand them without having access to any other part of the native's language. And for this reason, these are the sentences with which he begins his translation. This holds equally for the child learning his first language who must begin with those sentences which can be taught by ostension. As Quine puts it, ". . . observation sentences are the ones we are in a position to learn first, both as children and field linguists."[32]

In addition to native observation sentences the linguist has evidence for translating native truth-functional connectives. Negation has the effect of changing an occasion sentence to which the native assents to one to which he would dissent or vice-versa. Conjunction can be identified as a native locution which forms compound sentences such that a native would assent to the compound if and only if he would assent to both of the constituent sentences. And native alternation is an expression which forms a compound from which the native would dissent if and only if he would dissent from each of the constituent sentences. Similar criteria can be constructed for the other truth functions.

By going bilingual the linguist can broaden the scope of what he has evidence to translate to include non-observation occasion sentences. Let us suppose the native sentence corresponding to 'Bachelor' is 'Ungkar'. The reason the linguist cannot translate this sentence is that the set of stimulations which the native would assent to or dissent from on being queried with 'Ungkar' is different from the set to which the linguist would assent to or dissent from on being queried with 'Bachelor?' It is highly unlikely that the linguist and native would take the same set of people to be bachelors. By becoming bilingual the linguist can overcome this problem. For the bilingual linguist 'Bachelor' and 'Ungkar' have the same stimulus meaning. And consequently, he can translate 'Ungkar' and all other non-observation occasion sentences.

The Quinean bilingual linguist can translate native

(10)   occasion sentences

(11)   truth-functional connectives

and can determine which native sentences are

(12)   stimulus analytic.

Notably missing from our list are native standing sentences, which we shall discuss shortly. Even if these could be translated using Quine's behavioral criteria, we would hardly have a translation manual. We have no way of translating the native's words. Ordinarily translation from a foreign language to English does not proceed by equating sentences with sentences, but by replacing native words with synonymous English words and by transforming the native sentence structure into English sentence structure. This requires a bilingual lexicon and a description of native grammar. Is it possible to construct criteria analogous to Quine's to broaden the linguist's translation to include native words? Surprisingly, Quine argues that it is not. He claims that (10)–(12) are the limits of what can be determinately translated on the basis of what he regards as the available evidence. There are two reasons for this. First, native words, in particular what Quine calls the apparatus of objective reference, terms, quantifiers, demonstratives, articles, et cetera, cannot be determinately translated. And second, neither can standing sentences. We shall begin with his argument for the former claim.

4   *Translational Indeterminacy of Terms*

Consider the native sentence 'Lo gavagai' and suppose that the linguist has divided it into two words, 'lo' and 'gavagai', neither of which he has yet translated and that he has translated the one-word sentence, 'Gavagai', as 'Rabbit'. Can he conclude from this that 'gavagai' is a native term true of rabbits and thus to be translated by 'rabbit'? Quine argues that the linguist can draw no such inferences.

> Stimulus synonymy of the occasion sentence 'Gavagai' and 'Rabbit' does not even guarantee that 'gavagai' and 'rabbit' are coextensive terms, terms true of the same things.
>
> For, consider 'gavagai'. Who knows but what the objects to which this term applies are not rabbits after all, but mere stages, or brief temporal segments of rabbits? . . . Or perhaps the objects to which 'gavagai' applies are all sundry undetached parts of rabbits; again the stimulus meaning would register no difference. When from the sameness of stimulus meanings of 'Gavagai' and 'Rabbit', the linguist leaps to the conclusion that a gavagai is a whole enduring rabbit, he is just taking for granted that the native is enough like us to have a brief general term for rabbits and no brief general term for rabbit stages or parts.[33]

Quine's claim is that stimulus synonymy of 'Gavagai' and 'Rabbit' does not enable the linguist to tell whether 'gavagai' is true of rabbits, undetached rabbit parts, rabbit stages, or even manifestations of rabbithood. And, thus, it does not give the linguist a way of determining whether 'gavagai' should be translated into English by 'rabbit', 'undetached rabbit part', 'rabbit stage', or 'manifestation of rabbithood'.

One might think that this only shows that Quine's behavioral criteria are defective and need adjustment. It seems easy enough to fix up the criteria. To translate 'gavagai' all we need do is to point and to ask some questions. Quine argues that this will not settle the translation.

> Point to a rabbit and you have pointed to a stage of a rabbit, to an integral part of a rabbit, to the rabbit fusion, and to where rabbithood is manifested. Point to an integral part of a rabbit and you have pointed again to the remaining four sorts of things; and so on around. Nothing not distinguished in stimulus meaning itself is to be distinguished by pointing. . . .[34]

So pointing cannot achieve the necessary discrimination among the different possible translations of 'gavagai'. What about asking questions? Cannot the linguist ask in the native's language, 'Is this gavagai the same as that gavagai?' pointing to one part of the rabbit on the 'this' and another on the 'that'? If the native assents, the linguist can rule out 'undetached rabbit part' as a translation for 'gavagai'. But the linguist's being able to ask and understand the question presupposes that he has translated the native locutions corresponding to 'this', 'that', and 'the same'. However, Quine maintains that

> We cannot even say what native locutions to connect as analogues of terms as we know them, much less equate them with our term for term, except as we have also decided what native devices to view as doing in their devious ways the work of our own various auxiliaries to objective reference; our articles and pronouns, our singular, and plural, our copula, our identity predicate. The whole apparatus is interdependent. . . . The native may achieve the same net effects through linguistic structures so different that any eventual construing of our devices in the native language and vice-versa can prove immaterial and largely arbitrary. Yet the net effects, the occasion sentences and not the terms, can match up in point of stimulus meanings as well as ever for all that. Occasion sentences and stimulus meaning are general coin; terms and reference are local to our conceptual scheme.[35]

Consider again our English native hybrid, 'Is this gavagai the same as that gavagai?'. Quine's point is that the decision to translate some native expressions as 'this', 'that', or 'the same', is tied up with the decision to translate 'gavagai' as 'rabbit'. The linguist asks quite a different question, if he translates the native expression he takes to correspond to 'the same' as 'part of the same thing'. The question becomes 'Is this gavagai part of the same thing as that gavagai?', assent to which is compatible with translating 'gavagai' as 'undetached rabbit part'. There are, then, different manuals of translation compatible with (10)–(12), one of which translates 'gavagai' as 'rabbit' and the other of which translates it as 'undetached rabbit part'. There must be, of course, different translations for the native copula and other apparatus of objective reference in the two manuals of translation. We can now understand why Quine defines stimulus meaning and stimulus synonymy in terms of stimulations rather than objects. Stimulations are neutral with respect to there being rabbits or undetached rabbit parts and so do not impose on the native the linguist's beliefs about what there is.

The first conclusion Quine draws from the above considerations is that the linguist cannot uniquely determine what 'gavagai' means in English, whether it means 'undetached rabbit part', 'manifestation of rabbithood', 'rabbit', and so on. Secondly,[36] and more surprisingly, he concludes that the linguist cannot determine to what the native is referring when he says 'Lo gavagai'—that is, whether 'gavagai' is true of rabbits, manifestations of rabbithood, or undetached rabbit parts. As Quine puts it, "reference itself proves behaviorally inscrutable."[37] To keep these theses distinct we shall call the first *indeterminancy of translation* and the second *inscrutability of reference*. The two theses are obviously related. If the linguist cannot determine what 'gavagai' is true of, then he cannot fix its meaning in English.

What is surprising is that Quine offers no direct argument for either thesis. He does not give us two incompatible manuals of translation both of which are compatible with (10)–(12). Rather, he argues from analogy. He compares natural languages with formal systems, in particular the laws of natural numbers.[38] But the comparison is rather complicated, and the same point can be made with a much simpler example. Consider the following formula:

(13) $(x)(Nx \supset (\exists y)(Ny \cdot (x \neq y \cdot Lyx)))$

Now let us suppose that (13) constitutes a language which consists of only this one sentence. We assume we know the following about (13). Jones, the only speaker of (13), assents to (13), if to anything, given any stimulation. That is, it is stimulus analytic. '(x)' and '$(\exists x)$' are, respectively, universal and existential quantifiers, and 'x' and 'y' are variables. Our problem is to decide upon a translation of 'L' and 'N' into English. We know very little about (13). The only constraint, and one that hardly deserves the name, is that (13) is stimulus analytic and so the translation of 'L' and 'N' into English should yield as a translation of (13) a stimulus analytic sentence. Given this minimal condition, there are a large number of predicates which could be equated with 'N' and 'L' among which are, respectively, 'is a number' and 'is larger than' and also, respectively, 'is a person' and 'is a parent of'. Clearly, the two interpretations are not equivalent. Moreover, on the former interpretation in uttering (13), we would take 'N' and 'L' to be true of natural numbers and on the latter of persons. Consequently, there is no way to tell determinately what 'N' and 'L' are true of and what they mean in English. Of course, this is on the assumption that neither Jones's behavior nor his language provides us with additional evidence for further restricting the interpretation of 'N' and 'L'. Thus, the referents of the terms 'N' and 'L' are inscrutable, and their translation into English is indeterminate.

There are obvious parallels between this simple example and translation from the native language into English. The translation of the term 'gavagai' into English, like 'N' or 'L', is indeterminate. It could be translated as either 'rabbit', 'manifestation of rabbithood', or 'undetached rabbit part'. There are differences, however. There are more constraints on the translation of the native language into English, for the linguist can translate determinately native occasion sentences and truth connectives and mark native analytic sentences. But, still, according to Quine, these constraints are not sufficient to single out a unique interpretation of 'gavagai'. And as a result, we do not know exactly what it is true of and what it means in English.

If we accept Quine's conclusion, we are in the awkward position of being unable to translate native terms, quantifiers, the copula, and so forth. At least the translation of native observation and occasion sentences is determinate; their translation is based upon solid behavioral evidence. Or so it seems. But Quine claims that the evidence is not as solid as it appears to be. Each of Quine's behavioral criteria depends upon the linguist's prior translation of native assent and dissent. We saw earlier in the chapter that Quine identifies assent with the more serene response to the linguist's query 'Gavagai?'. As was pointed out, there is no reason to connect assent with serenity rather than with agitation. To do so, Quine argues, is to project our cultural biases onto the native. Consequently, indeterminancy of translation applies to assent and dissent as well. And, thereby, stimulus meaning, stimulus synonymy, and stimulus analyticity are infected with indeterminacy.[39] But the translational indeterminancy of terms and of assent and dissent are not on a par. Suppose there are several hypotheses about native assent and dissent compatible with native behavior and stimulation patterns, but incompatible with one another. There is no non-arbitrary way to choose among them. For translation to get off the ground we must choose one of these hypotheses and use it to translate native occasion sentences and truth-functional connectives and to determine native stimulus analytic sentences. Even then the translation of native terms and the other apparatus of reference would be indeterminate. As Quine remarks, "the indeterminancy of translation comes in degrees."[40]

If Quine is right about translation, why do not linguists give us six or seven manuals for translating a language rather than one? In translating a remote language linguists sometimes do offer alternative translations for parts of the language, but not for all of it. The reason is that

> . . . Linguists adhere to implicit supplementary canons that help to limit their choice of . . . [manuals of translation]. For example, if a question were to arise over equating a short native locution to 'rabbit' and a long one to 'rabbit part' or vice-versa, they would favor the former course, arguing that the more conspicuously segregated wholes are likelier to bear the simpler terms.[41]

But Quine argues that these supplementary canons should not be confused with evidence for translation, for on (10)–(12) it is just as likely that the short native expression should be associated with 'rabbit part' rather than with 'rabbit'. These canons, then, are just as much an imposition onto the native's language of the linguist's beliefs as is the linguist's decision about what to regard as native assent and dissent.

Might the bilingual clear up indeterminacy of translation? One would think that if anyone could translate terms from the native language to English, a bilingual could. For, surely, a bilingual knows what the terms mean in each of the languages he speaks. And to translate terms from the native language to English all he need do is equate terms from the two languages which mean the same. But, indeterminancy of translation is not so easily turned aside. How does the bilingual know what terms to equate? Take 'gavagai'. The bilingual's task is to translate it into English. The bilingual is now in exactly the same position as the linguist. He too can translate 'gavagai' into English in a variety of ways each of which is incompatible with any of the others. In fact, standing in English, the bilingual is not even able to determine what 'gavagai' is true of. For all he knows when he says 'Lo gavagai', he could be referring to a rabbit, an undetached rabbit part or a manifestation of rabbithood. The bilingual, then, is not able to surmount either inscrutability of reference or indeterminacy of translation.

Inscrutability of reference and indeterminacy of translation are a serious business. We are forever unable to tell to what people who speak a radically different language from our own are referring and what they mean by the terms of their language. Consequently, we can never know whether they count among the objects of their universe ideal types, whole enduring objects, or stages. To put the matter in a more philosophical tone of voice, we cannot discover the ontology of such speakers. However, it seems that we can be relatively confident about the ontology of people whose language is related to our own or whose culture is similar to ours. Of course, the more distantly related the language or the more different the culture the less confident we can be. But about speakers of our own language who share our culture we can be absolutely certain. Or can we? The rub is that inscrutability of reference and indeterminacy of translation apply to our own language, though it is a bit odd to call it 'translational' indeterminacy. When you say something, I do not translate your words into my language, since we speak the same language. To see Quine's point what we must do is take it that we do not speak the same language even though the words we utter sound the same. Suppose you say 'There's a rabbit' pointing to something in your field of vision. Looking in the same direction, I see a rabbit. Should I take it from this that you are referring to a rabbit? According to Quine,

> . . . Radical translation begins at home. Must we equate our neighbor's English words with the same strings of phonemes in our own mouths? Certainly not. . . . We can systematically reconstrue our neighbor's apparent references to rabbits as really references to rabbit stages. . . . The problem at home differs none from radical translation. . . .[42]

So, you and I are in no different position than native and linguist. In understanding what you mean by what you say, on Quine's view, I have no more evidence to go on than your behavior and the stimulations I can surmise are impinging upon your sense receptors. Consequently, just as the linguist cannot determine what the native thinks there is, I cannot determine what you think there is.

One would think that this conclusion shows the absurdity of Quine's view, for normally we have no difficulty understanding one another. When you say 'There's a rabbit', I have every reason to take you to be referring to a rabbit. After all you did use the word 'rabbit', accompanied by a pointing gesture in the direction of something I would call a 'rabbit'. And here I have more to go on than just your behavior and stimulation patterns; I have your words. I can ask what you mean by 'rabbit' and most probably you will not say it is a manifestation of an ideal type, but rather that it is a physical object. What does this come to? I am afraid it does not come to much. It does not overcome intralinguistic inscrutability of reference or indeterminacy of translation. What it shows is that for all practical purposes we do not misunderstand one another. When you ask me to pass you a rabbit, I do not misunderstand you and pass you a gnu. I take your words at face value. But if I did not, if I were perverse, I could take you to be asking me to pass you a manifestation of a rabbithood. Even your proferred definition of 'rabbit' is no help in the face of such perversity. There is no reason why your 'physical object' cannot be taken to mean what I mean by 'manifestation of an ideal type'. Point to a physical object and you have pointed to a manifestation of an ideal type. Of course, if I did not take your 'rabbit' or 'physical object' at face value, I would have to reinterpret many other terms and expressions in your language. But, according to Quine, this could be done. So, even with my perverse interpretation of your terms, I would still be able to fulfill your request. In passing you a rabbit, I would be passing you a manifestation of rabbithood. No misunderstanding arises. Our normal activities get on without mishap, no matter how I construe your terms and referential expressions, as long as my construals are compatible with all the evidence obtainable from your behavior and stimulation patterns. Problems arise only when I ask philosophical questions about what you are referring to in saying 'That rabbit over there . . .'.

Though we cannot tell what objects people are really talking about, even people who speak the same language as we do, we could be worse off. We could fail to understand the referents and meaning of our own terms. But clearly *we* can tell to what we are referring. Or can we? Quine argues that we cannot, that we are in precisely the same position with our own language as we are with the language of others.

> . . . The inscrutability of reference can be brought even closer to home than the neighbor's case; we can apply it to ourselves. If it is to make sense even of oneself that one is referring to rabbits . . . and not to rabbit stages. . . . then it should make sense equally to say it of someone else.[43]

But since it does not make sense to say it of someone else, Quine concludes that it does not make sense to say it of ourselves.

It is natural to think that we are in a different position from others. Even if we do not know what others are referring to, we know what we are referring to. How could we not know that? We know what we mean, when we use 'rabbit'. We mean *a physical object which is a hopping rodent with long ears,* et cetera. And *that* is what we are referring to when we say 'That's a rabbit'. But just as we can reinterpret someone else's reply to 'What is 'rabbit' true of?' we can reinterpret our own answer; we can construe 'physical object' to mean *manifestation of an ideal type.* In doing so we would have to reinterpret the other words of objective reference in our own language. But if we can do it for another's language, we can do it for our own. Still, there seems to be something we can know when we say, 'That's a rabbit', which others cannot know. It is thought that when we utter this sentence, we can intro-spect and come to know what we mean by these words. And by understanding this we can tell to what we are referring in uttering the sentence.

What do we understand in such a case? Classical em-piricists, like Berkeley, claim that a mental image appears in the mind, when we utter or hear a word. And by under-standing this image we understand what we mean by the word.[44] But what image do we have when we say 'That's a rabbit'? Is it an image of a rabbit, of a rabbit stage, of a manifestation of rabbithood? If mental images, pictures in the mind, are no different from garden variety pictures, then there is no way to tell the difference among mental images of these different sorts of things. What would be the difference? Take a picture of a rabbit and you have thereby taken a picture of all the rest. So supposing our meanings to be mental images does not enable us to de-termine the referents of our terms.

Some philosophers suppose that when we say 'That's a rabbit', there are words which occur in our mind and by understanding these words we can determine to what we are referring in uttering the sentence. Of course, the mental sentence cannot be a duplicate of the uttered sentence, for then we could dispense with the duplicate and understand the sentence directly. Rather, if any sentence occurs, it must be something like, 'That's a physical object which has fuzzy hair, long ears, et cetera'. That is, it must be what we mean by the sentence we utter. There are various arguments against such a view. First, if our meanings, themselves, are words, then we face the problem of under-standing them. There must be other words, which express what we mean by these words. Obviously this would create an infinite regress. The second criticism is Quinean. The words which supposedly occur as our meaning of 'That's a rabbit' are open to interpretation. The mental occurrence of 'physical object' can be taken to mean *undetached rabbit part* or *manifestation of an ideal type*. As we have seen before, this would require the interpretation of other words, but according to Quine, it could be done. And we would once again have inscrutability of reference. The third and strongest criticism against such a view is that when we speak and understand our language there do not occur such mental words of which we are conscious.

Can Katz's semantic theory overcome inscrutability of reference? There are two reasons why it cannot do so. First, on Katz's view we are not conscious of the set of semantic markers which constitute the meaning of a word or sentence. But, then, we are not in a privileged position with special access to our meanings which others could not have. A psychologist or linguist could know as much about our unconscious semantic markers as we. Consequently, we would have no more evidence to go on than they in determining the referents of our terms. And according to Quine since paucity of evidence brings in its wake inscrutability of reference for the linguist, so would it for us as well. There is a second reason why semantic markers will not do the trick. Take 'rabbit' again. What semantic markers should we associate with it? If Quine is right about translation, then it should be possible, compatible with the available evidence, to assign as one of its semantic markers either (Physical object) or (Manifestation of an Ideal Type). Which of these we would associate with 'rabbit' would bring in its wake corresponding changes in the lexical entries of quantifiers, the copula, demonstratives, and so forth. Once again we would have inscrutability of reference.

It seems we have reached the paradoxical conclusion that we can never know the referents of our terms. But, then reference would seem to make no sense. This, however, creates the following difficulty for Quine's argument for inscrutability of reference. On the one hand, the argument purports to show that we cannot determine whether 'gavagai' is true of rabbit stages, manifestations of rabbithood, or undetached rabbit parts. On the other hand, we find that the same thing applies to the terms in our own language; we cannot tell what the terms of our own language are true of. But, if we cannot determine that 'rabbit', 'rabbit stage', 'manifestation of rabbithood', and 'undetached rabbit part' are true of different objects, what sense can we give to Quine's claim that 'gavagai' can be translated by mutually incompatible terms? For all we know they could be true of the same object. So in order to show that reference makes no sense across languages, Quine assumes that it makes sense within our own language. But, this assumption runs counter to his position that inscrutability of reference applies to the home language. Consequently, Quine's claim that in both our language and the native language, reference is inscrutable seems to be inconsistent.[45]

There is a way, however, to avoid the apparent inconsistency. Let us suppose we are at home in English using and understanding its apparatus of objective reference, in particular the logical expressions of quantification theory. With English as a background language, we can determine whether two terms are *coextensive*—that is, true of the same things.

'F' and 'G' are *coextensive* in English if and only if all F's are G's and vice-versa.[46]

Since all rabbits are not undetached rabbit parts and vice-versa, all undetached rabbit parts are not manifestations of rabbithood and vice-versa, and all rabbits are not manifestations of rabbithood and vice-versa, then 'rabbit', 'undetached rabbit part', and 'manifestation of rabbithood' are not coextensive terms. Now the claim that 'gavagai' can be translated into English by non-coextensive terms makes sense, but it only makes relative sense. That is relative to a background language which contains 'All . . . are . . . '.

What about the terms of our own language? How can we make out that they are inscrutable, when we must assume they are not in order to show the inscrutability of native terms? We can do this by switching languages, by going native. As native linguists, our task is to translate English terms into the native language. But now we shall have non-coextensive native terms which can serve equally well as translations for each English term. And, thus, from our vantage point as native linguists the referents of English terms are inscrutable. So it is only against our background language that we can make sense of the difference among 'rabbit', 'rabbit stage', et cetera. And it is against this background language that the terms of another language are referentially inscrutable. As Quine puts it

> Toward resolving the quandry, begin by picturing us at home in our language, with all its predicates and auxiliary devices. This vocabulary includes 'rabbit', 'rabbit part', 'rabbit stage', . . . ; also the two-place predicates of identity and difference, and other logical particles. In these terms we can say in so many words that this is a rabbit and that a rabbit part, this and that the same rabbit, and this and that different parts. *In just those words.* This network of terms and predicates and auxiliary devices is, in relativity jargon, our frame of reference, or coordinate system. Relative to *it* we can and do talk meaningfully of rabbits and parts. . . .[47]

Hence, as long as we are speaking English rather than speaking about it, 'rabbit', 'undetached rabbit part', and 'manifestation of rabbithood' are true of different objects and so do constitute alternative translations for 'gavagai'.

In our home language if we can settle questions of sameness and difference of reference can we also settle questions of sameness and difference of meaning? Our criterion for coextensiveness can determine whether two terms are true of the same thing, but not whether they mean the same. Take 'creature which had a heart' and 'creature which had a kidney'. These two terms are coextensive, for all creatures which had a heart are creatures which had a kidney. However, the two terms do not mean the same. It is easy enough to devise a criterion for term synonymy analogous with the criterion for coextensiveness.

> 'F' and 'G' are synonymous if and only if necessarily all
> F's are G's and vice-versa.

On this criterion, 'creature which had a heart' and 'creature
which had a kidney' are not synonymous, since clearly it is
not necessary that all creatures which had a heart are creatures which had a kidney. 'Bachelor' and 'adult unmarried
male who is not a widower' are marked as synonymous by
this criterion. So it appears that in English where we have
available 'all . . . are_____' and 'necessarily' we can determine whether a speaker regards two terms as coextensive
and as synonymous. But this seems to run counter to
Quine's claim that definitions of 'synonymous' ultimately
depend upon 'analytic' and vice-versa, and thus, are circular.

Before taking up this point, I want to distinguish between
the theory of meaning in which the leading notions are
'meaning', 'analyticity', 'synonymy', 'necessity', 'entailment',
and 'contradictoriness' and *the theory of reference* in which
the leading notions are 'reference', 'extension', 'satisfaction',
'true' and 'true of'. The theory of reference and the theory
of meaning treat different but related subject matters. The
referent of 'the natural satellite of earth' is the moon. But
it is possible for the moon to be destroyed and for the earth
to capture in its orbit another natural satellite, say Halley's
comet. Then, the referent of 'the natural satellite of the
earth' would be Halley's comet. However, the meaning of
this singular term has not changed. Meaning and reference
are related. If two different expressions have the same
meaning and can be used to refer, then they can be used
to refer to the same thing. And if two different expressions
can be used to refer only to different things, then they
differ in meaning.[48]

One of the differences between the terms in the theory
of reference and the theory of meaning is that a language
which does not contain any terms drawn from the latter is
extensional. A language is extensional if and only if coextensive expressions can be substituted one for the other in
any sentence of the language without altering the truth

value of the sentence. A language which is not extensional is *intensional*. We shall regard a *context* as extensional if and only if substitutivity of coextensive terms in that context does not alter the truth value of the sentence containing the context. We have defined 'coextensiveness' for general terms; coextensiveness for singular terms and sentences is similar.

Two singular terms '*a*' and '*b*' are coextensive if and only if *a* is identical to *b*.

Two sentences '*p*' and '*q*' are coextensive if and only if *p* if and only if *q*.

Let us apply the notions of extensionality and intensionality to sentences containing concepts drawn from the theory of reference and the theory of meaning. Consider the following two sentences, both of which are obviously true.

(14) 'Creature which had a heart' is true in English of creatures which had a heart.

(15) 'Creature which had a heart' means in English *creature which had a heart*.

Substituting 'creature which had a kidney' for the second occurrence of 'creature which had a heart' in (14) does not change its truth value, but so substituting it in (15) does. A language which contains 'means' is, then, intensional. We should notice in passing that 'All _____ are . . .' contains only extensional contexts, whereas 'Necessarily _____' contains an intensional context.

Quine rejects the terms from the theory of meaning as being unscientific, though his reasons for doing so are not altogether clear. There are places where he seems to reject them because their criteria cannot be grounded upon a speaker's behavior and stimulation patterns.

> When . . . we recognize with Dewey that "meaning . . . is primarily a property of behavior," we recognize that there are no meanings, nor likeness nor distinctions of meaning, beyond what are implicit in people's dispositions to overt behavior.[49]

Applying Dewey's dictum to the distinction between analytic and synthetic sentences, Quine holds that

> The distinction wavers as soon as we try to base it on verbal behavior. . . . The shortcoming that vitiates the notion . . . [is that it] is just insufficiently empirical. . . . It is . . . behaviorism that . . . looks askance at analyticity.[50]

Now these remarks are open to wide interpretation. One interpretation is that we cannot make sense of the distinction, because it cannot be drawn on the basis of speaker behavior and stimulation patterns. Generalizing from this, we might suppose that Quine rejects concepts from the theory of meaning, as he clearly does, because there cannot be any criteria for them in terms of behavior and stimulation patterns. But, if this is one of his reasons, then he must also reject those from the theory or reference, for they too cannot be so defined. That is, I believe, one of the lessons of inscrutability of reference. However, Quine does not find the concepts from the theory of reference as unclear and scientifically unacceptable as he finds concepts from the theory of meaning.

There is another reason, alluded to earlier in the chapter, which Quine gives for rejecting the latter and accepting the former. He claims that definitions of terms in the theory of meaning are circular. Take our criterion for the synonymity of 'F' and 'G' which turned on its being necessary that all F's are G's and vice-versa. How can we tell whether it is necessary? Certainly, it is necessary if and only if 'All F's are G's and vice-versa' is analytic in English. Little gain in insight here, for 'analytic' is no clearer than 'necessary'. Now 'All F's are G's and vice-versa' is analytic if and only if it can be turned into a logical truth by substituting synonyms for synonyms. We have come full circle without being able to tell whether 'All F's are G's and vice-versa' is necessary.[51]

A seemingly parallel criticism might be made against our criterion for coextensiveness. It depends upon our being able to tell whether all *F*'s are *G*'s and vice-versa. Someone might think that 'All . . . are _____', borrowing a phrase from Quine, is as much in need of clarification as 'coextensiveness'. But there is hardly a problem here and certainly no circle of definitions. We determine that all *F*'s are *G*'s and vice-versa by examining the *F*'s and seeing whether they are *G*'s and the *G*'s and seeing whether they are *F*'s. Similarly, to determine whether the two singular terms '*a*' and '*b*' refer to the same thing we must determine whether *a* is identical to *b*. To do this we go out and look. Sometimes, as with Venus and the evening star, it might take fiddling with telescopes and doing some calculations. According to Quine, there is no parallel procedure for telling whether two terms are synonymous or whether a sentence is analytic. In the last chapter we shall consider whether Katz's semantic theory circumvents Quine's criticisms.

Where does this leave us? Against a background of English we know that 'rabbit', 'undetached rabbit part', and 'manifestation of rabbithood' are true of different objects and so constitute alternative translations for 'gavagai'. So no paradox arises for Quine's argument for inscrutability of reference. In the face of these alternatives how does translation go on? For the linguist does provide us with native to English dictionaries and grammars. According to Quine, he does this by segmenting

> . . . heard utterances into conveniently short recurrent parts, and thus compiles a list of native 'words'. Various of these he hypothetically equates to English words and phrases, in such a way as to conform to [(10)–(12)]. Such are his *analytical hypotheses*.[52]

In addition, Quine claims, the linguist will need analytical hypotheses to equate native grammatical constructions with English grammatical constructions. Together these analytical hypotheses comprise the linguist's translation manual.

It is only in a loose sense, as Quine recognizes, that analytical hypotheses are hypotheses. A characteristic of genuine scientific hypotheses is that they can be confirmed or disconfirmed on the basis of available and future evidence. Not so with analytical hypotheses.

> . . . The linguist's finished jungle-to-English manual has as its net yield an infinite *semantic correlation* of sentences: . . . Most of the semantic correlation is supported only by analytical hypotheses, in their extension beyond the zone where independent evidence for translation is possible. That those unverifiable translations proceed without mishap must not be taken as pragmatic evidence of good lexicography, for mishap is impossible.[53]

The reason that mishap is impossible, according to Quine, is that there is no further evidence over and above (10)–(12) which has any bearing on the selection of analytical hypotheses. Consequently the selection of those parts of a manual of translation which goes beyond (10)–(12) is arbitrary. The linguist is free to choose any set of analytical hypotheses compatible with (10)–(12). That is, to equate the native's 'gavagai' with 'rabbit', 'undetached rabbit part' or 'manifestation of rabbithood'.

5   Translational Indeterminacy of Standing Sentences

We have seen the indeterminacy of translation of native terms. There is, as well, a similar thesis which applies to the native's standing sentences. They are those sentences response to which is not tied to present non-verbal stimulations. The theoretical sentences of science are paradigms of such sentences. One way, then, of viewing the task before the linguist in translating the native's standing sentences is that he must translate into English the native's theoretical sentences. Quine maintains that the translation of these sentences is indeterminate. There appear to be, at least, two different arguments for indeterminacy of standing sentences in Quine's work, neither of which are given in much detail. I will now sketch what seems to be Quine's central argument for indeterminacy but will hold off examining it closely and critically until the last chapter when I consider the consequences it has for transformational linguistics. In addition, in the last chapter I will take up Quine's other argument for indeterminacy which I believe is actually the stronger of the two.

Let us turn then to what seems to be Quine's main argument for the translational indeterminacy of standing sentences. He asks us first to consider the underdetermination of our own physical theory.

> . . . Physical theory is underdetermined . . . by all *possible* observations. . . . Consider all the observation sentences of the language: all the occasion sentences that are suited for use in reporting observable events in the external world. . . . Some of these . . . will be true and the others false, by virtue simply of the observable though unobserved past and future events in the world. Now my point about physical theory is that physical theory is underdetermined by all these truths. Theory can still vary though all possible observations be fixed. Physical theories can be at odds with each other and yet compatible with all possible data even in the broadest sense. In a word they can be logically incompatible and empirically equivalent.[54]

To put the matter schematically, let us suppose that O_1, O_2, . . . constitute all the possible observation sentences of English. Some of these sentences are true and some false. Let O_1', O_2', . . . be the true ones. To simplify matters let us suppose there are only two competing theories, A and B, both of which consist of a consistent set of theoretical or standing sentences. Now Quine's thesis about physical theories has two sub-theses. He claims first that it is possible that A and B are compatible with O_1', O_2', . . . and second that they can be logically incompatible with one another. These two theses are open to various interpretations. I will hold off, however, giving the reasons for my interpretation until the last chapter. I take the theses to be first, that if A is a physical theory of O_1', O_2', . . . , then there is at least another theory B of O_1', O_2', . . . , such that A is logically consistent with O_1', O_2', . . . , and B is logically consistent with O_1', O_2', . . . , and second, that A and B entail a contradiction.[55]

How does this have a bearing on translation? According to Quine,

> . . . the starting point [of translation] is the equating of observation sentences of the two languages by an inductive equating of stimulus meanings. In order afterward to construe the foreigner's theoretical sentence we have to project analytical hypotheses, whose ultimate justification is substantially just that the implied observation sentences match up. But now the same old empirical slack, the old indeterminacy between physical theories recurs in second intension. Insofar as the truth of a physical theory is underdetermined by observables, the translation of the foreigner's physical theory is underdetermined by translation of his observation sentences. If our physical theory can vary though all possible observations be fixed, then our translation of his physical theory can vary though our translations of all possible observation reports on his part be fixed. Our translation of his observation sentences no more fixes our translation of his physical theory than our possible observations fix our own physical theory.[56]

Once again schematizing Quine's argument will help us understand it. Suppose the native observation sentences are NO_1, NO_2, . . . and his theoretical sentences NT_1, NT_2, . . . Further there is a finite subset of the NT's to which the native assents constituting what Quine calls his physical theory. These are the theoretical sentences the native believes. According to Quine, we can correctly pair each NO with its corresponding English observation sentence, EO, with only inductive uncertainty by using the criterion for stimulus synonymy. Now Quine's theses of the translational indeterminacy of standing sentences is that it is possible to devise different analytical hypotheses, compatible with all the data, but which pair some of the NT's with logically incompatible English theoretical sentences. Suppose the two analytical hypotheses are *HA* and *HB* and that they yield translations compatible with the data obtained by stimulus criteria.[57] That is, they both give as English translations for each *NO* its stimulus synonymous English counterpart. But, for the native's physical theory, the theoretical sentences to which he assents, *HA* and *HB* yield respectively the logically incompatible *A* and *B* as its translations into English. This has two consequences. First, we cannot tell which physical theory the native holds, whether he holds one which corresponds to *A* or to *B*. And second we cannot tell what the sentences of the native's physical theory mean, whether they mean the same as *A* or as *B*. That is, there is both an indeterminacy of native beliefs and of native meanings.

Translational indeterminacy might be perfectly acceptable, if the sentences which could not be determinately translated were limited to highly theoretical sentences. We would not find it surprising or distressing if sentences far removed from observation could not be determinately translated, if there were alternative interpretations offered for them. Such things are common in translating poetry and more abstract prose and there is no reason not to expect comparable indeterminacy in translating the theoretical sentences of a language radically different from our own spoken by a people having an exotic culture. But Quine holds open the possibility that such indeterminacy affects not only the upper reaches of theory, but talk about ordinary middle-sized objects as well. His intention in presenting the above argument is

> . . . to persuade anyone to recognize the indeterminacy of translation of such portions of natural science as he is willing to regard as underdetermined by all possible observations. If I can get people to see this empirical slack as affecting not just highly theoretical physics but fairly common-sense talk of bodies, then I can get them to concede indeterminacy of translation of fairly common-sense talk of bodies.[58]

Of course, whether talk of ordinary objects is underdetermined by available evidence is a highly debatable question. However, one might look upon Quine's argument for the inscrutability of reference as showing that talk about such objects does go beyond what Quine regards as the available evidence.

One question, which Quine leaves open, is whether indeterminacy of standing sentences applies to English as well. I think that it does. If the linguist can construct analytical hypotheses which give divergent translations of native standing sentences into English standing sentences, then a native linguist can devise analytical hypotheses which give incompatible translations of English standing sentences into the native language.[59]

6   Translational Indeterminacy and Propositions

In discussing inscrutability of reference and indeterminacy of translation of terms and of standing sentences, we touched on many philosophical issues. But we have yet to discuss Quine's central motivation for presenting these theses which is, I believe, to show that there are difficulties with mentalist theories of language use and acquisition. As I pointed out in the beginning of the chapter, Quine does not directly criticize the views of Chomsky and Katz. Rather, he calls into question the existence of such things as propositions, ideas, concepts, intentions, and beliefs, the stock in trade of mentalism. And the arguments he gives for doing so are based on the theses mentioned above. In what follows I want to consider Quine's arguments against there being propositions. First, I will briefly present some arguments philosophers have given for thinking there are such objects. Second, I will consider what sort of an object a proposition is. Third, I will give Quine's criticisms of the arguments for propositions, concentrating in particular on his arguments which turn on the translational indeterminacy of standing sentences. Finally, I will show the relationship between Quine's attack on propositions and his behaviorism.

In Chapter II, I distinguished among three different uses of 'proposition'. It is used to refer to the meanings of sentences, to the objects of the propositional attitudes, and to the bearers of truth value. I believe that these should be kept distinct, but Quine does not do so. He uses 'proposition' in the sense of 'the meaning of a sentence' to apply to all three classes of putative entities. In what follows I shall adopt this use of 'proposition'. That Quine does not carefully distinguish among the different uses of 'proposition' does not, I believe, affect his arguments against there being propositions. Before turning to these arguments, I shall reconsider four arguments adduced for the existence of propositions. First, we appear to refer to them. Second, supposing that they exist seems to explain some facts about inter- and intralinguistic synonymy. Third, they are posited as the bearers of truth value. And fourth, they are taken to be the objects of the propositional attitudes. Let us begin with the first two. Consider the sentences:

(16)   (a)   Selma is a pediatrician.
       (b)   Selma is a baby doctor.
       (c)   Selma er en barnespesialist.

These sentences mean the same and the meaning they have in common is taken to be a proposition. Why should we think there are such things? One reason is that we refer to them. For example, we say such things as, 'The meaning of (16) (a) is unclear'. And in doing so we appear to be referring to the meaning of (16) (a) and saying something about it. Moreover, we seem to be able to tell when the meaning of two sentences is the same or different. And, we can determine this across languages; we can tell that in (16) the two English sentences express the same proposition as the Norwegian sentence. One of the criteria philosophers use to determine identity of propositions is synonymy.

(17)   Two sentences express the same proposition if and only if they are synonymous.

This in turn gives us an explanation for our ability to translate sentences from different languages.

(18) Two sentences are translations of one another if and only if they express the same proposition.

We have, then, the following arguments for the existence of propositions. First, in our ordinary conversations with one another we appear to refer to them; and second, facts about inter- and intralinguistic synonymy seem to warrant our supposing they exist.

The third reason for positing propositions is to serve as the bearers of truth value. However, as I showed in Chapter II, there are difficulties with this. Consider

(19) The man who saw Liberty Valence was here yesterday.

Suppose Harry says (19) in the morning referring to Ransom, and Fred says it in the afternoon referring to Jake. And what Harry says is true, while what Fred says is false. Since both Harry and Fred have uttered the same sentence which has the same meaning on both occasions, the meaning of the sentence—that is, the proposition which it expresses—would be both true and false. Consequently, the proposition which it expresses cannot be the bearer of truth value. To avoid this unpalatable result, we could adopt E. J. Lemmon's proposal and relativize assignment of truth values to times.[60] The proposition expresesd by (19) is true when Harry utters it in the morning and false when Fred utters it in the afternoon. No more difficulty arises here than with a chair's being red in the morning and blue in the afternoon. But suppose Harry and Fred utter (19) at the same time. Then, the proposition expressed by (19) would be both true and false. Consequently, relativizing truth value to times does not enable us to take propositions to be the bearers of truth value.

The reason that a sentence, such as (19), can be used to say something true on one occasion and false on another is that it contains referential devices, such as definite descriptions, locative and temporal adverbs, and proper names, all of which can vary in their referent from occasion to occasion. To prevent referential variation such expressions could be expanded to have a unique referent. For example, the definite description in (19) can be augmented so that it can be used to refer to only one person, 'the tall, dark, thin-lipped man who saw Liberty Valence on August 16, 1889, at 10:00 P.M. at Joe's saloon who is named Ransom Stoddard'. If all referential expressions in a sentence are treated in this way, it results in what Quine calls an *eternal sentence*.[61] Now there is no shift in the truth value of what is said from instance to instance in uttering an eternal sentence. So, we could take the propositions expressed by such sentences to be the bearers of truth value.[62]

There are several difficulties with this theory. Suppose you utter (19) and I say

(20)   (a)   That's true

       (b)   What you say is true

In Chapter II, we supposed that the 'That' of (20) (a) and the 'What you say' of (20) (b) were referring expressions and that in uttering (20) (a) or (b) I am referring to something and saying of it that it is true. It is fairly clear that if I am referring to anything, I am not referring to an eternal sentence which is an expansion of (19), nor to the proposition expressed by such a sentence. This, of course, is clearer in my saying (20) (b), for what I am referring to, if to anything, is what you said, and you certainly said neither the eternal sentence expansion of (19) nor the proposition it expresses. An additional problem is that we need an account of how and by whom an expansion of (19) into an eternal sentence is to be carried out.

We shall consider two suggestions for a solution to the latter problem, neither of which is successful. Katz, claiming to paraphrase Quine, proposes that it can be done on the basis of the information in the context in which (19) is uttered.[63] As we have seen, to eternalize (19), it is necessary to expand the definite description which functions as subject of the sentence. Suppose that you say (19) to me and that neither you nor I nor anyone else in the context in which you utter (19) knows the name or the whereabouts or much else about the man who saw Liberty Valence. You could pick him out of a lineup if you had to, but you could not describe him, at least not very well. So, there is insufficient information in the context to carry out the eternalization of (19), and probably not enough information is available in the context in which most sentences are uttered to eternalize them. The second suggestion, which is Quine's for the eternalization of sentences, is different from the one Katz attributes to him, but does not fare much better than Katz's proposal. Quine claims that

> . . . the eternal sentence will be one that the original speaker could have uttered in place of his original utterance in those original circumstances without detriment, so far as he could foresee, to the project he was bent on.[64]

But in the case I have described above there is no eternal sentence you could have uttered in place of (19), since you do not know very much about the man who saw Liberty Valence. As Quine recognizes, there is much room for improvement here.[65] Despite these problems, we will suppose that the thesis that the bearers of truth value are propositions expressed by eternal sentences is at least plausible, since our goal here is to consider Quine's arguments against there being such entities and not to determine what the bearers of truth value are.

Lastly, some philosophers take propositions to be the objects of the propositional attitudes. Consider

(21)   Sam believes that the girl is a thief.

One view about the logical form of this sentence is that it consists of two names, 'Sam' and 'that the girl is a thief', and a relation, 'believes'. A speaker in uttering (21), then, is said to refer to the two objects bearing these names and to be saying of Sam that he stands in the relation of believing to the object named by 'that the girl is a thief'. But what object is this? It cannot be the sentence 'The girl

is the proposition expressed by any sentence which could be used to state the theorem. Now the theorem would clearly exist if I did not know it. In fact, it would exist even if no one knew it. Moreover, both you and I, if we know the Skolem-Lowenheim Theorem, know the same thing. Consequently, the Skolem-Lowenheim Theorem, the propositional object of my knowledge, is not a mental object, though it is an abstract object.[69] Now it might be wondered how propositions, if they are not mental objects, can be objects of thought. The answer to this question is that not all objects of thought need to be mental objects. For example, physical objects which by (23) are clearly not mental objects can be objects of thought. Take Scott, the boy cutting my lawn. I am thinking about Scott and because I am, he is an object of thought. Similarly for propositions. I think that Scott is cutting the lawn and, as a consequence, that Scott is cutting the lawn is an object of thought.

Let us reconsider the arguments we have given for the existence of propositions with an eye to evaluating them. The arguments are of two sorts. The first, which is hardly an argument, is that we appear to use such expressions as

(24) (a) The meaning of the first sentence on this page

      (b) That the yard needs to be raked

      (c) What Harry and Sam believe

to refer to propositions. The second turns on their putative explanatory value. By supposing that there are such entities we are able to explain certain facts about meaning, truth, and the propositional attitudes. The status of their existence, so it is said, is no different from the existence of electrons, curved space, or gravitational fields. Quine does not find the first argument very persuasive. He correctly points out that we would be misled in thinking that there are meanings and beliefs just because there are expressions like those in (24).[70] After all, no one thinks there is an average American family or possibilities even though we can say meaningfully

(25)   (a)   The average American family has 2.4 children.

         (b)   The possibility that it will rain is slim.

Quine finds the second sort of reason somewhat more convincing. We would be committed to there being propositions if supposing there were enabled us to explain facts about meaning, translation, truth, and the propositional attitudes. But Quine claims that either propositions obscure the facts that they are supposed to explain, or the facts can be explained without them. Take truth. Instead of the propositions expressed by eternal sentences, Quine takes the sentences themselves to be the bearers of truth value. Everything about truth explained by the former, he claims, can be explained by the latter.[71] There is a difficulty, however, with Quine's proposal. Suppose that the eternal sentence uttered is ambiguous and under one meaning it is true and the other false. There is no switch in truth value from occasion to occasion. The sentence is eternally true and eternally false, a consequence, I am sure, unacceptable to Quine. This problem aside, Quine finds that, rather than clarify matters about meaning and translation, assuming there are propositions only falsifies the situation. Suppose we have two standing sentences, A and B, the former native and the latter English, which express the corresponding propositions $[A]$ and $[B]$. Our criterion in (17) provides a way of determining whether these are identical. $[A]$ and $[B]$ are identical if and only if A and B are synonymous. But because of translational indeterminacy, there is no way in principal to tell whether A and B are synonymous and consequently, no way for determining whether $[A]$ and $[B]$ are identical. So, supposing A and B express propositions, gives us the illusion that there is a fact about synonymy to be explained. But Quine claims that there is no fact of the matter; there is no synonymy to be explained. Consequently, we have no reason to suppose that A and B express propositions.

One should be a little less sanguine about giving up the objects of the propositional attitudes, for we seem to be able to explain a great deal of human behavior in terms of beliefs, intentions, hopes, wishes, wants, desires, and thoughts. But just as there is an indeterminacy of native sentence meanings there is an indeterminacy of native intentions, hopes, wishes, et cetera. Consider the native standing sentence *A* to which the native assents, and suppose it can be translated into English by either *B* or *C*. What does the native believe? Does he believe [*B*] or [*C*]? There is no way to tell. Since we cannot determine what the translation of *A* is into English, there is no way to determine what belief the native holds, no way to choose between [*B*] and [*C*] as the translation of *A*. And consequently, to suppose there is some determinate proposition which the native believes in assenting to *A* is once again to falsify matters. Thus, the propositional attitudes give us no grounds for believing there to be propositions.

When someone claims that there are objects of a certain kind, the burden of proof is on him. It is not up to us to show that there are not or could not be such things. The arguments of Quine we have considered to this point purport to show that the evidence advanced to support the claim that there are propositions does not do so. Quine, however, goes one step further. He claims that difficulties arise in supposing there to be propositions. The problem is in their individuation. He argues that we cannot tell when one proposition is the same as or different from another, as we can, Quine contends, with abstract objects such as numbers and sets, and physical objects, such as planets and flowers. And Quine maintains that

> Little sense has been made of the term ['proposition'] until we have before us some standard of when to speak of propositions as identical and when as distinct.[72]

But according to Quine, no such standard can be given. A few pages back in (17) I proposed a criterion for propositional identity. [*A*] and [*B*] are identical propositions if and only if *A* and *B* are synonymous. Now suppose *A* and

B are native and English standing sentences, respectively. Because of translational indeterminacy, there is no way to tell whether *A* and *B* are synonymous. For to suppose that we can is

> . . . to suppose that among all the alternative systems of analytical hypotheses of translation which are compatible with the totality of dispositions to verbal behavior on the part of the speakers of [the] two languages, some are "really" right and others wrong on behaviorally inscrutable grounds of propositional identity. . . . The very questions of conditions for identity of propositions present not so much an unsolved problem as a mistaken ideal.[73]

Switching to one language does not help, since, as we have seen, there would be indeterminacy even if *A* and *B* were both English sentences. So, according to Quine, not only are there no reasons for believing there are propositions, but there is a reason for believing that there are not any. In reply to Quine some philosophers have argued that propositions are no worse off than physical objects, for no one has given a satisfactory criterion for their individuation either. I think there is a difficulty with this criticism. That there is to date no criterion of identity for physical objects does not mean that one could not be given. In contrast, if it is sound, Quine's argument against there being a criterion of identity for propositions shows that in principle there could not be such a criterion.

Perhaps we have been too hasty in accepting Quine's argument against propositions. It rests on the assumption that 'proposition' only makes sense if we are supplied with a criterion for their individuation. We could give up this assumption. As Quine puts the point,

> The precept "No entity without identity" might simply be relaxed. Certainly the positing of first objects makes no sense except as keyed to identity; but those patterns of thing talk have in fact enabled us to talk of . . . propositions in partial grammatical analogy without an accompanying standard of

identity for them. Why not just accept them thus, as twilight half-entities to which the identity concept is not to apply?[74]

Quine's argument against this is that "What might properly count against such half-entities . . . is a certain disruption of logic."[75] What Quine has in mind by 'disruption of logic', I believe, is the following. Consider

(26)   Sam loves Miriam.

This sentence consists of the two singular terms 'Sam' and 'Miriam' and the two-place predicate 'loves'. Suppose further that

(27)   Sam is the father of Nathan.

It follows from (26) and (27) that

(28)   The father of Nathan loves Miriam.

The principle being applied here is the *substitutivity of identicals*. That is, two referring expressions which refer to the same thing can be replaced one for the other in any sentence without changing the sentence's truth value. The point behind the principle is that truth supposedly should not be affected by what a thing is called.

But there are well-known counter-examples to the principle. Consider

(29)   Kathy believes that Shorter is Shorter.

In accordance with the view that propositions are the objects of the propositional attitudes, this sentence is analyzed as consisting of the two-place predicate 'believe' and the singular terms 'Kathy' and 'that Shorter is Shorter' which refers to a proposition. Now suppose that

(30)   Shorter is the winner of the marathon

and that Kathy does not believe that he is. But from the substitutivity of identicals and (29) and (30) it should follow that

(31)   Kathy believes that Shorter is the winner of the marathon.

However, by hypothesis she does not. And since by hypothesis (29) and (30) are true and (31) false, we must either revise the principle of the substitutivity of identicals or our analysis of (29). Both cause a 'disruption of logic'.

We have been supposing that 'that Shorter is Shorter' in (29) is a complex singular term containing the singular term 'Shorter' and that 'Shorter' in this context refers to the famous marathon runner. Following Frege, we could take 'Shorter' in (29) not to refer to Frank Shorter, the marathon runner, but rather to what Frege calls the *sense of* 'Shorter'. That is, to this term's meaning. In this case, 'the winner of the marathon' could not be substituted for 'Shorter' in (29), since they do not have the same referent. This modification of our analysis of (29) saves the substitutivity of identicals, but involves an increase in the complexity of our logic. We no longer have a uniform treatment of the referring function of singular terms. In some contexts a given term refers to an individual, in others it refers to its sense. To incorporate this we must add to our logic a criterion which distinguishes such contexts.

Rather than complicate our treatment of singular terms, we could take them to refer to individuals wherever they occur, but alter the principle of the substitutivity of identicals so that it would not apply to the positions occupied by terms like 'Shorter' in (29). This would require a criterion similar to the one needed above to mark such positions. To preserve on the one hand our analysis of (29) and propositions as the objects of the propositional attitudes and on the other the substitutivity of identicals, we must either modify this principle or treat the occurrence of singular terms differently depending on the context in which they occur. In either case our logical theory is made more complex by introducing objects for the propositional attitudes. However, complexity of theory itself is no bar to admitting an object to our ontology, if it serves some explanatory function. But since propositions seem to serve no such purpose and ". . . causal science gets on well without them,"[76] Quine argues that we can dispense with them in trying to explain truth, meaning, and the propositional attitudes.

Dropping propositions as the objects of the propositional

attitudes might lead us to seek other objects for them. An alternative is to take the logical form of sentences like (29) as consisting of 'Kathy' and the unanalyzed predicate 'believes that Shorter is Shorter' in which 'Shorter' would occur as a part as does 'dog' in 'dogged'. The substitutivity of identicals could not, then, apply to 'Shorter', since it would not occur as a term in the predicate. This still leaves us with the mental acts of believing, wishing, hoping, et cetera, if not with their objects, to use in our theories about language acquisition and use. But Quine finds most of the propositional attitudes themselves to be just as unsuited for scientific purposes as he does their objects.[77] Can we tell what the native believes, wishes, hopes for, or even says? To think that we can go beyond what we are able to determine using stimulus meaning and stimulus synonymy is to suppose that we have evidence to choose among the rival analytical hypotheses all of which are compatible with the native's behavior and stimulation patterns. But, Quine claims that translational indeterminacy shows this to be impossible. He draws the conclusion that we have no evidence for attributing the propositional attitudes to the native, nor to others, nor even to ourselves, except those which can be grounded in stimulus conditions and behavior. According to Quine,

> If we are limning the true and ultimate structure of reality, the canonical scheme for us is the austere scheme that knows . . . no propositional attitudes but only the physical constitution and behavior of organisms.[78]

So, we have come full circle to what I have called in the beginning of the chapter Quine's soft core behaviorism. That is, human behavior, including speech, if it is to be explained at all, is not to be explained in terms of a speaker's beliefs, intentions, or meanings, but is to be explained in terms of his behavior and stimulation patterns. Now this conclusion does not tell us that the particular theory developed to explain human behavior will be Skinnerian. Consequently, one has not turned aside Quine's soft core behaviorism by showing that Skinner's behaviorism does not account for the data. The only way this can be done, I think, is to show either that Quine's arguments against propositions and propositional attitudes are bad arguments or that they lead to results which Quine himself cannot accept. In the next chapter after considering the consequences translational indeterminacy has for transformational linguistics, I will consider some criticisms of Quine's arguments.

VI

Transformational Linguistic Theory and Translational Indeterminacy

Introduction

The views of Quine on the one hand and Chomsky, Katz, and Austin on the other are clearly in conflict on many philosophical issues. The one on which I shall concentrate attention in this chapter is ontological. The latter three accept such objects as propositions, internalized grammars, illocutionary acts, illocutionary act contents, intentions, and so forth, all of which Quine rejects as being scientifically unacceptable. And because of this, he rejects their theories of language and speech which are committed to such objects. In what follows I will take propositions as paradigmatic of the objects Chomsky, Katz, and Austin accept, and present Quine's arguments against their existence. If these arguments are sound one would suppose that they could be applied *mutatis mutandis* to the other objects.

At the heart of Quine's criticisms of propositions is his claim that there are no criteria for individuating them— that is, for determining whether two sentences express the same or different propositions. And without a criteria for individuation, Quine holds that propositions have no place in a scientific theory of language and language use. There are two sorts of arguments against propositions in Quine's work. First, he argues that the criteria philosophers have traditionally used to individuate propositions are based upon a cluster of related terms contained in what we called in the last chapter the 'theory of meaning', including 'analyticity', 'synonymy', and 'necessity', all of which Quine finds unclear. Second, he holds that the translational indeterminacy of standing sentences shows that in principle there cannot be a way of individuating propositions. There are actually two arguments based upon indeterminacy one of which I discussed briefly in the last chapter which I will reconsider in more detail in this chapter. My first task is to present Quine's criticisms of definitions of terms from the theory of meaning which are used in criteria to individuate propositions. Second, I will apply these criticisms to Katz's definitions of these terms. And lastly, I will show that Katz's definitions are not subject to these criticisms.

1   Quine on 'Analyticity', 'Synonymy', and 'Necessity'

There are three kinds of criticisms Quine raises against traditional definitions of 'synonymy', 'analyticity', 'necessity', and related terms. He holds that these definitions are inadequate because either they are circular, contain an undefined term, or lack generality. There are two kinds of circularity. The first is the quite trivial sort in which a term in the definiendum is contained in the definiens. The second is the more usual kind which arises when a set of terms is to be defined. Suppose we have a set of definitions $A_1 \ldots . A_n$ where a_i is the definiendum and b_i the definiens of A_i. Further, let $b_i = a_j$, where a_j is the definiendum of A_j and where $i \neq j$. A set of definitions meeting this condition is to be called *connected*. A connected set of definitions is circular if and only if $b_n = a_1$. The second of Quine's criticisms can also be divided into two types. It arises either when the definiens contains a non-technical term, such as 'necessary', which, according to Quine, is as much in need of clarification as 'synonymous', 'analytic', et cetera, or when the definiens contains a technical term, such as 'semantical rule', which we do not understand. The last sort of criticism applies to definitions of terms in the theory of meaning which cover only one language. Since the purpose of defining these terms is to provide a criterion not only for intra-linguistic, but interlinguistic propositional identity, definitions applicable to only one language and, hence, lacking generality, are inadequate.[1]

For our purposes the importance of these criticisms is the bearing they have on criteria for propositional identity. A condition on the adequacy of any such criterion is that it mark

(1) (a) Matilda chews gum bands.

      (b) Matilda chews rubber bands.

as expressing the same proposition. As we saw in (17) in the last chapter, a standard way of determining propositional identity is in terms of sentential synonymy.

(2) S and S' express the same proposition if and only if S and S' are synonymous.

But, how do we determine whether (1) (a) and (b) are synonymous? A suggestion in the spirit of Leibniz is that

(3) S and S' are synonymous if and only if they are interchangeable *salva veritate*.

That is, S and S' can be replaced one for the other in any sentence without changing the sentence's truth value. (1) (a) and (b) can be replaced one for the other in

(4) It is true that _____.

without changing (4)'s truth value. But substitutivity *salva veritate* in (4) which is an extensional context is clearly not sufficient to guarantee interchangeability in all contexts. Any two English sentences having the same truth value can be interchanged in (4) without affecting its truth value. But clearly such sentences cannot be interchanged in an intensional context *salva veritate,* for example in

(5) Necessarily _____.

In order to assure substitutivity of two sentences in all contexts they must necessarily have the same truth value. That is

(6)   *S* and *S'* are interchangeable *salvae veritate* if and only if it is necessary that *S* if and only if *S'*

This enables us to rule out sentences which contingently have the same truth value from being interchangeable *salva veritate,* for their biconditional is not necessary. But how can we tell whether it is necessary that *S* if and only if *S'*? As I pointed out above, Quine regards 'necessary' to be as unclear as 'synonymous'. And so if we stop with (6), we would fall afoul of Quine's second criticism. We need, then, a criterion for determining whether a sentence is necessary. A standard criterion is that

(7)   It is necessary that *S* if and only if '*S*' is a logical truth.

and

(8)   '*S*' is a logical truth if and only if '*S*' is true under every possible replacement of its non-logical expressions.

For example,

(9)   Matilda flies gliders or Matilda does not fly gliders

is a logical truth, since replacing any of its non-logical expressions, that is:

(10)   (a)   Matilda flies gliders
         (b)   Matilda
         (c)   flies
         (d)   gliders

with any expression of the same type yields a true sentence. The problematic sentences are ones like

(11)   Matilda chews gum bands if and only if Matilda chews rubber bands

which, as it stands, is not a logical truth, for it consists of (1) (a) and (b). Replacing these *different* sentences with

(12)   (a)   Sugar dissolves in water
         (b)   Lead dissolves in water

produces a false bi-conditional and, thus, on the basis of (8), (11) is not a logical truth. However, (11) can be converted into a logical truth by replacing synonyms for synonyms—that is, by replacing 'rubber bands' with 'gum bands'. By doing so we obtain

(13)   Matilda chews gum bands if and only if Matilda chews gum bands

which is obviously a logical truth. In light of this we should change (7) to

(14)   It is necessary that S if and only if 'S' is a logical truth or 'S' can be turned into a logical truth by substituting synonyms for synonyms.

But, how do we know that 'gum band' and 'rubber band' are synonymous? As we saw in Chapter V, the definition for term synonymy belongs to a circular set of definitions. Thus, (14) belongs to such a set. Since (2), (3), (6), (7), (8), and (14) are connected but not circular, what we have rather than a circular set is a closed loop of definitions. Consequently, the definition of propositional identity contained in (2) is not very illuminating.

2   Katz on 'Analyticity' and 'Synonymy'

It will help in seeing the force of Quine's criticisms applied to Katz's semantic theory to have a brief review of the theory of transformational grammar presented in Chapter IV. On this theory a grammar is divided into syntactical, semantical, and phonological components. In turn the syntactical component is divided into a base and a transformational component. The base component which contains a set of context-free phrase structure rules and a lexicon has as its output labeled phrase markers. These phrase markers, the deep structures of sentences, have as their lowest nodes lexical items with accompanying sets of syntactic and phonological features and semantic markers. The latter represent the meaning(s) of the lexical items. The deep structure of a sentence is the level which indicates a sentence's constituent structure and which determines the grammatical relations among its lexical items. Because this information is necessary for the operation of the semantical component, deep structures are part of its input. In addition they are the input to the transformational component which contains an ordered set of transformational rules. These rules operating on deep structure phrase markers map them into surface structure phrase markers which have at their lowest nodes a sequence of lexical items which constitute a sentence. Since the changes transformations make on the constituent structure of P-markers affect meaning, surface structure information is, also, required as input to the semantic component. The semantic component consists of a set of projection rules which operate on deep structures and surface structure information yielding a set of readings for a sentence which represent the sentence's meaning(s). In addition to providing information for the operation of the semantic component, surface structures serve as the input to the phonological component which supplies each sentence with a phonetic interpretation. We can view, then, a grammar as a device which pairs the sound pattern of a sentence with a representation of its meaning(s).

Besides specifying the form of a grammar of a possible human language, the linguistic theory we are considering provides criteria for linguistic properties of constituents of sentences, sentences, and sets of sentences, such as 'grammatical', 'synonymous', 'paraphrase', 'structurally ambiguous', 'analytic', and 'contradictory'. These criteria operate on the outputs of a grammar's components assigning linguistic properties to the sentences and their constituents which are generated by the grammar. For example, Katz defines 'synonymy' in the following way.

> (15)   A sentence S is fully synonymous with S' just in case the set of readings assigned to S is identical to the set of readings assigned to S'.[2]

(15) applies to the readings of sentences which constitute the output of the semantic component.

The adequacy of any theory is judged in part by whether it correctly predicts the range of data which the theory is constructed to explain. This of course applies equally to grammars. According to most transformational grammarians, the data used in constructing a grammar of a language consists of the judgments speakers make about that language. Now 'judgment' can be used to refer to both an act of judging and to the judgment made. It is the latter sort of linguistic judgment for which a grammar is supposed to give an account. For example, speakers of English judge that

(16) (a) (1) (a) and (b) are grammatical
    (b) (1) (a) and (b) are synonymous.

And it is claimed that a grammar of English to be adequate must predict (16) (a) and (b). Strictly speaking, however, such a grammar cannot account for these facts. All that a transformational grammar does is generate a set of phrase markers and a set of sentences with accompanying phonetic and semantic interpretations. Only the definitions of linguistic properties operating on the outputs of a grammar's components can make predictions of the sort contained in (16) (a) and (b). Consider (16) (b). A grammar of English assigns identical readings to (1) (a) and (b). Operating on these readings, (15) predicts that these sentences are synonymous which accords with (16) (b), thereby confirming not the grammar of English which supplied the readings, but this grammar in conjunction with (15). So, if judgments of the sort contained in (16) (a) and (b) constitute the linguist's data, the theory he constructs to account for this data consists of a grammar of English and definitions of linguistic properties. Of course, for a theory of this sort to be fully adequate it must account not only for judgments like (16) (a) and (b), but for all the linguistic judgments speakers make about their language.

In the beginning of this chapter I described three of Quine's criticisms of definitions of terms belonging to the theory of meaning. According to Quine, these definitions either are circular, contain an undefined term, or lack generality. Are the criteria for semantic properties such as (15), which are given in transformational linguistic theory, also subject to these criticisms? I think they are not. It is fairly clear that these criteria do not lack generality; they are supposed to cover all possible human languages. But does not Katz's definition of 'synonymy' (15), upon which we shall concentrate our attention, contain an undefined technical term, 'reading of a sentence', which we do not understand? It is easy enough, however, to provide a definition:

(17) $<(SM_1) \ . \ . \ . \ . \ . \ (SM_n)>$, an ordered set of semantic markers, is a reading of S of L if and only if the projection rules of G of L operating on the semantic markers of the lexical items of S and S's deep structure associate $<(SM_1) \ . \ . \ . \ . \ (SM_n)>$ with S.

S is a sentence, L the language to which S belongs, and G the grammar of L. (17), however, contains many undefined terms in its definiens, for example, 'projection rule', 'deep structure', and 'semantic markers of lexical items'. Consider the last of the three. How do we determine the pairings of lexical items and semantic markers? N. L. Wilson, a critic of Katz, claims that without an answer to this question we can have no general definition of 'analyticity in L' or 'synonymy in L'. And without a general definition for the latter we have no criterion for propositional identity. What Wilson demands is a general definition of 'X is a semantic marker for E in L' where E is a lexical item. And since, according to Wilson, Katz does not provide this, any definitions of semantic terms which depend upon pairings of semantic markers and lexical items are inadequate.[3]

Katz's way around this criticism is to propose a theoretical account of intuitions speakers have about the linguistic properties of their language.

> If we cannot eliminate information from the lexical reading of a word W without losing predictions and explanations of semantic properties and relations of expressions and sentences in which W occurs, then such information belongs in the dictionary entry for W and is hence rightly deemed semantic; and if we can simplify the dictionary by excluding

a certain piece of information from all of them, then it is rightly deemed non-semantic.[4]

What Katz describes above for linguistics is no different from other sciences. The linguist's task is to describe a language, *L*. His data are the speakers of *L*'s linguistic judgments, J_1, J_2, ... Equipped with a theory about grammars and with definitions of linguistic properties which together constitute his linguistic theory or universal grammar, *UG*, the linguist constructs the rules and the lexicon of *L* which constitute the grammar, *G*, of *L*. *G* is an adequate description of *L* if and only if in conjunction with *UG* it predicts J_1, J_2, ... The question raised above about the pairings of semantic markers and lexical items can now be answered. A lexical item of *L* is to be paired with a set of semantic markers just in case such a pairing is included in a lexicon which is part of an adequate grammar of *L*. Now this gives the linguist no mechanical way of discovering the pairings of lexical items with semantic markers. That is, Katz does not give a general definition of '*X* is a semantic marker of *E* in *L*' which Wilson demands. But it does provide a way of determining whether the pairings of semantic markers and lexical items he proposes are correct or not. So, Katz's definitions of semantic terms avoid the criticisms which Quine raises against others. They neither are circular, lack generality, nor contain an undefined term.

It would seem as though we are now in a position to provide a criterion for propositional identity based on (2) and (15).

(18) *S* and *S'* express the same proposition if and only if the reading, *R*, associated with *S* is identical to the reading, *R'*, associated with *S'*.[b]

However, we still have to consider whether Quine's argument against propositions, which is based on the purported translational indeterminacy of standing sentences, cuts against (18). Before doing so, I shall reconsider this argument in more detail.

3   *A Reconsideration of the Translational Indeterminacy of Standing Sentences*

Quine first asks us to consider an indeterminacy which he believes affects physical theories. He claims

> Physical theories can be at odds with each other and yet compatible with all possible data even in the broadest sense. In a word, they can be logically incompatible and empirically equivalent.[6]

This can be divided into two theses about physical theories:

(19) (i)   Physical theories can be at odds with each other [or in other words] logically incompatible.

(ii) Physical theories can be compatible with all possible data [or in other words] empirically equivalent.

To simplify interpreting these theses I will use the following notational conventions used in the last chapter. Subscripted O's and T's stand for observation and theoretical sentences, respectively, and O'_1, O'_2, . . . for all the true observation sentences which report all possible data. Instead of considering 'physical theories' in general we shall narrow our discussion to two, A and B, each of which is composed of a consistent set of T's.

There are two difficulties in interpreting Quine's thesis, the first of which applies to both (19) (i) and (ii). Does Quine presuppose that there *are* physical theories of the events reported in O_1', O_2', . . . which are empirically equivalent and logically incompatible? Or is he claiming more cautiously that *if* there is a physical theory of the events reported in O_1', O_2', . . . , then there are others which are empirically equivalent and logically incompatible with it? Since a good principle of interpretation is to attribute the more cautious view, I will suppose Quine holds the second of the two. The second difficulty arises in (19) (ii). It contains 'compatible' and 'empirically equivalent' which can be construed in various ways. Let me first give my interpretation of (19) and then my reasons for it. I take Quine to be making the following claims. If there is an A which is a physical theory of the events reported in O_1', O_2', . . . , then

(20)   (i)   There is a B which is a physical theory of the events reported in O_1', O_2', . . . and

        (ii) A and B entail a contradiction and

        (iii) A is logically consistent with O_1', O_2', . . . and B is logically consistent with O_1', O_2' . . .

One might argue that (20) (iii) is too weak an interpretation of (19) (ii) and that what it means is that

(21) A entails O_1', O_2', . . . , except those O''s which report quantum phenomena, and B entails O_1', O_2', . . . , except those O''s which report quantum phenomena.

My reasons for not interpreting (19) (ii) as (21) are, first, that it stretches the meaning of 'compatible' quite out of shape to interpret it as 'entails', and second, it commits Quine to the untenable position that there could be no other observation sentences, besides those which report quantum phenomena, which are not entailed by a physical theory of all observable events. And lastly the principle of caution also applies here. (21) implies (20) (iii). So if one can show that there are difficulties with (20) as it stands, they will apply to (20) in which (20) (iii) is replaced by (21).

Regardless of the bearing (20) has on translation, it is important to determine its truth, for it has important ramifications for scientific theories. Suppose we have a theory A of the events reported in O_1', O_2', ... Now Quine's point about physical theories is that there would be another theory, B, which explains the events reported in O_1', O_2', . . . as adequately as does A, but which is logically incompatible with it. That is, A and B are different theories about the universe. Which do we choose, A or B? If Quine is right about physical theories, there is no rational basis for selecting one over the other, assuming of course neither

A nor *B* is the simpler of the two. Which of them we select is arbitrary, a matter of convention, since the set of observation sentences, O_1', O_2', . . . , constitutes all the possible evidence that has a bearing on selecting between *A* and *B*, and both *A* and *B* are consistent with this evidence.

The next step in Quine's argument for indeterminacy is to apply (20) to translation. But caution is in order here, for he does not claim, as I think some have interpreted him, that translational indeterminacy of standing sentences follows merely from the underdetermination of theories by their evidence. To see this let us accept uncritically Quine's (20) and apply it directly to translation. Suppose that using Quine's behavioral criteria we have collected all possible data for translating the native's language which is reported in the observation sentences O_1', O_2', ... Applying (20) to translation in a straightforward manner, we obtain the following. If there is a translation manual, *HA*, which is a theory of O_1', O_2', . . . , then

(22)   (i)   There is a translation manual, *HB*, which is a theory of O_1', O_2', ...

(ii)   *HA* and *HB* entail a contradiction

(iii)   *HA* is logically consistent with O_1', O_2', . . . and *HB* is logically consistent with O_1', O_2', . . .

The difficulty with (22) is that it does not have as a *consequence* the translational indeterminacy of native standing sentences. *HA* and *HB* can be inconsistent without giving logically incompatible translations of native standing sentences. *HA* and *HB* include a native-to-English dictionary and syntax. Now we can imagine the syntax in *HA* to identify some native sentences as passives, while *HB* denies this. Yet the translations which *HA* and *HB* yield for these sentences can turn out to be identical, if we add compensatory rules to the semantics of either *HA* or *HB*. *HA* and *HB* would then be logically incompatible, but would not give logically incompatible translations for any native standing sentence. In fact they could give the same translation.

Quine's application of (20) to translation is a bit more subtle than what is given in (22). Consider again radical translation. Suppose we are able to identify the native's theoretical and observation sentences and, as well, determine to which of these the native assents—that is, those sentences the native believes. The theoretical sentences which the native believes we shall take to be his physical theory. The native's observation sentences are easy enough to translate into their corresponding English counterparts using stimulus synonymy. And once we have done this, there is no problem finding out which observation sentences he believes.[7] But how do we translate the native's physical theory? According to Quine, the only data we have to go on is our translation of the observation sentences the native believes. Let us suppose that the native is enough like us that his physical theory is a theory of the events reported in the observation sentences he believes. And let us suppose that, unlike us, he believes only true observation sentences, NO_1', NO_2', ...[8] If (20) is applicable to our physical theories, it also applies to the native's physical theories. If there is a native physical theory, NA, of NO_1', NO_2', . . . , then

(23) (i) There is an NB which is a theory of NO_1', NO_2' . . . .

(ii) NA and NB entail a contradiction.

(iii) NA is consistent with NO_1', NO_2' . . . . NB is consistent with NO_1', NO_2' . . . .

The translation of NO_1', NO_2', . . . via stimulus meaning is our O_1', O_2' . . . . But what is our translation of the native's physical theory? Both A and B are compatible with our translation of the observation sentences he believes. However, our translation of these sentences—the only evidence Quine regards to be relevant for translating the native's physical theory—provides insufficient evidence for choosing between the two. And consequently, we have no way of knowing whether the native's physical theory is to be translated by A or by the logically incompatible B. Thus, the translation of the native's physical theory into English is indeterminate.

It is a short step from this conclusion to the more general thesis of translational indeterminacy of the native's standing sentences. If we were able to give a unique translation for these, then we could translate uniquely the native's physical theory, for his physical theory would just consist of the standing sentences to which he assents. But, if we accept the preceding argument, we cannot uniquely translate the native's physical theory. And thus, it follows that we cannot determinately translate the native's standing sentences. As a consequence, a modified (22) does apply to translation. (22) (ii) must be changed to

(24) HA and HB give logically incompatible translations for the native standing sentences.

Consequently, if Quine is right about physical theories and about their ills' infecting translation, then we can neither tell what physical theory the native believes nor tell what he means by his theoretical sentences.

4   Transformational Linguistic Theory and Translational Indeterminacy

We must now consider whether the above argument affects transformational linguistic theory and the definition of propositional identity in (18) based upon the theory. To see whether it does, let us consider the linguist's task in light of transformational linguistic theory. His job is to construct a transformational grammar of the native's language, NTG, and of English, ETG. Each will provide readings for the native's sentences and for English sentences and thereby give us a criterion for translation. An English sentence, ES, and a native sentence, NS, are translations of one another if and only if the readings assigned to ES by ETG and the readings assigned to NS by NTG are identical. This is to do no more than to apply (15) interlinguistically. And by virtue of (18), if *ES* and *NS* have the same readings, they would express the same propositions. If Quine's indeterminacy is correct, the linguist, on the basis of the evidence available to him, can construct two grammars of the native's language, *NTG* and *NTG'*, which are compatible with all the data but which give incompatible translations for the native's standing sentences. The incompatibility would arise in the following way. Suppose *NTG* and *NTG'* assign to *NSS*, a native standing sentence, the readings *RNSS* and *RNSS'*, respectively. And further suppose that *ETG* assigns to *ESS* and *ESS'*, two logically incompatible English standing sentences, the readings *RESS* and *RESS'*. The translation of *NSS* into English is indeterminate, if *RNSS* and *RNSS'* are identical respectively to *RESS* and *RESS'*. If this were so, we would then have no way of knowing what proposition *NSS* expresses, whether it is the proposition expressed by *ESS* or by *ESS'*. And consequently, (18) could not provide us with a criterion for propositional identity.

We have kept the transformational grammar for English fixed in arguing for the translational indeterminacy of native standing sentences. But the same underdetermination which affects construction of a transformational grammar for the native's language also applies to the construction of a transformational grammar for English. Quine's thesis applied to our home language is that we can construct two different transformational grammars *ETG* and *ETG'* which are compatible with the data yet give logically incompatible readings for English standing sentences. That is, for some English standing sentence, *ESS*, there would be associated two different readings, *RESS* and *RESS'*, the former assigned to *ESS* by *ETG* and the latter by *ETG'*. And further, *RESS* and *RESS'* would be the readings respectively of two standing sentences in another language, the native's language for example, which were logically incompatible. As a consequence, we would be unable to tell what proposition *ESS* expresses. Thus, to suppose that *NSS* or *ESS* express a determinate proposition is to hold either of two mistaken beliefs: that is, that there is only one transformational grammar compatible with the data for English and for the native's language or that if there is more than one, they are logically compatible. And on Quine's view since these beliefs are mistaken, there is reason to hold that neither *ESS* nor *NSS* express propositions.

Up to this point I have concentrated my attention on applying Quine's argument for translational indeterminacy to one aspect of transformational grammar. That aspect is Katz's claim that his semantic theory provides a basis for determining synonymy uniquely for all sentences and, thus, gives us grounds for telling when the propositions expressed by any two sentences are the same or different. I believe Quine intends his argument to call into question more than the existence of propositions.[9] In Chapter III, I outlined Chomsky's claim that in learning a language speakers internalize a specific set of rules constituting the grammar of their language which they tacitly use in speaking and understanding. Now on Chomsky's view the function of a grammar of *L* is to generate all and only the sentences of *L* and the correct grammatical descriptions of these sentences. The grammatical descriptions of the sentences of *L* are correct if and only if they predict the facts which speakers of *L* know about the sentences of their language. As we see, it is a consequence of Quine's argument for the translational indeterminacy of standing sentences that it is possible to construct ". . . appreciably unlike and still comparably manageable systems of rules for generating the same infinite totality of well-formed sentences."[10] If this is so, there is no telling which set of rules a speaker has internalized, nor whether two speakers of the same language have internalized the same set or different sets of rules. And it follows that the same sort of difficulty in individuating propositions applies to internalized grammars. That is, we have no criterion of identity for such grammars. To claim that a speaker has an internalized grammar which he unconsciously follows is, first, to suppose that one of the alternative but yet incompatible grammars is the right one, though there is no evidence for selecting one rather than the other and, second, to abandon the standards of identity employed elsewhere in science. Quine finds both these consequences unpalatable and regards it as being far less costly to forgo Chomsky's and Katz's mentalism.

In Chapter III, I indicated that the mind-body problem appears within transformational linguistic theory. On Katz's view of communication a speaker selects a message he wants to convey to a hearer. Using in part his internalized grammar, he chooses a sentence which expresses his message and, then, encodes it in a signal which causes him to utter the sentence.[11] The question is how does the 'mental' message which the speaker wishes to express play a role in a causal explanation of the physical movement of the speaker's articulatory system? Katz's answer to the problem is to identify mental states with brain states. He claims that

> The theoretical constructions used by a mentalist linguist in building his theories are intended by him to have psychological reality. . . . *Reference* to mental states is construed as reference to brain states. This is why the events to which the mentalist's constructions refer can stand as links in the causal chain that contain vocalizations and sound waves.[12]

One might think that this meets Quine's objections to mentalism, for we can formulate our linguistic theory in mentalistic terms, but any reference our theory makes to mental events, capacities, states, et cetera can be read as a covert reference to brain states and processes.

I am afraid, however, that if Quine's indeterminacy thesis is correct, Katz's identity theory does not meet Quine's objections. I take Katz's thesis to be that for every distinct mental state which linguistic theory attributes to a speaker there is a brain state to which it is identical. Let us consider the native and his physical theory. What mental state are we to attribute to him?—the one which corresponds to his believing his correlate of our physical theory *A* or our physical theory *B*? The conclusion of Quine's indeterminacy argument is that there is no grounds for attributing one rather than the other to the native. Consequently, there is no way to connect the native's putative mental state which constitutes his belief of his physical theory with the brain state which Katz supposes the native to have. As Quine puts a similar point,

> To expect a distinctive physical mechanism behind every genuinely distinct mental state is one thing; to expect a distinctive mechanism for every purported distinction that can be phrased in traditional mentalistic language is another. The question is whether . . . [the native] really believes *A* or believes rather *B*, is a question whose very significance I would put in doubt.[13]

5   Some Criticisms of Quine's Argument for Translational Indeterminacy

I want now to turn to several criticisms of indeterminacy of translation, the first of which, I believe, Quine can answer. Quine claims that indeterminacy affects both physical theory and linguistic theory. But, then, argue Chomsky and Katz, the latter is no worse off than the former, and since Quine holds that it is meaningful to speak of the truth of hypotheses in physical theory, Chomsky and Katz claim that it should be equally meaningful in linguistic theory.[14] I think the answer to this criticism is in a heirarchy of indeterminacy. As Quine puts the point,

> The indeterminacy of translation is additional. Where physical theories A and B are both compatible with all possible data, we might adopt A for ourselves and still remain free to translate the foreigner either as believing A or as believing B.[15]

To see the force of this suppose we believe a theory *A* of $O'_1, O'_2. . . .$ That is, we ascribe to a theory of all true observation sentences. Quine's point about the indeterminacy of translation is that even given our choice of A and all the truths we can determine by means of that theory, we still cannot determine whether the native believes A or B. And since by hypothesis, A is a theory of all we can observe to be true about the world, there is no additional evidence we can bring to bear to choose between A and B as our translation of the native's physical theory. Consequently, our translation of his physical theory is indeterminate.

The second criticism I wish to raise for Quine is one, I believe, he has not answered. His argument for translational indeterminacy and his subsequent attack on propositions do not have the far-reaching consequences he attributes to them. Let us suppose we have a physical theory, A, of O_1', O_2', . . . such that A contains the theoretical sentences, S. Now (20) is satisfied, if there is another theory, B, of O_1', O_2', . . . which is identical to A except that B contains $\sim S$ instead of S.[16] A and B, then, would be compatible with all the data, but logically incompatible with one another. To apply this to translation suppose that on the basis of our translation of the observation sentences the native believes, our translation of his physical theory is A. But, if (20) is true, B should be an equally good translation of the native's physical theory. However, the only difference between A and B is that the former contains S and the latter $\sim S$. Our translation of the native's physical theory is indeterminate, but the indeterminacy does not turn out to have very serious consequences, for there would be only one sentence, *NSS*, in the native's theory which could be translated by S or by $\sim S$ and as a result would not be determinately translated.

This does not seem to accord with what Quine has in mind. He claims that

Rival systems of analytical hypotheses can conform to all speech dispositions within each of the languages concerned and yet dictate, in *countless cases,* utterly disparate translations; not mere mutual paraphrases, but translations each of which would be excluded by the other system of translation.[17]

However, it is not difficult to extend the above argument to yield an infinite number of incompatible translations. If (20) applies to translations as I have indicated, so too does (22). That is, there would be two translation manuals *HA* and *HB* which give *A* and *B*, respectively, as translations of the native's physical theory. Moreover, they would also give an infinite number of incompatible translations of native sentences. The native's language contains not only *NSS*, but *NSS • NSS*, *NSS • NSS • NSS*, and so on, where '•' is native conjunction. Now *HA* would translate these sentences as *S*, *S and S*, *S and S and S*, and *HB* would translate them as $\sim S$, $\sim S$ and $\sim S$, $\sim S$ and $\sim S$ and $\sim S$ and so on. These translation manuals would give, then, incompatible translations of native standing sentences in "countless cases," but would be, I believe, a trivialization of (22).

The work of most anthropologists and linguists would not suffer if only *NSS* and its related ilk could not be determinately translated. It would seem, however, that the philosophical thesis that every sentence expresses a determinate proposition must go by the board. But, there is a way to circumvent this. To preserve the neatness of our propositional theory, in a Quinean spirit we could choose to ignore *NSS* and its relations. We could round off the native's language by declaring *NSS* et cetera to be non-sentences. As Quine has taught us, this would be to do no more than the physical scientist does when he chooses to disregard some putative recalcitrant datum and hold onto his theory. For Quine to make his case against propositions, I think he would have to show that for any native standing sentences there could be incompatible translations. But, if this is to be established via (20), then he would have to show that for every theoretical sentence, *T*, of *A* where *A* is a theory of O_1', O_2', . . . there is another theory *B* of

O_1', O_2', . . . which contains or implies $\sim T$. Quine might well have wide agreement on (20), as he expects, but there is no reason for him to expect such agreement on this more radical thesis about physical theories.

6   The Peirce-Duhem Argument for Translational Indeterminacy

In Chapter V, I indicated that there is another argument which Quine alludes to, but does not give in any detail for translational indeterminacy. I think that this argument to which I now want to turn my attention avoids the criticisms raised against the argument for translational indeterminacy based on (20). In "Epistemology Naturalized" Quine claims that translational indeterminacy follows from two theses, one of which he attributes to the American philosopher Charles Sanders Peirce and the other to the French philosopher Pierre Duhem.

> If we recognize with Peirce that the meaning of a sentence turns purely on what would count as evidence for its truth and if we recognize with Duhem that theoretical sentences have their evidence not as single sentences but only as larger blocks of theory, then the indeterminacy of translation of theoretical sentences is the natural conclusion. . . . This conclusion conversely, once it is embraced seals the fate of any general notion of propositional meaning.[18]

There are two difficulties with Quine's statement of Peirce's thesis. First, it cannot apply to all sentences, since questions, imperatives, and performatives, though they have a meaning, do not have a truth value and so do not have any evidence for their truth. Peirce's thesis, if it is true at all, can apply only to indicative sentences. Second, as Quine presents it, there is a problem in the interpretation of Peirce's thesis. It is not altogether clear what Quine has in mind when he says that the meaning of a sentence *turns purely* on the evidence for its truth. One interpretation of Quine's claim is to identify the meaning of a sentence with the evidence for its truth. Let 'S' stand for any indicative sentence and '$O_1, O_2, \ldots$' for a set of observation sentences. A plausible interpretation of Quine's Peircean thesis is that

(25) The meaning of 'S' is $O_1, O_2, \ldots$ if and only if $O_1, O_2, \ldots$ is the evidence for the truth of 'S'.

This in turn gives us a criterion for synonymy and thereby propositional identity.

(26) S and S' are synonymous if and only if S and S' have the same evidence for their truth.

Duhem's thesis, which Philip Quinn calls the *Separability Thesis*,[19] Quine regards to be "the crucial consideration behind [his] argument for the indeterminacy of translation."[20] Using the notation introduced above, Quinn states the separability thesis in the following way.

(27) For all T there is no O such that T entails O.[21]

One can see immediately that if (27) were true, (25) could not apply to theoretical sentences, for no theoretical sentence by itself would entail any observation sentence. Hence, if we suppose the meaning of a declarative sentence is the evidence for its truth and the separability thesis holds, there would be no way to tell either what the meaning of any particular theoretical sentence is, whether two such sentences are synonymous, or whether they express the same proposition.

The reason Quine argues for translational indeterminacy is to call into question the existence of propositions. The argument we are now considering does just that without a detour through translation. Translational indeterminacy, however, does not go by the board, for it follows from (25) and (27), as one might expect. If there are no criteria of identity for propositions expressed by theoretical sentences of the same language, one would hardly think there to be such criteria for propositions expressed by sentences of two different languages. This can easily be shown in more detail. Suppose we have a pair of native standing sentences NT_1 and NT_2 which conjointly entail $NO_1, NO_2, \ldots$ and a pair of English standing sentences 'T and R' which conjointly entail O_1, O_2, . . . Further, let us suppose that each NO_i is paired with its stimulus synonymous correlate O_i such that the pairings exhaust the native and English observation sentences entailed by (NT_1 and NT_2) and by (T and R), respectively. That is, the evidence for the truth of (T and R) is the same as for (NT_1 and NT_2). Assuming that we have no behavioral criteria for translating NT_1 or NT_2, except for the translation of the observation sentences they conjointly entail, we have no way of pairing either native standing sentences with T or with R. Hence the translation of NT_1 and of NT_2 into English is indeterminate.

Of course, the argument we are considering, which I shall call the *Peirce-Duhem argument,* depends for its soundness on the truth of (25) and (27). There seems to be little doubt that (27) is true. On the standard reconstruction of scientific theories, theoretical sentences—that is, those sentences containing only theoretical terms—do not by themselves entail observation sentences. Rather it is the conjunction of theoretical sentences with *statements of initial conditions* and *rules of correspondence* which has observational consequences.[22] Suppose we wish to explain the trajectory of a particular rocket. To do so we must state the initial causal conditions which play a role in the rocket's trajectory. In addition, we must have a theory which explains the trajectory of rockets. And lastly, we must have a set of rules which relate the theoretical sentences of our theory to observational consequences and, thereby, give an interpretation of the theoretical terms contained within the theory.

To relate this to the Peirce-Duhem argument for indeterminacy, we shall streamline our discussion a bit and drop out the statements of initial conditions, supposing that they are available when we need them. We shall consider a limiting case of a theory which contains one theoretical sentence, T, and one rule of correspondence, R, relevant to T. Given the relevant antecedent conditions on the standard reconstruction of scientific theories

(28) $(T$ and $R)$ entail $O_1, O_2, \ldots$

where the set of observation sentences, $O_1, O_2, \ldots$, is the evidence for the truth of $(T$ and $R)$.[23] We are now in a better position to understand the Peirce-Duhem argument. Because $O_1, O_2, \ldots$ are entailed by $(T$ and $R)$ together and, thus, are the evidence for the joint truth of $(T$ and $R)$, this evidence cannot be distributed between them. According to Peirce's thesis, the evidence for the truth of an indicative sentence is its meaning. But there is no evidence for T or for R alone. And hence, we can neither assign it a meaning, determine whether it is synonymous with another theoretical sentence, nor whether it and another theoretical sentence express the same proposition.

There would be a way around this argument, if R were analytic, for then $O_1, O_2, \ldots$ would be evidence for the truth of T, since the truth of R would be determined by the meaning of its terms and its syntax. But Quine argues that we have no grounds for attributing analyticity to R and, thus, R and T have their evidence together. One consequence of this, quite congenial to Quine, is that if any of the observational consequences of R and T turn out to be false all that we can conclude is that R is false or T is false. And assuming there is no reason to believe one over the other, we could hold either R to be true or T to be true. As Quine puts it, "Any statement can be held true come what may, if we make drastic enough adjustments elsewhere in the system."[24]

We have, then, two arguments against propositions and for translational indeterminacy. The first which Quine gives in some detail depends upon a putative indeterminacy of physical theories. The second to which Quine only alludes has as its premises theses of Peirce and of Duhem. We have seen that the first argument cuts against Katz's semantic theory, but that two criticisms have been raised against it. What about the second argument? First, the criticisms. Since it does not depend upon an indeterminacy of physical theory, it is not open to Katz and Chomsky's criticism. And because it applies to every theoretical sentence, it cannot be trivialized in the way the first argument can be.

It is obvious that if Peirce and Duhem's theses are true and the arguments based on them against propositional identity are sound, a Katzian semantics cannot be constructed which covers theoretical sentences. There are two possible rejoinders. First, one could reject Peirce's thesis and claim that the meaning of a theoretical sentence is not its observational consequences. But, then, one would have to give readings for the theoretical terms of science along Katzian lines. This has not been done. And given what we know about such terms, there is some doubt that it could be done. Second, one could argue that the terms and sentences of science do not fall within the purview of linguistics. And so it is not the linguist's task to provide an account of their syntax or semantics. But Quine has an answer to this way out. He claims that many of the sentences about our garden variety middle-sized objects are theoretical. Consequently, the same ills which befall the theoretical sentences of science infect these sentences which are clearly within the domain of linguistics.[25] On Quine's account of theoretical sentences it is easy enough to show that many sentences about ordinary objects are theoretical. But, I suppose any linguist who attempts to exclude the theoretical sentences of science from the domain of linguistics would, also, reject Quine's account of sentences about the non-theoretical objects amidst which we live our daily lives.

Conclusion

I have focused my attention in the last two chapters on Quine's eschewal of propositions and the propositional attitudes. This, I take to be the major point of difference between Quine's behaviorism and Chomsky's mentalism, not that Chomsky's mentalism has as a central feature the traditional notion of 'proposition'. However, as I tried to show,

Quine's arguments against propositions can be applied to many of the objects to which transformational linguistic theory is committed. There is no dispute between Chomsky and Quine, as some might think, on the doctrine of innate abilities. Both behaviorist and mentalist theories of language acquisition impute to the child innate principles and structures. Rather, the difference is in the character of these principles and structures which the two theories attribute to the child, although Quine holds that transformational linguistic theory goes beyond what the evidence warrants.[26] In fact the notion of evidence which Quine employs is at the root of his attack on mentalist theories. Quine avers that all the evidence we have to go on in obtaining knowledge about the world, including knowledge about language, ours as well as others, is the evidence of our senses. No one, Quine thinks, who considers himself to be an empiricist would dispute this. Switching to the linguistic mode, Quine's explication of 'the evidence of the senses' is encapsulated in his 'observation sentences'. It is the relationship between the true observation sentences and our theoretical sentences which gives rise to Quine's arguments for the translational indeterminacy of standing sentences. And in turn this indeterminacy leads to Quine's calling into question the existence of the putative propositions expressed by such sentences. My criticisms of Quine's views have centered on his arguments for indeterminacy and the conclusions about propositions he draws from them. However, I think there is room for further critical analysis of his account of evidence in terms of observation sentences. But, I shall leave this for a later time.

Notes

Chapter I

1. The interested reader should consult the Bibliography for reference to the important contributions these philosophers have made to the philosophy of language.

2. Russell's theory of definite descriptions is found scattered throughout his writings, but the main sources for it are in the Bibliography under 'Russell'.

3. B. Russell, *Introduction to Mathematical Philosophy* in *Readings in the Philosophy of Language,* ed. J. F. Rosenberg and C. Travis (Englewood Cliffs, N.J.: Prentice-Hall, 1971), p. 171.

4. B. Russell, "On Denoting," in *Problems in the Philosophy of Language,* ed. T. M. Olshewsky (New York: Holt, Rinehart and Winston, 1969), p. 303.

5. Ibid.

6. Ibid., p. 309.

7. Ibid.

8. Ibid., p. 174.

9. This view is substantially that of J. R. Searle in "Proper Names" in *Readings in the Philosophy of Language,* pp. 212–218.

10. This and the following criticism are due to K. S. Donnellan, "Proper Names and Identifying Descriptions," *Synthese* 1970, pp. 352–353.

11. P. F. Strawson, "On Referring," in *Readings in the Philosophy of Language,* p. 185.

12. Ibid.

13. Ibid., p. 179.

14. P. F. Strawson, *Introduction to Logical Theory* (London: Methuen, 1964), pp. 170–179, 184–190. L. Linsky, *Referring* (London: Routledge and Kegan Paul, 1969), pp. 85–100 and note 11.

Chapter II

1. C. K. Ogden and I. A. Richards, *The Meaning of Meaning* (London: K. Paul, Trench, Trubner and Co., 1938); T. C. Pollock, *The Nature of Literature, Its Relation to Science, Language and Human Experience* (Princeton: Princeton University Press, 1942); C. A. Mace, "Representation and Expression," in *Analysis* (1934), pp. 33–38; H. Feigl, "Logical Empiricism," in *Twentieth Century Philosophy*, ed. D. D. Runes (New York: Philosophical Library, 1943), pp. 373–416; C. L. Stevenson, *Ethics and Language* (New Haven: Yale University Press, 1944); C. Morris, *Signs, Language, and Behavior* (New York: Prentice-Hall, 1946). The Bibliography in this note is taken from C. Morris, *Signs, Language, and Behavior*, p. 261.

2. Hans Reichenbach, *Elements of Symbolic Logic* (New York: Free Press, 1966), Chapter I.

3. J. L. Austin, *How To Do Things With Words* (Cambridge: Harvard University Press, 1962). The two other sources for Austin's views are in "Performative Utterances," in *Philosophical Papers*, ed. J. O. Urmson and G. J. Warnock (Oxford: Oxford University Press, 1961) and "Performative-Constative," in *Philosophy and Ordinary Language*, ed. C. E. Caton (Urbana: University of Illinois Press, 1963).

4. Reichenbach, p. 17.

5. Ibid.

6. Ibid., p. 19.

7. Austin, *How To Do Things With Words*, pp. 99–131, pp. 144–150, pp. 101–131.

8. Ibid., p. 5.

9. Ibid., p. 84. We can perform certain illocutionary acts by using signals, such as bidding at an auction. But, these cases are derivative on language and in what follows we shall not consider them.

10. Ibid., p. 57.

11. Ibid., p. 121. This scheme is not identical to Austin's. There are difficulties with this test. Cf. p. 121f.

12. Ibid., p. 14.

13. Ibid., p. 18.

14. Ibid., pp. 14–15.

15. Ibid., p. 15.

16. Ibid., pp. 133–134.

17. Ibid., p. 136.

18. Ibid., p. 137.

19. Ibid.

20. Ibid.

21. Austin considers these sorts of conditions when he discusses 'issuing an utterance' which he calls a 'locutionary act'. Ibid., pp. 92–98. However, his treatment of locutionary acts is rather brief and confusing and for this reason I will not discuss it. John Searle in "Austin on Locutionary and Illocutionary Acts," *Philosophical Review*, 1968, pp. 405–424, points out some difficulties with the notion of 'locutionary act'.

22. Austin, *How To Do Things With Words*, pp. 141–142.

23. Reichenbach, p. 19.

24. It is possible to substitute adjectives and nouns for ϕ in (23) (ii) generating perlocutionary descriptions, for example, 'overjoyed'. But, there is no corresponding substitution instance of (23) (i). In addition (23) (ii) lacks generality. It should probably be revised changing '*H* to be ϕ' to '*H* to $\left\{ \begin{array}{c} be\ \psi \\ \phi \end{array} \right\}$ where ψ takes adjectives, verbs, and noun phrases as substitutions instances and ϕ takes verb phrases.

25. Austin, *How To Do Things With Words*, pp. 108–119.

26. P. F. Strawson, "Intention and Convention in Speech Acts," *Philosophical Review*, 1964.

27. Austin, *How To Do Things With Words*, pp. 104–105. Ludwig Wittgenstein, *Philosophical Investigations* (Oxford: Basil Blackwell, 1953), pp. 11–12.

28. Searle, pp. 405–424.

29. Austin seems to recognize this point in "Truth," *Philosophical Papers*, 1961, pp. 88–89. But he goes on to concentrate his attention on the truth of statements.

30. Richard Cartwright, "Propositions" in *Analytical Philosophy*, ed. R. J. Butler (Oxford: Basil Blackwell, 1966), pp. 87–88.

31. Cf. Alvin Goldman, *A Theory of Human Action* (Englewood Cliffs, N.J.: Prentice-Hall, 1970), Chapter I.

32. (36) can be used to perform other illocutionary acts besides promising. It can be used to say what one habitually does. I shall disregard this use of (36).

33. 'Sentence type' is being used here in its grammatical rather than logical sense. The different sentence types in English are questions, declaratives, and imperatives.

34. P. F. Strawson, "Truth," in *Philosophy and Analysis*, ed. Margaret MacDonald (Oxford: Basil Blackwell, 1954), pp. 260–277.

35. Ibid., p. 273.

36. Ibid., p. 274.

37. Ibid., pp. 274–277. Strawson considers other uses besides confirming, such as agreeing, conceding, and endorsing, but for ease of presentation I shall disregard these other uses.

38. Ibid., p. 270.

39. Ibid., p. 274.

40. Austin, "Truth," p. 86.

41. Austin, *How To Do Things With Words*, p. 141 and "Truth," p. 89.

42. '*' indicates an ungrammatical string of words.

43. Strawson, "Truth," p. 275. Hare, *The Language of Morals* (Oxford: Basil Blackwell, 1954), p. 272.

44. Strawson, "Truth," p. 275.

45. J. R. Searle, "Meaning and Speech Acts," in *Knowledge and Experience*, ed. C. D. Rollins (Pittsburgh: University of Pittsburgh Press, 1962), pp. 28–37.

46. W. P. Alston, *The Philosophy of Language* (Englewood Cliffs, N.J.: Prentice-Hall, 1964), pp. 32–49.

47. Ibid., p. 36. For various reasons Alston complicates this and the following definition. The criticism I raise against these definitions is not affected by these changes.

48. Ibid., p. 37.

49. Ibid., p. 42.

50. Austin, "Other Minds," *Philosophical Papers*, 1961, pp. 70–71.

51. Cf. C. E. Caton, "On the General Structure of the Epistemic Qualification of Things Said in English," *Foundations of Language*, 1967, pp. 37–66, for a discussion of epistemic qualifiers.

Chapter III

1. Noam Chomsky, *Syntactic Structures* (The Hague: Mouton & Co., 1957); *Aspects of a Theory of Syntax* (Cambridge: M.I.T. Press, 1965); *Cartesian Linguistics* (New York: Harper and Row, 1969).

2. Chomsky, *Aspects of a Theory of Syntax*, pp. 3–4.

3. Ibid., p. 4.

4. Ibid., p. 27.

5. Ibid., p. 8.

6. Ibid.

7. Ibid., p. 9.

8. Noam Chomsky, "Linguistics and Philosophy," in *Language and Philosophy*, ed. Sidney Hook (New York: New York University Press, 1969), p. 63.

9. Ibid., p. 64.

10. Chomsky, *Aspects of a Theory of Syntax*, p. 25.

11. Chomsky, "Linguistics and Philosophy," p. 83.

12. G. Harman, "Psychological Aspects of the Theory of Syntax," *Journal of Philosophy*, 1967, pp. 81–82.

13. Ibid., pp. 81–82.

14. Ibid., p. 82.

15. Chomsky, "Linguistics and Philosophy," p. 87.

16. G. Harman, "Reply to Arbini," *Synthese*, 1968, p. 425.

17. J. J. Katz, "Mentalism in Linguistics," in *Readings in the Philosophy of Language*, ed. J. F. Rosenberg and C. Travis (Englewood Cliffs, N.J.: Prentice-Hall, 1971), p. 369.

18. Ibid., pp. 373–374.

Chapter IV

1. Chomsky, *Aspects of the Theory of Syntax* (Cambridge: MIT Press, 1965); J. A. Fodor and J. J. Katz, "The Structure of a Semantic Theory," *The Structure of Language: Readings in the Philosophy of Language*, ed. Fodor and Katz (Englewood Cliffs, N.J.: Prentice-Hall, 1964), pp. 479–519.

2. N. Chomsky, "Deep Structure, Surface Structure, and Semantic Interpretation," in *Semantics—An Interdisciplinary Reader in Philosophy, Linguistics, Anthropology, and Psychology*, ed. D. D. Stein-

berg and Leon A. Jakobovits (London: Cambridge University Press, 1971); R. C. Dougherty, "An Interpretive Theory of Pronominal References," pp. 488–519, and R. S. Jackendoff, "An Interpretive Theory of Negation," pp. 218–241, both in *Foundations of Language,* 1969.

3. For a basic bibliography of generative semantics, see J. D. McCawley, "Interpretive Semantics Meets Frankenstein," *Foundations of Language,* 1971.

4. Chomsky, *Aspects,* p. 60.

5. These rules are due to J. R. Ross and M. Halle.

6. The symbols are to be read in the following way: $S =$ sentence, $NP =$ noun phrase, Aux = auxiliary, $VP =$ verb phrase, Adv = adverb, Prt = particle, Adj = adjective, $P =$ preposition, Det = determiner, $N =$ noun, Tns =tense, M = modal, Perf = perfect, Prog = progressive, Pass = passive, Pres = present, Pst = past, Pre $S =$ Pre Sentence, $Q =$ question, Imp = Imperative, Neg = Negation, Emp = Emphasis.

7. At the end of the chapter, rules (7)(k)–(o) will be replaced with other devices for introducing lexical formatives into a derivation.

8. '# #' indicates sentence boundary.

9. Obviously, there is more than one way to derive (8); (c) could read 'NP-Tns-M-V-NP'. Two derivations will be said to be identical if and only if they map into the same P-marker, a notion which we shall introduce shortly.

10. It has been argued by Postal that a context-free phrase structure grammar cannot generate all and only the sentences of Mohawk. Consequently, according to Postal a general linguistic theory which contains as its only syntactic rule schemata a context-free schemata is inadequate. A. Hazen in private communication has shown Postal's argument to be invalid. However, no one to date has shown that context-sensitive grammars cannot generate the set of sentences of any human language.

11. There is not a perfect fit between (11) and (13). Neither 'present may' nor 'present' appears in (10). However, 'present may' is the same as 'may'.

12. These definitions of grammatical relations are due to Chomsky. Cf. *Aspects,* pp. 68–73. However, they cannot be generally applied to sentences derived from a grammar which consists of the rules in (7). Notice that application of (7)(b) can produce a tree in which VP dominates two NP's. If these rules were used in deriving a sentence, we would not be able to determine the direct object for the sentence.

13. We divided phrase structure rules into two kinds: context sensitive and context free. It is an open question whether a context-free grammar can generate all and only the sentences of English. There is no question that a context-sensitive grammar can do so.

14. Transformations are classified as substitution, deletion, or adjunction depending upon whether their main function is to substitute, delete, or adjoin.

15. This rule is a simplified version of a rule from J. R. Ross and M. Halle.

16. (29) (30) contain 'it' because there are sentences such as

        Jones thought Sam was a hero.

        It was thought by Jones that Sam was a hero.

which are syntactically related.

17. The object of the embedded S is not uniquely determined by the rules previously given. These rules, also, designate 'to Alice' as the object of the embedded S.

18. J. R. Ross, "Constraints on Variables in Syntax," Ph.D. dissertation, M.I.T., 1967.

19. J. J. Katz, "Recent Issues in Semantic Theory," *Foundations of Language*, 1967, p. 133.

20. Fodor and Katz, "The Structure of a Semantic Theory," pp. 481–482.

21. We distinguish between 'a semantics', 'universal semantics', and 'semantic theory'. The first is a component of a particular grammar, the second a part of universal grammar, and the last, a theory about the first two.

22. J. J. Katz, *Semantic Theory* (New York: Harper and Row, 1972), pp. 36–37.

23. This P-marker is simplified by leaving out the phonological and syntactical features associated with the lexical items.

24. A semantic marker has been added for a sense of 'past'.

25. G. Lakoff, "On Generative Semantics," in *Semantics—An Interdisciplinary Reader in Philosophy, Linguistics, Anthropology, and Psychology*, p. 234.

26. Since sentences can be structurally ambiguous, the meaning of such sentences is determined with respect to one of its derivations.

27. Fodor and Katz, "The Structure of a Semantic Theory," p. 504.

28. I. Kant, *Prolegomena to Any Future Metaphysics*, trans. Mahaffy-Carus, ed. L. W. Beck, Library of Liberal Arts, 1954, p. 14.

29. The general supposition underlying the point is contentious. In knowing that all unicorns are one-horned one does not have to know whether there are unicorns.

30. Katz, *Semantic Theory*, p. 50. This is a simplified version of Katz's definition.

31. J. R. Ross, "On Declarative Sentences," in *Readings in English Transformational Grammar*, ed. R. A. Jacobs and P. S. Rosenbaum (Waltham, Mass.: Ginn, 1970), pp. 222–273.

32. Ibid., pp. 229–230.

33. Cf. Chapter II for a discussion of the possible relationships between performative verbs and illocutionary acts.

34. J. D. McCawley, "Interpretive Semantics Meets Frankenstein," *Foundations of Language*, vol. 7, no. 2, p. 285. McCawley calls what I am calling the logical form of a sentence its semantic structure. My use of 'logical form' follows G. Lakoff, in *Linguistics and Natural Logic* (Ann Arbor: University of Michigan, Phonetics Laboratory, 1970), p. 18.

35. Fodor and Katz, "The Structure of a Semantic Theory," p. 486.

36. Ibid., p. 497.

37. Katz, "Recent Issues in Semantic Theory," p. 129.

38. Jackendoff, "An Interpretive Theory of Negation," pp. 223–228.

Chapter V

1. W. V. O. Quine, *Word and Object* (Cambridge: M.I.T. Press, 1960).

2. Ibid., p. 28.

3. Ibid., p. 81.

4. G. S. Reynolds, *A Primer of Operant Conditioning* (Glenview, Ill.: Scott, Foresman and Company, 1968).

5. Quine, *Word and Object*, p. 82.

6. Ibid.

7. Ibid., p. 83.

8. A. N. Chomsky, "Review of B. F. Skinner's *Verbal Behavior*" in *The Structure of Language*, ed. J. A. Fodor and J. J. Katz (Englewood Cliffs, N.J.: Prentice-Hall, 1964), pp. 547–578.

9. Quine, *Word and Object*, p. 10.

10. Ibid., p. 9.

11. W. V. O. Quine, *Philosophy of Logic* (Englewood Cliffs, N.J.: Prentice-Hall, 1970), p. 17.

12. Quine, p. 83.

13. W. V. O. Quine, *Words and Objections*, ed. Donald Davidson and Jaacko Hintikka (New York: Humanities Press, 1969), p. 306.

14. See Chapter IV.

15. Quine, *Word and Object*, p. 83.

16. Ibid., p. 84.

17. Ibid., p. 27.

18. Ibid., p. 29.

19. A *wh-question* is one which begins with 'who', 'what', 'when', 'why', etc. A *yes-no question* is one which has a 'yes' or 'no' answer.

20. Quine, *Word and Object*, p. 31.

21. Ibid.

22. Ibid., pp. 32–33.

23. Ibid., p. 66. Paul Ziff in "A Response to Stimulus Meaning," *Philosophical Review*, 1970, pp. 63–74, presents a range of similar criticisms, but gives the mistaken impression that Quine has not recognized these difficulties.

24. Quine, *Word and Object*, p. 28.

25. Ibid., p. 38.

26. W. V. O. Quine, "Two Dogmas of Empiricism," *From a Logical Point of View* (Cambridge: Harvard University Press, 1961), p. 23.

27. Ibid., p. 37.

28. Quine, *Word and Object*, p. 55.

29. Ibid., pp. 35–36.

30. W. V. O. Quine, "Epistomology Naturalized," *Ontological Relativity* (New York: Columbia University Press, 1969), pp. 86–87.

31. As Dreben has pointed out to Quine, allowances must be made for the color blind and insane. Ibid., p. 89.

32. Ibid.

33. Quine, *Word and Object*, p. 50.

34. Ibid., p. 52.

35. Ibid., p. 53.

36. Quine, "Ontological Relativity," in *Ontological Relativity*, p. 35.

37. Ibid.

38. Ibid., p. 43.

39. Quine, *Words and Objections*, p. 312.

40. Ibid.

41. Quine, *Word and Object*, p. 74.

42. Quine, "Ontological Relativity," pp. 46–47.

43. Ibid.

44. An obvious criticism to the theory is that it does not provide an account of what we mean by words like 'the', 'or', 'when', etc. For there is no plausible image which could be associated with them.

45. S. Davis, "Translational Indeterminacy and Private Worlds," *Philosophical Studies*, 1967, pp. 38–47.

46. The definition can be relativized to speakers and times, but the fine points are not necessary for our purpose.

47. Quine, "Ontological Relativity," p. 48.

48. Katz's semantic theory presented in Chapter IV is a theory of meaning, not a theory of reference.

49. Quine, "Ontological Relativity," p. 29.

50. W. V. O. Quine, "Philosophical Progress in Language Theory," *Metaphilosophy*, 1970, pp. 6–7.

51. Quine, "Two Dogmas," p. 29.

52. Quine, *Word and Object*, p. 68.

53. Ibid., p. 71.

54. W. V. O. Quine, "On the Reasons for the Indeterminacy of Translation," *Journal of Philosophy*, 1970, p. 179.

55. I leave open the question of what it is for both A and B to be theories of O_1', O_2' . . . I take it that Quine's view is that whatever the relationship is, his theses about physical theories hold.

56. Quine, "On the Reasons for the Indeterminacy," pp. 179–180.

57. We should also include here that HA and HB yield the same pairings for all data obtained by behavioral criteria.

58. Quine, "On the Reasons for the Indeterminacy," p. 183.

59. Another question Quine does not leave open is whether inscrutability of term reference always entails indeterminacy of standing sentences. He claims wrongly, I believe, that ". . . the inscrutability of terms need not always bring indeterminacy of sentence translation in its train, . . ." in, "On the Reasons for the Indeterminacy," p. 182.

60. E. J. Lemmon, "Sentences, Statements, and Propositions," in *British Analytical Philosophy*, ed. B. Williams and A. Montifiore (New York: The Humanities Press, 1966), p. 96.

61. Quine, *Word and Object*, pp. 193–194.

62. J. J. Katz holds this view in *Semantic Theory*, pp. 125–126.

63. Ibid.

64. Quine, *Word and Object*, p. 208.

65. Ibid.

66. Ibid., p. 193.

67. This definition is incomplete. One would like a criterion for

the verbs in (23) (c) and a specification of what it is to be a physical property in (23) (a).

68. See G. Frege, "The Thought," in *Logic and Philosophy,* ed. G. Iseminger (New York: Appleton-Century-Crofts, 1968), pp. 7–19, for a view of the sort presented here.

69. See A. Church, "Propositions and Sentences," *The Problem of Universals* (South Bend, Ind.: Notre Dame University Press, 1956), pp. 3–11.

70. Quine, *Word and Object,* p. 242.

71. Ibid., p. 208.

72. Ibid., p. 200.

73. Ibid., p. 206.

74. Quine, "Speaking of Objects," *Ontological Relativity,* p. 23.

75. Ibid.

76. Quine, "Speaking of Objects," p. 24.

77. Quine, *Word and Object,* p. 218.

78. Ibid., p. 221.

Chapter VI

1. These criticisms can be found in W. V. O. Quine, "Two Dogmas of Empiricism," in *From a Logical Point of View* (Cambridge, Mass.: Harvard University Press, 1961), pp. 20–46.

2. J. J. Katz, *Semantic Theory* (New York: Harper and Row, 1972), p. 48. This is a slightly modified version of Katz's definition.

3. N. L. Wilson, "Linguistic Butter and Philosophical Parsnips," *The Journal of Philosophy* (1967), p. 67.

4. Katz, *Semantic Theory,* p. 286.

5. For the sake of simplicity we shall suppose S and S' to be unambiguous.

6. W. V. O. Quine, "On the Reasons for the Indeterminacy of Translation," *The Journal of Philosophy* (1970), p. 179.

7. Actually what Quine ("On the Reasons for the Indeterminacy," p. 179) says is that our only data for translating the natives physical theory is our translation of his observation sentences, including both those he believes and those he does not believe. But, I would think that translating observation sentences the native does not believe has no bearing. on translating theoretical sentences he does believe.

8. This assumption is not necessary to the argument, but it simplifies presentation of it.

9. W. V. O. Quine, "Methodological Reflections," *Synthese* (1970), pp. 386–398.

10. Ibid., p. 387. There are some who claim that this is what has occurred in the development of interpretive and generative semantic theories.

11. J. J. Katz, "Mentalism in Linguistics," in *Readings in the Philosophy of Language,* ed. J. F. Rosenberg and C. Travis (Englewood Cliffs, N.J.: Prentice-Hall, 1971), pp. 374–375.

12. Ibid., p. 371.

13. Quine, "On the Reasons for the Indeterminacy," p. 181.

14. Katz, *Semantic Theory*, p. 290 and N. Chomsky, "Quine's Methodological Assumptions," *Synthese* (1968), pp. 53–68.

15. Quine, "On the Reasons for the Indeterminacy," p. 180.

16. This criticism and the criticism of indeterminacy of translation which depends upon it could be turned aside, if it could be shown that no two theories A and B which differ only in that one contains the contradictory of the other could both be theories of O_1', O_2', . . . As Philip L. Quinn has pointed out to me in private communication this could not be shown since both $(((T \cdot S) \supset O) \cdot ((T \cdot \curlywedge S) \supset O))) \equiv (T \supset O)$ and $(((T \cdot S) \to O) \cdot ((T \cdot \curlywedge S) \to O))) \equiv (T \to O)$ are tautologies, where $(A \to B) =_{df} \square(A \supset B)$. One could argue against this that '___ is a theory of ___' means neither '___ materially implies ___' nor '___ strictly implies ___', but anyone who did so argue would have to provide another relationship between theory and evidence.

17. W. V. O. Quine, *Word and Object* (Cambridge, Mass.: M.I.T. Press, 1960), p. 73. Emphasis is my own.

18. W. V. O. Quine, "Epistemology Naturalized," in *Ontological Relativity* (New York: Columbia University Press, 1969), pp. 80–81.

19. Philip Quinn, "What Duhem Really Meant," unpublished manuscript, p. 5.

20. Quine, "Epistemology Naturalized," p. 82

21. 'T' must be taken to be non-conjunctive.

22. Ernest Nagel, *The Structure of Science* (New York: Harcourt, Brace and World, 1961), pp. 97–105. Carl G. Hempel and Paul Oppenheim, "The Logic of Explanation," in *Readings in the Philosophy of Science*, ed. H. Feigl and May Brodbeck (New York: Appleton-Century-Crofts, 1953), pp. 319–352.

23. Christopher Hill has suggested that if we could tell which of NT_1 and NT_2 and of T and R are rules of correspondence, then the translation of NT_1 and NT_2 into English would not be indeterminate. But this solution is not available if we drop our simplified theory and replace it with actual theories which contain more than one theoretical sentence and one rule of correspondence.

24. W. V. O. Quine, "Two Dogmas of Empiricism," in *From a Logical Point of View* (Cambridge, Mass.: Harvard University Press, 1953), p. 43.

25. Quine, "On the Reasons for the Indeterminacy," p. 183.

26. N. Chomsky and J. Katz, "On Innateness a Reply to Cooper," *The Philosophical Review* (1975), pp. 74–87.

Select Bibliography

Additional bibliographical material may be found in the Notes.

1. *Collections:* These books contain many of the most important recent articles in philosophy of language and in linguistics.
   a. Caton, C. E., ed. *Philosophy and Ordinary Language.* Urbana: University of Illinois Press, 1963. Includes Austin's "Performative—Constative."
   b. Fodor, J. A. and Katz, J. J. eds. *The Structure of Language: Readings in the Philosophy of Language.* Englewood Cliffs, N.J.: Prentice-Hall, 1964. Contains Fodor and Katz's seminal article, "The Structure of a Semantic Theory," which provides the first semantics for transformational grammars.
   c. Jakobovitz, L. A. and Steinberg, D. D., eds. *Semantics.* Cambridge: Cambridge University Press, 1971. Sections on philosophy, psychology, and linguistics.
   d. Olshewsky, T. M., ed. *Problems in the Philosophy of Language.* New York: Holt, Rinehart and Winston, 1969. Has an excellent bibliography.
   e. Rosenberg, J. F. and Travis, C., eds. *Readings in the Philosophy of Language.* Englewood Cliffs, N.J.: Prentice-Hall, 1971.
   f. Searle, J. R. *The Philosophy of Language.* Oxford: Oxford University Press, 1971. Contains an important symposium on Chomsky's doctrine of innate ideas with contributions by N. Chomsky, N. Goodman, and H. Putnam.

2. *Classics of Philosophy of Language:* See also the entries under Austin, Chomsky, Quine, and Russell.
   a. Carnap, R. *Meaning and Necessity.* Chicago: University of Chicago Press, 1960.
   b. Frege, G. *Philosophical Writings of Gottlob Frege,* ed. and trans. P. Geach and M. Black. Oxford: Basil Blackwell, 1960.
   c. Tarski, A. *Logic, Semantics and Metamathematics.* London: Oxford University Press, 1956.
   d. Wittgenstein, L., *Philosophical Investigations.* New York: Macmillan, 1953.
   e. Wittgenstein, L. *The Tractatus Logico-Philosophicus,* trans. D. F. Pears and B. F. McGuiness. London: Routledge, 1961.

3. *B. Russell:* Russell's writings on the philosophy of language are scattered throughout his rather extensive writings. I have listed here the main sources for his theory of definite descriptions.
   a. Russell, B. *Introduction to Mathematical Philosophy.* London: Allen and Unwin, 1920. See "Descriptions" in 1e.
   b. Russell, B. "On Denoting," in *Problems in the Philosophy of Language* in 1d.
   c. Russell, B. and Whitehead, A. N. *Principia Mathematica.* Cambridge: Cambridge University Press, 1925.

4. *J. L. Austin:* Austin's contributions to the philosophy of language are in 1a, 4a, and 4b.
   a. Austin, J. L. *How to Do Things with Words,* ed. J. O. Urmson. London: Oxford University Press, 1962.
   b. Austin, J. L. *Philosophical Papers,* ed. J. O. Urmson and G. J. Warnock. London: Oxford University Press, 1961. The articles on the philosophy of language are "The Meaning of Words," "Truth," "Unfair to Facts," "How to Talk—Some simple ways," and "Performative Utterances."
   c. Fann, K. T., ed. *Symposium on Austin.* New York: Humanities Press, 1969. Part IV contains articles on Austin's philosophy of language.
   d. Furberg, Mats. *Locutionary and Illocutionary Acts: A Main Theme in J. L. Austin's Philosophy.* Toronto: Toronto University Press, 1969.
   e. Searle, J. R. *Speech Acts, An Essay in the Philosophy of Language.* Cambridge: Cambridge University Press, 1969. To date the most important extension of Austin's views on the philosophy of language.

f. Strawson, P. F. "Intention and Convention in Speech Acts." *Philosophical Review,* 1964. An important discussion of the application of the notion of 'convention' to illocutionary acts.

5. *N. Chomsky:* The literature on transformational linguistic theory is vast, and a good deal of the current work in the area circulates in mimeographed and typescript versions before being published, which often occurs some years after their appearance. There are now many places from which one can obtain these articles before publication, the most important of which are the Chicago Linguistic Society, Linguistics Department, University of Chicago, and the Indiana University Linguistics Club, Linguistics Department, Indiana University, Bloomington.

This Bibliography concentrates its attention on the linguistic theory currently held by Chomsky, the revised standard theory, leaving aside generative semantics. For bibliographical references to the latter theory see the notes to Chapter IV.

a. Chomsky, N. *Aspects of a Theory of Syntax.* Cambridge: M.I.T. Press, 1965. The main theoretical discussion of the standard theory.

b. Chomsky, N. *Language and Mind.* New York: Harcourt Brace Jovanovich, 1970. A good introduction to transformational linguistic theory and its philosophical implications.

c. Chomsky, N. *Syntactic Structures.* The Hague: Mouton and Co., 1965. First published in 1957, this book is the seminal work in transformational linguistic theory.

d. Hook, S., ed. *Language and Philosophy.* New York: New York University Press, 1969. Contains important critical discussions of the philosophical implications of transformational linguistic theory by N. Chomsky, G. Harman, T. Nagel, W. V. Quine, and R. Schwartz.

e. Jackendoff, R. S. *Semantic Interpretation in Generative Grammar.* Cambridge: M.I.T. Press, 1972. A revision of the theory proposed in 4a. Argues that surface structure information must be part of the input to the semantic component and that all transformations are not meaning preserving.

f. Katz, J. J. and Postal, P. M. *An Integrated Theory of Linguistic Description.* Cambridge: M.I.T. Press, 1964. Integrates the Fodor and Katz semantics of 1b into the theory in 5a and advances the hypothesis that transformations are meaning preserving.

g. Katz, J. J. *Semantic Theory*. New York: Harper and Row, 1972.   A revision of the Katz-Fodor semantic theory of 1b.

h. Katz, J. J. *The Underlying Reality of Language*. New York: Harper and Row, 1971.   A general introduction to the philosophical presuppositions of transformational linguistic theory.

i. Lyons, J. *Chomsky*. London: Fontana/Collins, 1969.   A very readable basic introduction to transformational linguistic theory.

For further bibliographical references see 1b, 1c, and 1f.

6. *W. V. O. Quine:* Quine's central work in the philosophy of language, *Word and Object,* is perhaps the most influential work in the field in the last fifteen years. I have made no attempt to assay the extensive secondary literature on Quine's philosophy of language.

a. Davidson, D. and Hintikka, J., eds. *Words and Objections: Essays on the Work of W. V. Quine*. Dordrect: D. Reidel, 1969.   Contains criticisms of Quine's philosophy and his replies. It has a complete bibliography of Quine's work to 1969.

b. Harman, G. "Quine on Meaning and Existence." *Review of Metaphysics,* 1967.   One of the standard interpretations of Quine's metaphysics and philosophy of language.

c. Quine, W. V. O. *From a Logical Point of View*. Cambridge: Harvard, 1961.   Contains "Two Dogmas of Empiricism," one of the most important articles on philosophy of language in the twentieth century.

d. Quine, W. V. O. *Ontological Relativity and Other Essays*. New York: Columbia University Press, 1969.   Contains "Speaking of Objects" which is a good introduction to 6g.

e. Quine, W. V. O. "On the Reasons for the Indeterminacy of Translation." *The Journal of Philosophy,* 1970.

f. Quine, W. V. O. *The Roots of Reference*. La Salle: Open Court, 1974.   The material in this book has not been incorporated into the chapters on Quine, since it appeared after they were submitted for publication. It contains substantial revisions of Quine's views in *Word and Object* on many important points.

g. Quine, W. V. O. *Word and Object*. Cambridge: M.I.T. Press, 1960.

h. Ziff, P. "A Response to Stimulus Meaning," *Philosophical Review*.   A criticism of Quine's behaviorism in 6g.

Index